Embedded Computer Systems, Introduction and Architecture

(c) 2012

Patrick H. Stakem

8th in the Computer Architecture Series

Table of Contents

Roadmap..5
   Organization 15
Elements of Embedded Computers....................................19
   Central Processing Unit...19
      The fetch/execute cycle...20
      RISC and MultiCore..26
      FPGA and SOC 36
   Memory in embedded..41
      Memory organization...45
      Caches..45
      Memory Management..48
   Input/Output..50
      I/O Schemes..50
      Busses..53
         Software bus..60
   Embedded Peripherals...78
   Sensors and sensor interfacing..84
   Actuator and Mechanism Interfacing................................103
   Software...107
      Instruction Set Architecture...107
      Open Source versus Proprietary....................................110
      Operating system..112
         Process...119
         The bootstrap ("boot") process.................................123
         Opsys in hardware..125
      IP Cores..125
Real-Time Embedded...127
Embedded Systems Standards...132
Architecture of some embedded systems and chips...........140
   Arduino..140
   ARM 142
   The Intel Microcontrollers...149
   Texas Instruments..159
   Analog Devices..162

    Motorola..163
    PIC..166
    The CADC..170
    Whirlwind...171
    Embedded Microprocessors in space applications............172
        Remote debugging...188
Embedded Case studies..190
    Apollo Guidance Computer.....................................190
    LG Electronics Internet Refrigerator 192
    Samsung HomePad Refrigerator 193
    Smart Washing machine..193
    Athena Missile Guidance Computer........................194
    Ford Sync Telematics System..................................197
    Implantable medical devices....................................198
    Mars Science Laboratory Curiosity.........................198
    Nikon Exspeed..200
    NASA Standard Spacecraft Computer -1.................200
    IBM pc keyboard and mouse...................................203
    QES-III Locomotive computer................................204
    Smart Meter/Smart Grid..205
Embedded System Failures Case studies.....................................207
    Ariane 5 Launch Vehicle...207
    Big Bay Boom...209
    Mars Climate Orbiter...210
    Mars Rover Pathfinder..211
    Montgomery County (MD) traffic light system.....................213
    Patriot Missile..215
    Therac-25 216
    USS Yorktown...217
    NEAR spacecraft...218
    Clementine Spacecraft 220
    Dive Computer fault..221
Appendix – Binary System and Math operations........................222
Appendix - Floating Point...239
Glossary of Embedded System Terms and Acronyms................250
Selected Bibliography on Embedded..269

If you enjoyed this book, you might also be interested in some of these...305

Roadmap

This section describes how the book is organized. Feel free to skip around. I am assuming a basic knowledge of computer architecture, but most of what you need to know is also included. The details of computer math are presented in an appendix. I have collected together a representative list of reference books and interesting titles in the bibliography. There is a glossary of terms in embedded computing. In a quickly evolving field such as embedded computers, new and relevant material is emerging all the time. This book represents a current snapshot of the field. The plan is to update the material at reasonable intervals. A second volume will address the specifics of implementing embedded systems.

Most of the technology is what it is, because of the path that was taken. Computers started out as mechanical devices, were then implemented in relay and vacuum tube technology, and then in semiconductors. It is useful to review how we got where we are. The author acknowledges that not all of the readers will have stored data on punch cards or paper tape, or transmitted data via Teletype at 300 baud. I expect that the readership has grown up in a world that has always had an Internet, even a World-Wide Web, and in which, one could always lift their own computer. It was not always so.

The book starts out with a top-level discussion of the structure and organization of embedded computers as computers, the fetch-execute cycle, memory, Input/output. We focus on classical cpu architectures, while also looking at Field Programmable Gate Array (FPGA) and System on Chip (SoC) approaches. This leads us to the discussion of software for embedded. There are several differences between embedded software and software in general. Most embedded systems are resource-constrained, but this is becoming less of an issue. Embedded systems generally require real-time response, and operate in a world where the timing of the result is as or more important than its accuracy. The correct answer, late, can be worse than an approximate answer on time.

Embedded systems have elements of hardware and software, and these are brought together into a working system. The systems engineering process, from requirements to testing and post-deployment support is discussed. There are known approaches that work. Software is a different animal than hardware, but the top-level principles for developing and testing derive from the same principles. Programmable hardware, in terms of FPGA's and SoC's introduce complexity, but can be addressed by the same engineering best practices.

Embedded systems have their own set of standards, and their own unique issues in security, but an embedded computer is also a computer. Virtualization and multicore technology have added new capabilities to embedded systems.

We will look at some real commercial products, both chips and systems. We will also consider failure cases, to learn, ideally, from others' mistakes. We learn more from failures than from successes. This book discusses the "what" of embedded systems, and the follow on volume will discusses the "how". There is necessarily some overlap in the material. Enjoy the journey.

This second edition has been expanded, revised, and updated. Thanks go to the graduate and undergraduate students who slogged through my embedded systems courses, and made suggestions.

Special thanks

To all those who supplied information, reviewed text, spotted errors, misspellings and grammatical flubs, and supported my efforts. Richard Ibbotson, UK; Bruce Eyrich; Marco Figueiredo, Conor McGinn, Trinity College; Ray Lloyd; Fred Stakem; John Culver at cpushack.com; my past students in course 525.415,

Microprocessor Systems, at Johns Hopkins University; and many others.

Author

The author received his BSEE from Carnegie Mellon University, and Masters in Computer Science and Applied Physics from the Johns Hopkins University. He has worked in the aerospace sector, supporting projects at all of the NASA Centers. He has taught for the graduate Engineering Science and Computer Science Departments at Loyola University in Maryland, and teaches Embedded Systems for the Johns Hopkins University, Whiting School of Engineering, Engineering for Professionals Program, and Capitol Technology University

Photo credits

All photos are from the author's collection, or courtesy, John Culver, www.cpushack.com.

Introduction

This book is an introduction to the subject of embedded computers. The topic refers to special purpose computers that are a part of a larger system, as opposed to generic desktop computers, tablets, and servers. Embedded systems are for specific purposes; they are not necessarily general purpose. They may have a limited or no human interface, but usually support complex I/O.

The goal of this book is to present embedded computers in the context of system design. This will include discussions of system architecture, taxonomy of available systems, hardware and software, design, security, standards, debugging and testing, and many other topics. The reader will be introduced to the concept to embedded systems, what they are, what they are not, and how they are used. The reader should be moderately familiar with computer architecture. No particular knowledge of programming languages is required. After reading this book, the reader will be familiar with embedded computer architectural features and peripherals and what types of applications they can enable. The reader will be brought to understand what is different about embedded systems.

Besides cpu's, we will touch upon the topics of the memory architectures and types that are used and the interfaces with devices. We will cover analog conversion, because most of the world is analog. We will look at embedded systems standards and security, and the emerging multicore architectures, and what this enables. Numerous case studies drawn from industry will be used to illustrate embedded systems concepts.

System, as I use the word here, refers to the computer, memory, input-output, and the associated devices that the embedded computer controls or communicates with.

Embedded systems weren't always based on microprocessors. The first embedded systems were large mainframes, but evolved to minicomputers, and then microcomputers, when these became available. The first embedded system may have been the IBM Whirlwind computer in the 1940's which was designed to be real-time. Single chip solutions are now the norm. For most applications, a single-chip microcontroller solution is used. This combines the central processing unit, the memory, and the input-output on a single chip. This has the advantage of simplifying the circuit board design, minimizing the size, power consumption, and heat generation.

The embedded computer can be characterized by the parameters of its central processing unit (CPU), memory, and input/output (I/O). The CPU parameters of importance are speed, power consumption, word size, and price. The memory parameters include power consumption, volatility, and size or capacity. I/O characteristics must be matched to external systems components.

A microprocessor has come to mean a monolithic CPU, wholly contained on a single chip. Embedded microcontrollers usually include memory and input-output circuitry as well. The first microprocessors were designed for calculators. They were 4-bit units that handled binary-coded decimal encoded digits, and did serial-by-digit calculations. They did it fast! In fact, the result appeared almost instantaneously to our eyes, unless you asked for something really hard, like 70-factorial. Then the calculator blinked. Texas Instruments and Hewlett-Packard repeatedly outdid each other in producing hand-held calculators with more functionality and less cost. But the 4-bit chips evolved into 8-bit models, and were made more general purpose.

Automobiles have used microprocessor-based controllers since the 1970's. There was a desire to reduce emissions, and simultaneously increase both fuel economy and performance. This was not going to happen with mechanical systems such as carburetors. Analog controllers were tried, but were troublesome. Then, 8-bit, and later 16-bit embedded processors used look-up tables in memory to determine the exact optimal operating time for the fuel injectors, based on multiple input parameters from engine sensors. 32-bit processors allowed for the function to be calculated in real-time, and the look-up table was no longer required.

32-bit processors could also do the required calculations for anti-lock brakes. With anti-lock brakes, you can get traction control and stability control almost for free.

The trend now is to include more than one CPU on the chip, called Multicore technology. In addition, specialized processor units for floating point, vector processing, and digital signal processing are included. Multicore changes the game.

Embedded versus Desktop and Server

Most microprocessors sold, by volume, are destined for embedded applications as opposed to desktop or server use. Embedded systems have limited or no human intervention. They are purpose-built, and self-contained. Many include the features of BIST – built-in self-test.

Embedded systems can be found in most consumer products. Embedded systems, as opposed to traditional general-purpose desktop computers or tablets, are targeted toward a specific application or market, have specialized I/O, and limited user interfaces.

Embedded systems are generally dedicated to a single task or small set of related tasks; have limited human interface; have special purpose interfaces; and are mostly self-contained.

Many embedded systems are required to be real-time - they have strict deadlines. Others are event-driven - a trigger event kicks off a predetermined sequence of responses. Embedded systems are almost always resource constrained. The resources might be size, weight, power, throughput, heat generation, reliability, deadlines, etc. Embedded systems have a high non-recurring engineering (NRE) cost (development cost), but are generally cheap to produce in volume. Embedded computers do not usually host their own development system. These are generally hosted on a pc.

Although the thrust of early Reduced Instruction Set Computing (RISC) development was enhanced computation that usually found itself in engineering workstations, the market for such endeavors was limited in scope. A much larger market, and, more importantly, a volume market, was found in embedded control. Volume markets are cost driven.

An important concept emerges here: although we usually associate RISC with 32- or even 64-bit machines, this is not necessarily always true. For a counterexample, consider the Microchip PIC, which represents a minimalist 8-bit approach to RISC for embedded control. More importantly, conventional RISC manufacturers, who might produce 50-100,000 units for the workstation market, are finding the multi-million piece embedded systems market appealing. This is a production environment, with the customer hand-holding done once, at development time. After that, the process involves turning out product and shipping it. Volume embedded control markets include laser printers, fax machines, cellular communication devices, set-top boxes, sewing machines, large and small appliances, keyless entry systems, etc. Emerging markets are automotive engine and transmission controls, smart appliances, antilock brake/traction/stability control systems, high-end video games, and more. Volume markets include cell phones and tablets, and smart automobiles. These devices have created a volume market larger than any traditionally known.

In automotive applications of embedded systems, the market has exploded. This includes sensors, memory, and device control. Embedded automotive processors can be found in airbag/crash systems, roll-over and stability control, engine control and monitoring, transmission control and monitoring, *infotainment* systems, driver assist systems, and systems monitoring and management. Hybrid (gas-electric) vehicles feature advanced battery management, "fuel state" calculation, and powertrain control. Cars can park themselves now, and self-driving cars are appearing. It is no longer a technology issue, but a regulatory and legal one.

Some of the parameters of importance in embedded computing include interrupt latency, integrated solutions for low chip count, and good development tools for quick time to market. The processor is usually characterized by its word size (number of bits), its clock speed, and its instruction set.

Although virtual memory is a feature that is not usually needed in embedded applications, memory management units (MMU's) can provide memory protection mechanisms even with a simple 1:1 mapping. The possibility of remapping over failed memory units (hot redundancy) is also a possibility.

We will explore the hardware and software aspects of embedded computing, and discuss the design and test/verification environment. This will include the Integrated Design Environments (IDE's) and a discussion on the choice of programming languages and operating systems.

After reading through this book, you will be generally familiar with embedded systems, and how they differ from desktop and server systems. You will be able to select appropriate solutions for particular embedded problems. Actually, purchasing a small embedded board such as the Raspberry Pi or Leaflabs Maple at around $50, and getting hands-on experience, would be an excellent idea. This will provide expertise in setting up and using the integrated development environment for embedded software development. You will have an overview of the various interfaces used with embedded devices, and the sensors and actuators that they interface to. You will understand the software environment, and the hard real time and soft real time domains. You will have seen various optimization strategies, trade-off's for hardware versus software-based solutions, a system engineering approach to embedded system design, standards, security, the application of multicore, and virtualization. You will see some approaches to debugging, but hands-on experience is really the key to that facet of the systems development process. Hopefully, you will know what to look for in selecting a hardware platform, a software package, or intellectual property for an embedded system. Right now, 98% of processor production goes into embedded systems. You will have a new appreciation for the pervasiveness of this technology into everyday life. You are surrounded by embedded computers.

Standard platforms

The advantage of using a commodity mass-produced platform is that it is readily available and cheap. At the same time, it may need additional hardware resources, and it may not be well adapted to real-time operations. The use of industry standard interfaces such as USB further reduces costs and simplifies the design. The real-time issues may be addressed by the proper choice of operating system.

Commodity pc's

The pc platform, in a variety of form factors, is cheap and readily available. There is a wide variety of existing operating systems and software environment for this platform. A *pc* will include the CPU, memory slots, built-in cache, an interrupt and dma controller, timers, and a bus architecture. Standard I/O interfaces such as USB can be assumed. Standard pc interfaces can be re-tasked. For example, the printer port is a high speed, bidirectional parallel port, and the old joystick port is a simple analog to digital interface.

The bus structure would likely be the PCI or the faster PCI Express. Some of the smaller form factor boards (nano-ITX) do not support a bus architecture. The pc BIOS supports device initialization and functional verification, as well as bootstrap from a variety of devices.

Tablet/phone architectures trend around the Apple interface, based on the ARM hardware, or the Android market, also using ARM processors. Pc's on a chip allow for tapping the legacy pc market with hand-held devices. Non-pc small boards, using various processor architectures such as x86, ARM, Rabbit, Pic, and others, are also players.

Definitions are necessary, so we all have the same meaning in mind for the technical terms. A glossary of terms is included at the back of the book, and Wikipedia is always useful for these as well.

A *bit* is the smallest unit of binary information. It represents a yes/no, on/off, left/right type of decision. It can be represented in mathematics as the digits zero or one. Any technology that can represent two states can represent a bit. Red/green, voltage or no voltage, current or no current, light or darkness, north magnetic or south magnetic, etc. We have to be careful to distinguish between the mathematical concept of a bit (one of two possible states) and its implementation.

Also, we don't need to use base-2 for computers, but it matches the implementation in microelectronics fairly well. Early computers (and calculators) used base-10, which we use because we have ten fingers. Without the development of shoes, we may have evolved a base 20 numeric system.

The choice of a base number in mathematics will influence how easy or hard it is to manipulate the numbers. If we just want to know that we have 1 sheep, 2 sheep, or many sheep, we don't need very sophisticated math. The ancient Babylonians used a base-60 math, which survives in the way we tell time (seconds, minutes, and angles). They also had computers, abacus units designed to handle their representation. The Romans did not use a positional number system, which is why it is very hard to do long division in Roman numerals.

A *positional number system* allows us to choose a base number, and use the number digits to represent different orders of magnitude, even fractions. In Roman numerals, we have a specific symbol for fifty, and that is L. In decimal, we use "50." That is to say, 5 x 10 (the base) and 0 times 1.

We need to consider the important concept of zero, which was used in Mesoamerica, China, India, and other places. The Romans had the concept of zero, just not a specific symbol for it. The zero symbol become important in positional notation, to keep the symbols in the right place, not just to indicate that we have no sheep.

We like to use ten as a base, because we have ten fingers. Actually, we can use any number for a base. The ones of interest to use in computing are base-2 and base-16. For microelectronics, the base-2 is used, because the physics of the devices allow for representation and recognition of two different states easily and efficiently. Base-16 is for our convenience (keep telling yourself that.)

Since we like to use base 10 and computers like to use base 2, we will need to discuss how to convert numbers between these bases. That will be covered later.

Organization

We will first discuss the elements of embedded computers, the central processing unit, the memory, and the input-output. We'll review the classic fetch-execute cycle of control flow computers. Feel free to skip ahead if this is a repeat for you. In Appendices, we look at more detail on some topics such as binary system, math, and implementation of these functions in logic circuits. We also cover floating point, and vector and SIMD (single instruction, multiple data) operations and structures. Back to the mainstream, we mention dataflow architectures, and the FPGA approach, as well as parallelism.

The memory discussion includes organization and types of memory, caches, and memory management. The input/output section includes the various I/O schemes, busses, a discussion of serial versus parallel communication, a section on serial I/O and standards. We then have sections on sensors as input devices, and actuators and mechanisms as output devices.

In the software section, we discuss the concept of the instruction set architecture, and programming languages and the development process. We look at the operating system, and the boot process. We then discuss the specifics of embedded software, and optimizations.

The design process for embedded systems is presented. This applies to the overall systems architecture, with its component levels of hardware and software, and their integration. The section covers hardware/software trades, and various design methodologies unique to embedded.

So my goals here are to present embedded systems in their context of dedicated applications, and to compare and contrast them with desktop, tablet, and server systems that operate in different environments and with different requirements. There is a lot of real-world engineering captured here.

Desktops and servers can confuse your database entries, deny access to the Internet, and refuse to play your latest game or video. Embedded computers can recycle traffic lights, the electrical grid, the nuclear power plant controls, the water and sewer system, or bring down airplanes. These systems are pervasive, hidden, and often ignored. Designers and architects have to be aware of the inherent safety and security of the systems they implement. A lot of infrastructure is at risk.

If you are familiar with Computer Architecture in general, you can skip the first couple of chapters. Embedded I/O has some unique issues, though, that are discussed there. You should generally understand instruction execution and digital logic, and experience with a programming language or two would not be a bad thing.

My goals in writing this book were:

• To introduce the readers to basic concepts of embedded computing systems.

• To introduce the readers to an IDE (Integrated Design Environment) for building software for embedded systems.

• To show readers the Systems Engineering approach to design, implementation, and testing.

• To teach the readers about device interfacing and programming.

• To teach the readers to match system requirements to architectural features in the computer.

• To teach the readers to select and implement appropriate software solutions for particular required functions.

• To show the readers how to make engineering trade-offs in system implementation.

• To expose the readers to the unique design challenges of embedded robotics and space applications.

Brief list of topics to be covered:

- Embedded systems versus desktop/server architecture.
- Embedded operating systems and software design.
- Hard and soft real time systems.
- Embedded processor architecture.
- Integrated development environments.
- Sensors and actuators.
- Virtualization applicability to embedded.

- Embedded standards and security.
- Software complexity.
- Radiation effects on semiconductors and mitigation techniques.
- CPU versus FPGA versus SoC implementation approaches.
- Case studies illustrating importance of the topics.

Elements of Embedded Computers

Over the history of computing hardware, it has been observed that the number of transistors on integrated circuits doubles approximately every 18 months. This is referred to as *Moore's Law*.

The elements of an embedded computer are the standard computer architecture ones of central processing unit (CPU), memory, and Input/output. Each element will be discussed in turn. Feel free to skip ahead if you are familiar with these topics, and refer back as needed.

Central Processing Unit

A *computer* performs arithmetic and logic functions on data, and provides flow of control. The arithmetic functions we would like to have performed are additional, subtraction, multiplication, and division. Actually, as we will see later, if we can subtract, we can do any of these operations. Multiplication can merely be repeated addition. The logical operations on binary data include inversion, AND, OR, Exclusive OR, and derivative functions such as Negated-AND (NAND), Negated-OR (NOR), and Negated-Exclusive OR (NXOR). Actually, for two binary symbols, there are 16 possible functions. Only some of these have names (and are useful). As with the mathematical functions, some can be represented as combinations of others. We'll look at mathematical and logical functions applied to binary data, and how the mathematical functions can be expressed in terms of the logical ones.

The *VonNeuman Architecture* says there is no distinction between the code and the data. This was an observation by John von Neumann of the Institute for Advanced Studies at Princeton University. While consulting for the Moore School of Electrical Engineering at the University of Pennsylvania, von Neumann wrote a "First Draft of a Report on the EDVAC" (computer). The paper described a computer architecture in which the data and the program are both stored in the computer's memory in the same address space. Before this, it was the custom to have separate code and data storage (the Harvard architecture), and they were not necessarily the same size or format. Von Neumann observed that the code is also data. Most modern microprocessors are this style. For speed, especially in digital signal processors, designers revert to the older *Harvard* architecture, with separate code and data stores, as this gives a speed-up in accessing from memory. In a Harvard architecture, it is difficult to have self-modifying code, which is a good thing from the debugging standpoint.

The fetch/execute cycle

This section discusses how an instruction gets executed. The basic process is referred to as the *fetch/execute cycle*. First the instruction is fetched from memory, and then the instruction is executed, which can involve the fetching and writing of data items.

Instructions are executed in steps called *machine cycles*. Each machine cycle might take several machine clock times to complete. If the architecture is pipelined, then each machine cycle consists of a stage in the pipeline. At each step, a memory access or an internal operation (ALU operation) is performed. A state machine in the CPU logic, driven by a clock source, sequences machine cycles.

A register called the *program counter* contains the location in memory of the next instruction to be executed. The contents of the program counter get automatically updated as the instruction executes. The address of the next instruction to be executed (not necessarily the next adjacent instruction) is put in the program counter. A *register* is a temporary holding memory for data, and is part of the CPU. At initialization time (boot), the program counter is loaded with the location of the first instruction to be executed.

After that, it is simply incremented, unless there is a change in the flow of control, such as a branch or jump. In this case, the target address of the branch or jump is put into the program counter.

The first step of the instruction execution is to fetch the instruction from memory into a special holding location called the *Instruction Register*. At this point, the instruction is decoded, meaning a control unit figures out, from the bit pattern, what the instruction is to do. This control unit implements the *ISA*, the instruction set architecture. Without getting too complicated, we could have a flexible control unit that could execute different ISA's. That's possible, but beyond the scope of our discussion here.

With the instruction decode complete, the machine knows what resources are required for instruction execution. A typical math instruction, for example, would require two data reads from memory, an Arithmetic Logic Unit (ALU) operation, and a data write. The data items might be in registers, or memory. If the instruction stream is regular, we can pipeline the operation. We have stages in the pipeline for instruction fetch, instruction decode, operand(s) read, ALU operation, and operand write. If we have a long string of math operations, at some point, each stage in the pipeline is busy, and an instruction is completed at each clock cycle. But, if a particular instruction requires the result of a previous instruction as an input, the scheme falls apart, and the pipeline *stalls*. This is called a *dependency*, and can be addressed by having the compiler optimizing the code by re-ordering. This doesn't always work. When a change in the flow of control occurs (branch, jump, interrupt), the pipeline has to be *flushed* out and refilled. On the average, the pipeline speeds up the process of executing instructions at the cost of complexity.

A special purpose hardware device, purpose-built, will always be faster than a general-purpose device programmed or configured for a specific task. This means that purpose-built hardware is the best, yet least flexible choice. Programmability provides flexibility, and reduces the cost of change. A new approach, provided by *FPGA* technology, gives us the ability to reconfigure the hardware and well as the software.

The optimization might be in a different data type, floating point or vector data as opposed to integers, or in the types of operations required.

Besides the integer processor, we can have a specialized floating point unit (FPU) that operates on floating point operands, or other specialized architectures.

Microcontrollers

A microcontroller is a simple CPU plus some memory and input-output. The idea is to have a single-chip solution to minimize costs. Microcontrollers are not used as general number crunchers, but in dedicated control applications such as elevators, gas pumps, and cell phones.

Where the modern CPU would include several levels of cache memory and multiple computer cores because the fabrication technology would support that level of complexity, a microcontroller would contain the cpu(s) memory, and I/O to support a single chip solution. This simplifies the rest of the system design, and reduces the parts count, which leads to lower costs.

Graphics Processing Unit (GPU)

A GPU is a specialized computer architecture to manipulate image data at high rates. It can be a single chip, or incorporated with a general purpose CPU. The GPU devices are highly parallel, and specifically designed to handle image data, and operations on that data. They do this much fastest than a programmed general purpose CPU. Most desktop machines have the GPU function on a video card or integrated with their CPU. Originally, GPU's were circuit card based. GPU operations are very memory intensive. The GPU design is customized to SIMD type operations.

The instruction set of the GPU is specific to graphics operations on block data. The requirements were driven by the demands of 2-D and 3-D video games on pc's, phones, tablets, and dedicated gaming units. As GPU units became faster and more capable, they began to consume more power (and thus generate more heat) than the associated CPU's.

Although designed to process video data, some GPU's have been used as adjunct data processors and accelerators in other areas involving vectors and matrices, such as the inverse discrete cosine transform. Types of higher-level processing implemented by GPU's include texture mapping, polygon rendering, object rotation, and coordination system transformation. They also support object shading operations, data oversampling, and interpolation. GPU's find a major application area in video decoding. Building on this, GPU's enable advanced features in digital cameras such as facial recognition, or eye tracking.

Vector Processor

Vector processing involves the processing of vectors of related data, in a *SIMD* (single-instruction, multiple-data) mode. For example, vector addition is an SIMD operation.

SIMD refers to a class of parallel computers that perform the same operations on multiple data items simultaneously. This is data level parallelism, which is found in multimedia (video and audio) data used in gaming applications. The SIMD approach evolved from the vector supercomputers of the 1970's, which operated upon a vector of data with a single operation. Sun Microsystems introduced SIMD operations in their SPARC architecture in 1995. A popular application of SIMD architecture is Intel's MMX (Multimedia Extensions) instruction set circa 1996 for the X-86 architecture.

In photography, the resolution of digital cameras exceeds that of film. The embedded processors in digital cameras enabled other features such as autofocus, auto-exposure, eye tracking, and faster image capture, comparable to and exceeding that for high definition movies. Using standard operating environments such as Android allow image manipulation software ("Photoshop") to be run on the camera itself.

Digital Signal Processor

Digital signal processors resemble computers in many ways, and come in embedded versions. They handle specialized data types, and include special-purpose operations derived from the digital signal processing realm. This includes the Multiply-and-Add (mac), a digital filtering primitive. Digital signal processing finds application with the processing of audio and video data. DSP for audio evolved from sonar processing, and video data processing evolved from radar.

A Digital Signal Processor (DSP) is similar to a general purpose CPU, but provides specialized operations for DSP-type operations on specialized data formats. Originally, the DSP function would be implemented by software running in a CPU. DSP operations usually have time deadline constraints (hard real time requirements).

Mobile phones and cable modems, to name two examples, drove the development of faster, dedicated hardware units. The first practical commercial product based on a DSP chip was Texas Instrument's Speak-n-Spell toy. Before that, the military applications of sonar and radar data processing drove the technology.

The nature of digital domain signal data and filtering in the digital domain require some unique architectural features. Hardware modulo addressing and bit-reversed addressing is used in digital filtering. Operations on data tend to be SIMD. The *Multiply-Accumulate* primitive is the basis for digital filter implementation. Saturation arithmetic is used to prevent overflow. Both fixed point and floating point data are used. A three-memory Harvard architecture allows simultaneous access of an opcode and two operands.

Multicore chips for DSP are now common. These fast DSP's have enabled new technologies and applications such as software-defined radio.

An illustrative device is Analog Devices' Blackfin series of embedded DSP's. These chips are supported by real-time operating systems. The Blackfin is a 32-bit RISC processor with dual 16-bit multiply/accumulate (MAC) units, and provision for 8-bit video processing in real-time.

Some ARM chips such as the Cortex-8 family, and the OMAP3 processors include both a general purpose CPU, and a DSP.

Viterbi Processor

A *Viterbi decoder* is used on a bit stream that has been encoded using a convolutional code for error correction to achieve reliable data transfer. The technique was developed by Andrew Viterbi in the late 1960's. Convolution codes operate close to the theoretical Shannon limit, although better codes have been developed. Viterbi encoded data is used with modems and hard drives, among other devices. It is applicable to speech recognition.

Originally implemented in software on a general purpose CPU, and later on DSP's, Viterbi-specific hardware chips are now available.

An example hardware instantiation is the Texas Instruments TMS320C6418 DSP chip, with Viterbi coprocessor. The chip has 0.5 megabyte of level 2 cache included with a DSP CPU, and the Viterbi unit. The DSP can achieve rates of 2.4 billion multiply-accumulate operations per second. The chip includes two serial ports, two audio ports, dual I^{2}C control ports, and the memory interface.

RISC and MultiCore

RISC approaches apply across the spectrum of computing. In RISC, instructions execute in one cycle. RISC machines tend to have a small instruction set, and complex instructions are built up from primitive ones. This follows the observation that, generally, the simple instructions are the most frequently used and the more complex instructions less so. The use of the RISC technique began around 1990, and has become mainstream. It evolved out of a time when memory was an expensive asset, and memory utilization was an issue.

Decoding instructionMicrocontrollers and addressing modes are a major bottleneck to speed, so simplified instruction encoding and few data addressing modes are preferable.

Single cycle execution improves interrupt latency and response determinism. A load/store architecture will have many on-chip registers to hold data currently in use. A RISC CPU is tightly coupled to memory, and achieves a high data bandwidth with a sophisticated cache. Instruction execution is pipelined. Instruction decoding is streamlined because there are fewer instructions, and they are relatively simple, with perhaps a single address mode.

Here's the top-level approach to a RISC implementation. Eliminate all instructions that can't execute in 1 clock cycle. Move complexity from hardware to software. Add more hardware, as feasible, to include more complex instructions. There are no "subroutines" or loops at the machine language level allowed. Don't slow down the majority of instructions for the minority.

The 90/10 rule says that about 90% of real code is simple instructions, such as load/store, alu ops, etc. Not much can be done to speed up the remaining 10% of complex instructions.

The instructions/task metric is low for CISC; high for RISC; i.e., RISC uses more instructions to get the job done, but they are faster instructions. Non-RISC instructions get more done, per instruction. For example, the string compare instruction in the IA-32 architecture is actually a loop in microcode. Since instructions usually have to complete before an interrupt can be recognized, these worst-case instructions interfere with or preclude real-time operation.

The Performance Equation

The amount of time to execute any particular piece of software can be expressed as:

$$T = N * C * 1/f$$

Where T = time required, N = number of instructions, C = clock cycles per instruction, and f is the clock frequency for the processor. The term instruction here refers to the number of machine instructions. An expression in a higher-level language can result in many machine instructions. Usually, an assembly language instruction maps directly to a machine instruction.

To minimize the time taken to do a software task, we can reduce N, reduce C, or increase f.

Increases in the clock frequency, and the frequency of operation of the hardware come with advances in technology, and can be assumed. There are numerous architectural approaches to reduce C, and the goal of the RISC approach is to reduce this term to 1. Unfortunately, this usually means a corresponding increase in N, the number of instructions to accomplish a task.

If we have very simple instructions, we may need more of them to accomplish a task. Simple instructions are easy to streamline and speed up by a variety of techniques. Some tasks are very difficult to reduce to the point of taking one cycle; the multiply and divide for example. Some tasks inherently need time to complete, particularly those with loops. Consider the block move instructions in the IA-32 architecture (sometimes called a software DMA). Here we have one instruction, N=1, but it can take hundreds of cycles to complete (C = 100's). Unless we have enough hardware to move hundreds of data items simultaneously, this is a problem. We can always throw more hardware at it. As technology rides the exponential complexity law, termed Moore's law, we have more hardware to work with. But we have to be clever about how this hardware is managed at run time.

Some RISC approaches to enhance speed of execution:

Load-Store Architecture

In a load-store architecture, memory is only accessed by a Load instruction (Read from memory), or a Store instruction (write to memory). All of the operational instructions (math, logical, etc.) operate only on data in registers.

Superscalar

The superscalar approach to instruction execution involves parallelism. It allows for execution of more than a single instruction per clock cycle, by using additional hardware to implement additional function units such as the ALU or multiplier. Multiple instructions at time are fetched and fed to separate execution pipelines. Additional hardware is required to check for data dependencies at runtime. In the case of a branch or change in the flow of control, the assumption of sequential execution is no longer met, and pipelines and other resources have to be reloaded. The superscalar approach dates from Cray's CDC 6600 machine in 1965. Superscalar was a natural fit for RISC architectures, and essentially all CPU's since 1998 on are superscalar.

Since the superscalar approach involves multiple parallel functional units, a key feature is the instruction dispatcher, which decides where the next instruction to be executed goes. The goal is to keep all of the hardware busy, all of the time. The sustained execution rate, without changes in context, is more than 1 instruction per clock. The performance depends on the intrinsic parallelism in the instruction stream; some sequences of instructions cannot be optimized. This is referred to as instruction-level parallelism. Sometimes, this can be corrected at the compiler level by instruction reordering. Branches and other changes in the flow of control are a problem.

As the level of hardware parallelism increases from 2 to 4 to greater, the cost of checking dependencies greatly increases. This is a cost in hardware. The practical limit to the number of simultaneously executing instructions is bounded by the complexity of checking dependencies, and is currently around six instructions.

In the limit, a multicore processor is superscalar, but the processors are not executing from the same instruction stream, and the entire CPU architecture is replicated, not just functional units within a CPU.

Scoreboarding

Scoreboarding is a technique to manage multiple resources such as pipelines, registers, and ALU's, to support dynamic scheduling. It was first used on the circa-1964 CDC 6400 mainframe. The technique implements a series of data tables that indicate the current use of resources. Resources can be idle, busy, or available. The hardware monitors the resources, and uses the next available resource for the currently executing instruction.

Speculative execution

In speculative execution, the CPU may proceed simultaneously down both paths of a data dependent branch (taken and non-taken) until the result is known, at which point one path of execution can be discarded. This takes additional hardware and resources, but saves time. Speculative execution reduces the time-cost of conditional branches. Branch prediction can also be used, and a history of branch addresses can be kept in a queue.

Register Windows

This technique was developed to optimize the performance of procedure calls, and was implemented in the Berkeley 32-bit SPARC architecture. It also found use in the AMD's 29k and Intel's i960.

Registers are a key resource, particularly in a load-store architecture. The allocation of registers dynamically at run time is the issue addressed by the concept of register windows. Registers are score-boarded. In the Berkeley design, only 8 registers are visible to the running program, out of a total of 64 available. The set of 64 is called the register file, and a set of 8 is called a register window. They are allocated as windows, and only 8 items (windows of registers) are tracked, not 64 (registers). Registers windows are a type of stack data cache.

In the AMD 29k, the windows could be of variable size. The SPARC architecture increased the number of register windows as technology allowed.

Other RISC techniques include:

Out-of-order execution is used as an approach to increase the work being done per clock cycle. Instructions are selected to be executed not necessarily in program order, but rather in the order that the associated data is available. This minimizes idle time in the CPU, and is an outgrowth of the dataflow approach in computer architecture. The first out-of-order RISC microprocessor was the floating-point unit of IBM's POWER-1, in 1990. It was also applied in the Intel PentiumPro, AMD K5, the PowerPC 601, SPARC64, Dec Alpha 21264, and MIPS R10000. The cost of out-of-order execution is increased complexity in the logic. The technique became mainstream around 1995.

The out-of-order approach relies on being able to find operations that have their associated operands ready. Read-after-write conflicts, branching, and interrupts complicate it. Sometimes, a pipeline stall is unavoidable. The logical ordering of the instructions has to be kept, to produce the correct results. Out of order processing has its best benefits when the pipeline is expanded. Register renaming is also used to support out-of-order execution. This technique maps the physical registers to a virtual register set.

Pipeline

We can break up instructions into sub steps, such as fetch opcode, decode, fetch operands, alu operations, and write result, with the idea of increasing throughput. In a pipeline architecture, more instructions are completed every clock time than in a simple architecture, where only one instruction is completed. This takes additional hardware, and complexity, to accomplish. Essentially parallel hardware allows for simultaneous sub-steps. More stages in the pipeline (the "superpipeline") require a lot more hardware, but vastly increases throughput. The Pentium-4 implemented a 20-stage pipeline. Ideally, a pipelined processor can fetch and complete an instruction every clock cycle. During the processing of an instruction, if the instruction has to wait for some item or results, the pipeline stalls as its steady-state flow is interrupted. This is called a bubble in the pipeline; essentially a pipeline NOP. Out-of-order execution of instructions can prevent bubbles from happening. Changes in the flow of control, due to a branch or interrupt disrupt the smooth functioning of the pipeline, and cause the pipeline to be reloaded. Conditional branches, where the path is not determined until the instruction has executed, are a particular problem. Sometimes this is addressed by speculative execution, which uses additional hardware to simultaneously follow both paths of the branch, until the results are known, at which point one path is discarded. Branch prediction techniques are also applied. The downside of a pipelined processor is that it may be difficult to determine exact latency in the case of interrupts, which is needed in a hard real time environment.

Within the pipeline, operand fetch and store are also problematic, as they involve memory operations, which are slower that the CPU. RISC architectures tend to employ a load/store approach, where registers can be loaded rom or stored to memory, but arithmetic and logical operations only operate on data in registers, which share silicon with the CPU.

Microcode

RISC machines tend to avoid microcode, and instead use hardwired instruction decode by combinatorial logic for speed. In a microcoded system, the instruction opcode is applied to a special read-only memory, and the sub-steps in the execution are read from the memory. This approach has the advantage that the instruction set can be extended to add new instructions, by extending the microcode. But it is not faster than using simple logic and state machines, producing a "hardwired" instruction set. Complexity in the instruction set, such as complex addressing modes, complicate the instruction decode. Above the microcode level is the "programmer-visible" level. If microcode is used, the decoding rom is referred to as the control store, and its contents define how instructions are executed. It is possible to have more than one interpretation (ISA) if the hardware allows it. The microcode concept goes back to the 1947 IBM Whirlwind computer.

Parallelism

The limitations to computer performance tend to be either the instruction rate of the cpu itself, or the channel capacity of the various data paths involved. One approach to increased performance is parallelism.

Multiprocessing allows us to apply the resources of multiple cpu's and their associated memory's to a single problem. If one cpu is fast, aren't more faster? Maybe.

Symmetric multiprocessing (SMP) involves multiple integral processor units with a common memory, and sharing an operating system. Processors are interconnected with busses, a mesh, point-point, or other communications methods. The bottleneck to scalability becomes the bandwidth of the interconnect. Mesh schemes avoid this bottleneck, at the cost of complexity, and can provide near linear scalability. The trick is in the programming. Different programming philosophies are required in the multiprocessing environment. If the problem is "embarrassingly parallel," it will scale in terms of the number of resources applied. Pathological non-parallel problems do not scale across multiple resources. Support for SMP is required at the operating systems level, and visibility of the parallelism is necessary at the language level. There is a required paradigm shift on the part of programmers, from the sequential, one thing at a time world, to the parallel, simultaneous approach.

The symmetric part of the architecture allows any processor to be assigned any task. The alternative is to have groups of different architectures, each optimized to a different data structure or task set. In SMP, tasks can be moved around for load balancing.

Up to about eight processors, a shared bus architecture can work well. Newer schemes use *NUMA*, non-uniform memory access, which allocates different sections of memory to different processors. Processor accesses to local memory are fast, and to another processor's memory more costly in time. Clustered multiprocessing makes use of large groups of commodity computing resources linked with a common operating system designed for the environment. If the multiprocessor is on one chip, we have multicore.

Some performance enhancements come from the architecture of the multiprocessor. For example, interrupt processing can be offloaded to a non-busy cpu. One issue is how interrupts are handled in multiprocessing. How are interrupts steered to the proper processor? It is a function of the operating system. In the same way that processes are assigned to certain processors, interrupts and their associated interrupt handling are also assigned. Binding interrupts to specific cpu's is not necessarily the proper approach, since this does not improves hits in cache memory. Multiple interrupts can overload the selected processor. Handling interrupts is a task, and task allocation is a function of the operating system. A multiprocessing operating system is required to manage the unique issues of multiprocessor hardware.

Another issue is cache coherency. In multicore architectures, each CPU core may have its own L1 cache, but share L2 caches with other cores. Local data in the L1 caches must be consistent with data in other L1 caches. If one core changes a value in cache due to a write operation, that data needs to be changed in other caches as well (if they hold the same item).

This problem is well known from the field of multiprocessing. The issues can be addressed by several mechanisms. In cache snooping, each cache monitors the others for changes. If a change in value is seen, the local cached copy is invalidated. This means it will have to be re-accessed from the next level before use. A global directory of cached data can also be maintained. Protocols for cache coherency include MSI, MESI, and others.

A *multicore processor* has multiple cpu and memory elements in a single chip. Being on a single chip reduces the communications times between elements, and allows for multiprocessing. Advances in microelectronics fabrication techniques lead to the implementation of multicores for desktop and server machines around 2007. It was becoming increasingly difficult to increase clock speeds, so the obvious approach was to turn to parallelism. Currently, in this market, quad-core, 6-core, and 8-core chips are available. Besides additional cpu's, additional on-chip memory must be added, usually in the form of memory caches, to keep the processors fed with instructions and data. There is no inherent difference in multicore architectures and multiprocessing with single core chips, except in the speed of communications. The standard interconnect technologies are applied to inter-core communications.

We can compare multicore devices to large parallel machines of some 10 years past, in the same sense that we can compare a single-chip cpu to large mainframe systems of 20-25 years ago. The architecture is similar, but the implementation is different due to changing technologies.

Multicore techniques are now being applied to embedded processors as well. This enables some techniques that were not previously available. In the embedded world, the cores do not necessarily need to be the same. Actually, this technique was used when to Intel floating point co-processor, the 80387, was incorporated onto the same chip as the integer processor, the 80386, in the design of the follow-on 80486 chip. Today, multiple integer cores can share the same silicon substrate with specialized floating point, digital signal and vector processing, and specialized media and video engines. The individual cores can implement superscalar, super-pipelined, or other optimization techniques. Essentially, we will shortly have a MIMD (multiple instruction, multiple data) parallel processing chip for embedded applications. Nothing is ever free, though. The challenge will be in the programming.

The latest ARM architecture for embedded supports multicore (currently, up to 8-core) 64-bit devices. Both symmetrical and asymmetrical implementations are included. Putting a lot of cores on a single substrate is challenging, and getting them to work together co-operatively and non-intrusively is difficult. The CoreLink cache coherent interconnect system, for use in multicore applications, is one emerging solution. Some problems are inherently parallelizable, but most are not. Not many problem domains scale linearly with the amount of computing horsepower available. Such *embarrassingly parallel* applications are rarely of practical interest.

FPGA and SOC

Field Programmable Gate Arrays are integrated circuits that are programmable or configurable at the hardware level. The devices are ideal for high density embedded designs. This configuration defines the interconnect between standard logic blocks on the device. The logic blocks can also be configurable. The device can be set up to be programmed once, or capable of being programmed multiple times. In the limit, the device can be reconfigured on the fly, as it is operating. An FPGA gives us configurable instead of fixed hardware. With a traditional CPU, we have fixed hardware from the manufacturer that we can direct with a software program in terms of operations on data, and the sequence of these operations. We can have data-dependent branches. With an FPGA, we have "programmable" or configurable hardware as well. Each reconfiguration results in a new and different architecture.

FPGA's consist of millions of logic gates. They are easily modified, and design changes have a small NRE cost. One can implement a CPU on an FPGA. This may not be the most efficient approach. Most of the designs involve the use of standard library components, or purchased or open source *IPC* – Intellectual Property Cores.

IP Cores are design files allowing for instantiation of standard components in an ASIC or FPGA. A large market has developed in the marketing and licensing of IP Cores. The advantage of the IP Core from a reputable source is the standardized design file that has been verified. Cores for I/O functions and complete processors are available. Cores can contain both analog and digital functions. Open source IP cores are available. These allow for modification of the design. The ARM processor, among others, is available as an IP core.

With an FPGA, we can match the architecture to the problem in a better way than applying a commodity CPU. For example, the input data format might require 13 bits. We can do this job with a 16-bit machine, or we can build a 13-bit ALU in the FPGA.

An *ASIC*, or Application Specific Integrated Circuit, gives us the ability to design and have fabricated a complex logic circuit. The design tools and simulator can be hosted on desktop tools, and we send the design tool to a semiconductor fabrication service. In return, we get packaged chips. The design better be right, as the cost of a design change in terms of dollars and time is high. The *non-recurring engineering* (NRE) can range into the hundreds of thousands of dollars. The advantage of the ASIC is that we get a custom hardware design for our particular problem. It is possible to include analog parts as well as digital. The ASIC will be purpose-built for the particular application. Complexity levels of 100 million gates have been achieved. Mixed-signal ASIC's permit both analog and digital devices on the same substrate. Standard design tools allow for output of design files to fabrication services such as *MOSIS* (Metal Oxide Semiconductor Implementation Service).

The ASIC is designed specifically for the application, and is "lean and mean," not containing anything else. The functionality is captured in a Hardware Description Language. An AISC can implement a CPU as part of its structure. With complexity at this level, the ASIC may be referred to a *System-on-Chip* (SoC) architecture. It can contain hundreds of millions of logic gates.

In mechanical terms, the ASIC represents a system cut from a single piece of metal. The FPGA would represent the same system constructed from standardized components and fasteners.

ASIC's have been around since the 1980's. Large libraries of functions have been developed that are purchasable or available in open source. Standard cells are used in the implementation, ensuring known and well-characterized devices.

Generally, FPGA's are slower and less energy efficient than ASIC's, but that is changing as FPGA technology matures.

For an FPGA or ASIC, with an embedded CPU core, the final device will be a chip on a board, so both the chip design and the board design need to be captured. The chip design pinout will influence the board design.

If the ASIC or FPGA includes a CPU core, there will be associated software. This development process is identical to that of any software programmable device, and is illustrated on the top of the diagram. We produce code in a higher-level language such as c, using library routines for common functions. Some assembly language may be included in-line or as separate modules. These are linked together into one software load of binary executable code.

We need a new word for the configuration information for the FPGA or ASIC. The preferred word is *configware*. It is not hardware, software, or firmware. The configware captures the device configuration. It is possible to translate c code to configware, essentially, compiling a program into hardware. This process is not always successful, and fails to exploit the inherent parallelism of the hardware, because of the lack of parallelism in the language. The hardware can also be specified directly in a hardware description language such as *VHDL* (Very High Level Design language). From this description, a synthesizer software tool produces a place-and-route description of the chip. FPGAs particularly use standardized logic blocks or modules, at a level of complexity above the gate level. The configuration of these modules, and their interconnect, is captured, as well as the I/O connection to the device's pins. This results in a binary file, akin to the binary machine language file from the software process. At this point, we have a definition of the synthesized hardware.

From the pinout of the device, we can design a printed circuit board (pcb) to hold the chips, using industry standard board layout tools. We also do a power and signal integrity analysis at this level.

This gives us an implementable design that is electrically and physically correct. From the pcb layout files, we can get a board manufactured.

VHDL code can be used to design the hardware of the chip for instantiation into a manufactured ASIC. This has a high NRE cost. We can also define a One-Time Configurable (OTC) FPGA target. Most interestingly, we can target a reconfigurable FPGA, which we can program at our own development facility. What is important to realize is that the device can also be reconfigured dynamically. If the ASIC is like ROM, then the FPGA is like flash. The software-based tools that produce software code from higher-level abstractions are called compilers. The software-based tools that produce configuration files from higher-level abstractions are called synthesizers.

The reconfiguration property is critical – reconfigurable FPGA's give us the ability to change the basic computing structure even on the fly. This opens new capabilities, but brings along with it a level of complexity that must be considered. If self-modifying code is a difficult concept, self-modifying hardware is even more so.

A system-on-chip (SoC) approach includes the processor, memory, and I/O on a single substrate. These may also be on different die in the same package. Analog and radio frequency parts can be included. The SoC is a "one-chip" solution. As semiconductor manufacturing technology advances, more functionality can be provided on a single chip. An alternative approach is the System in a Package (SiP), which integrates multiple chips in one package.

Most SOC design starts with IP cores and hardware blocks that are pre-qualified and tested. These can be combined in the design with memory cores, and specific I/O cores such as USB and CAN. Each core IP comes with its own license terms and restrictions. SOC's can be fabricated as full custom chips, in standard cells, and in FPGA's. The non-recurring engineering costs are higher for the

SOC approach, but it can result in a highly optimized design in terms of space, power, and reliability. Standard cell libraries are readily available. These have the advantage of having been tested in silicon, and target specific foundry's and processes.

An example of an ARM-based SOC is the Apple A5, used in the iPad-2 and iPhone-4S. This is an ARM V7 architecture, with the chip fabricated by Samsung. It can use a single or dual cpu core, and has dual L1 and L2 cache. It includes the NEON SIMD accelerator operating at 1 GHz, a custom image signal processor for face recognition, and 512 Mbytes of memory.

Memory in embedded

Parkinson's law: "in computers, programs expand to fill all available memory."

Embedded systems, although usually resource constrained, can make use of commodity static and dynamic random access memory (ram).

It is unusual to find mass storage in embedded systems, but it can certainly be included. This includes magnetic and solid state disks to hold large data sets. This storage can be made removable. Non-volatile RAM, such as battery-backed static memory can also be used.

There are many types of memory used with the current cpu's. Most memory types are supported, if the word sizes and timing match. There is a small amount of memory on the CPU chip itself. This would be the various registers, and in later versions of the chip, some cache memory. Most of the primary memory is placed on the same circuit board as the cpu, and can be soldered in place, or can take the form of plug-in modules. This memory is random-access. Some of it will be persistent, read-only memory, but more will be read-write, volatile memory. Secondary memory, with rotating magnetic disks, may be used along with optical disks for large offline storage. *Flash memory*, a type of persistent storage, is coming down in cost and up in capacity, and can be considered an alternative to disks. Non-volatile memory retains its contents without applied power.

Computer memory is organized in a hierarchy. We would like to have large amounts of low-power, fast, non-volatile storage. These requirements are mutually exclusive. The memory closest to the CPU is fast, random-access, volatile, and semiconductor-based, but expensive. Secondary storage, such as disk or flash, is slower, cheaper, persistent, and cheaper on a cost-per-bit basis. Backup storage, offline optical or magnetic, is still cheaper per bit, but may have a long access time.

Other characteristics of interest include memory latency, the time it takes to access the requested item, and throughput, the read or write rate of the memory device. Some memory may have a relatively slow latency, but a very high throughput, once things get going.

All-in-all, we have come a long way since computers stored bits as acoustic waves in a pool of mercury, and instructions were punched into paper tape.

RAM

In *RAM*, random access memory, any element accessible in the same clock time, as opposed to sequential media, such a tape or a disk. In *sequential media*, the access time varies, and depends on the order of access. This is true for disks, where the data item requested probably just went by the read heads, and another rotation of the platter is required. Of course, mechanical systems, in operation, tend to wear out due to mechanical causes.
A memory can be considered as a black-box with two functions, read and write. With the write function, we present the memory

with two inputs: the data item, and an address. There is no output. The memory associated the data item with the address and remembers it. On the read function, we present the memory with the address, and expect to get back the data item previously associated with it.

Other design choices in memory include volatility. The memory may forget after a period of time. That's not good. Although, depending on the timing, the data can be read out and written back just in time. More complicated, but cheaper.

Is there such a thing as totally non-volatile memory? One of the earliest memory types, magnetic core, was persistent when the power was turned off. It is unclear how long the data was retained. When compact disks, an optical media, first came out, the advertised lifetime was reported as 100 years. This has since been reduced, with some cd's and dvd's becoming unreadable in a period of several years. (A dvd is a cd with a greater capacity, because the wavelength of the laser light used is smaller, so the bits are smaller). If you want to see persistent color graphical information, the cave paintings at Lascaux in France are more than 17,000 years old, and still maintain their meaning. Magnetic hard disks do not forget their contents when the power is turned off. If they are properly stored, and not exposed to bumps, magnetic fields, and extremes of temperature, they seem to have the best data retention characteristics of currently available media. Exchangeable floppy disks have alignment problems in their readers, and magnetic and optical tape drives use a fragile media that is susceptible to damage and environmental effects.

Volatile memory includes static semiconductor ram and dynamic ram. Static ram uses a flip-flop architecture, and retains its contents as long as the power remains. Static ram is faster, less dense, and consumes more power than dynamic ram. *Dynamic RAM* is denser, usually by a power of 4, due to a simpler structure, but requires refresh. It forgets in fractions of a second, because the information is stored as a charge on a capacitor, which leaks away. Why would anyone use this as a storage media? It is cheap, easily mass-produced, the "forget" time is eons to a computer chip, and the overhead of the refresh operation is minimal. The CPU usually does the refresh, because the memory is not usable during that time. The memory can be organized into sections, so a refresh in one section still allows access in others. Some DRAM is self-refreshing. In the IBM-pc architecture, a fake-dma is used to signal a refresh operation in progress. .

Non-volatile memory includes various types of read-only memory, and battery-backed static ram, which has a life of several years, depending on the battery source.

Even *read-only memory* is written at least at once. Actually, a ROM (read-only memory) can be manufactured with a specific pattern of 1's and 0's built in. For prototyping, various types of programmable read-only memory are used. These can be written and erased multiple times. Earlier, ultraviolet light was used to erase the devices to an all-1's state. These chips had glass windows. Later, the contents became reprogrammable or alterable with higher voltage levels, and could be modified in-circuit. Both the *ultraviolet-erasable* versions (UV-PROM's) and the *Electrically alterable* forms (EEProms) tended to forget over a period of years. Before this phenomenon was understood, these types of parts were included in deployed systems that failed in later use. The early IBM AT's BIOS was one example, and similar embedded systems were used for subway fare card machines.

The follow-on to this is *flash memory*. Flash can be programmed in-circuit, and is random-access for read. To write flash, a block is erased to "1", and selected bits are written to "0". The write operation is slower than the read. In addition, although the device can be read indefinitely, there is an upper limit to the number of times it can be written. This is on the order of a million times in current technology, but this can be accomplished in under a second with the wrong application. Flash memory does wear out.

Write-only memory is of no particular interest.

Memory organization

Semiconductor memory, like all microelectronics, is a 2-dimensional structure. Thus, density usually goes up by a factor of four, as we double the width and the height. Memory is a very regular structure, amenable to mass production.

In random access memory we address bytes, or words. We get a collection of bits every time we read memory. To address individual bits within a word, we need to use the logical operations (AND, OR) within the alu to single out bits within a word.

Caches

This section discusses the concept of a cache in generic computer architecture terms. A *cache* is a temporary memory buffer for data. It is placed between the processor and the main memory. The cache is smaller, but faster than the main memory. Being faster, it is more expensive, so it serves as a transition to the main store. They may be several levels of cache (L1, L2, L3), the one closest to the processor having the highest speed, commensurate to the processor. That closest to the main memory has a lower speed, but is still faster than the main memory. The cache has faster access times, and becomes valuable when items are accessed multiple times. Cache is transparent to the user; it has no specific address. Temporary tables keep track of the mapping.

There can be different caches for instructions and data, or a unified cache for both. Code is usually accessed in linear fashion, but data items are not. In a running program, the code cache is never written, simplifying its design. The nature of accessing for instructions and data is different. On a read access, if the desired item is present in a cache, we get a cache hit, and the item is read. If the item is not in cache, we get a cache miss, and the item must be fetched from memory. There is a small additional time penalty in this process over going directly to memory (in the case of a miss). Cache works because, on the average, we will have the desired item in cache most of the time, by design.

Cache reduces the average access time for data, but will increase the worst-case time. The size and organization of the cache defines the performance for a given program. The proper size and organization is the subject of research.

Caches introduce indeterminacy into execution time. With cache, memory access time is no longer deterministic. We can't tell, a priori, if an item is or is not in cache. This can be a problem in real-time systems.

A *working set* is a set of memory locations used by a program in a certain time interval. This can refer to code or data. Ideally, the working set is in cache. The cache stores not only the data item, but also a tag, which identifies where the item is from in main memory. Advanced systems can mark ranges of items in memory as non-cacheable, meaning they are only used once, and don't need to take up valuable cache space.

For best performance, we want to keep frequently accessed locations in fast cache. Also, cache retrieves more than one word at a time; it retrieves a "line" of data, which can vary in size. Sequential accesses are faster after an initial access (both in cache and regular memory) because of the overhead of set-up times.

Writing data back to cache does not necessarily get it to main memory right away. With a *write-through* cache, we do immediately copy the written item to main memory. With a *write-*

back cache, we write to main memory only when a location is removed from the cache.

Many locations can map onto the same cache block. Conflict misses are easy to generate: If array A uses locations 0, 1, 2, ... and array b uses locations 1024, 1025, 1026, ..., the operation a[i] + b[i] generates conflict misses in a cache of size 1024.

Caches, then, provide a level of performance increase at the cost of complexity due to temporal or spatial locality of the data. The program is not aware of the location of the data, whether it is in cache or main memory. The only indication is the run time of the program. This can be an issue in real-time embedded.

Cache hierarchy

This includes the L1, L2, L3 caches. L1 is the smallest and fastest cache, located closest to the cpu, usually on the same chip. It is implemented in zero-wait-state static ram. Level 2 cache usually operates in burst mode. Some cpu's have all three levels on chip. Each of the levels of cache is a different size and organization, and has different policies, to optimize performance at that point. It is a cost issue and silicon real-estate issue.

A key parameter of cache is the *replacement policy*. The replacement policy strategy is for choosing which cache entry to overwrite to make room for a new data. There are two popular strategies: random, and least-recently used (LRU). In random, we simply choose a location, write the data back to main memory, and refill the cache from the new desired location. In the *least recently used* scenario, the hardware keeps track of cache accesses, and chooses the least recently used item to swap out.

As long as the hardware keeps track of access, it can keep track of writes to the cache line. If the line has not been written into, it is the same as the items in memory, and a write-back operation is not required. The flag that keeps track of whether the cache line has been written into is called the *dirty bit*. This book thus does discuss the dirty bits of computer architecture.

Note that we are talking about cache as implemented in random access memory of varying speeds. The concept is the same for memory swapped back and forth to rotating disk; what was called virtual memory in mainframes.

Cache organization

In a *fully-associative cache*, any memory location can be stored anywhere in the cache. This form is almost never implemented. In a *direct-mapped cache*, each memory location maps onto exactly one cache entry. In an *N-way set-associative cache*, each memory location can go into one of n sets. Direct mapped cache has the best hit times. Fully associative cache has the lowest miss rates.

TLB

The *Translation Lookaside Buffer* (TLB) is a cache used to expedite the translation of virtual to physical memory address. It holds pairs of virtual and translated (physical addresses). If the required translation is present (meaning it was done recently), the process is speeded up.

Caches have a direct effect on performance and determinacy, but the system designer does not always have a choice, when the caches are incorporated as part of the cpu. In this case, the system designer needs to review the cache design choices to ensure it is commensurate with the problem being address by the system.

Memory Management

Virtual memory is an abstraction. We pretend we have more memory than is available in the system, but we only see a portion of this memory at a given time. The contents of the physical memory that we do have are managed by hardware, and are swapped in and out from secondary storage. Data is transferred in blocks. The program can be written without worrying about how much memory is available. Actually, if we add more physical memory, the systems will run faster, because fewer swaps are required.

A *memory management unit* (MMU) translates memory addresses from logical/virtual to physical. This adds an overhead of translation to each memory access. In addition, the access time for the secondary storage may be a million times slower than for the primary memory, but it will be 100's of times larger, and certainly cheaper. There is also the energy consumption issue.

When the CPU accesses a desired item, it may be present in the memory, or not. If not, the process generates a Page fault, resulting in an interrupt, with a request for accessing the data item not currently resident. This requires clever programming to be an efficient process. Too many misses, and the process bogs down in overhead.

The scheme requires data structures to keep track of what range of data addresses is actually present in memory, and registers or tables to allow arbitrary mappings of logical to physical addresses. These data structures are usually not cachable.

There are two basic schemes: segmented and paged. The *paged* approach deals with fixed sized blocks of memory, and *segmentation* is more flexible in terms of size. Segmentation and paging can be combined, as in the x86 architecture.

The address translation process was originally handled by a separate MMU chip, although this function is now incorporated into the CPU. The operating system is in charge of the data structures and the details of virtual memory management.

Input/Output

Communication interfaces in embedded systems tend to be specialized, but can use industry-standard interfaces as well. The usual computer communications methods of polled I/O, interrupt-based I/O, and direct memory access are applicable. The data communication can be *serial* (bit at a time) or *parallel* (many bits at a time). There is an upper limit to the distance for parallel communications due to bit skew and cross-talk

Analog input and output is handled by digital to analog and analog to digital converters. Some embedded computer chips have these functions built in. Standard industry interfaces such as *USB* (Universal Serial Bus) are becoming standard in embedded systems as well. This provides access to a wide variety of devices, with no custom interfacing required.

Wireless networking approaching such as wifi and Bluetooth, and short-range infrared (IR) are also applicable to certain embedded systems. I/O pin limitations are found in embedded chips with built-in I/O functions. Serial I/O can actually be faster than parallel, because cross-talk (interference) issues can be eliminated. Serial I/O is bit-at-a-time, time-domain multiplexing of the signal.

I/O Schemes

Regardless how bits or signals come to a computer, there are several standards methods to sample them, or send them out. The various communication protocols define the physical connection (connectors) and electrical interface (voltages, etc.). Once we are at the processor chip boundary, and we are dealing with bits, there are three common schemes to read or write. These can be implemented in hardware or software. The three schemes are polled I/O, interrupts, or direct memory access. All of these schemes work with serial (bit-at-a-time) or parallel (many-bits-at-a-time) I/O.

In *polled I/O*, the computer periodically checks to see if data is available, or if the communications channel is ready to accept new output. This is somewhat like checking your phone every 5 seconds to see if anyone is calling. There's a more efficient way to do it, which we'll discuss next, but you may not have anything better to do. Polled I/O is the simplest method.

In *Interrupt I/O*, when a new piece of information arrives, or the communication channel is ready to accept new output, a control signal called an interrupt occurs. This is like the phone ringing. You are sitting at your desk, busy at something, and the phone rings, interrupting you, causing you to set aside what you are doing, and handle the new task. When that is done, you go back to what you were doing.

A special piece of software called an *interrupt service routine* is required. This is similar to a subroutine. The interrupt forces the next instruction to be a call to a predetermined location, the interrupt service routine. The return address is saved to resume executing the foreground program. You might jot down some notes to get back to what you were doing, when the phone call ends.

Exception

An *exception* is an internally detected error. Exceptions are like interrupts, but are synchronous with instructions. They are data dependent. There is an exception mechanism on top of the interrupt mechanism. Exceptions are usually prioritized and vectorized. A trap (software interrupt) is an exception deliberately generated by an instruction.

DMA

Direct Memory Access is the fastest way to input or output information. It does this directly to or from memory, without processor intervention or overhead. It is a way to block-move data in a rapid fashion, other than by cpu read followed by cpu write for each item.

Let's say we want to transmit a series of 32-bit words. The processor would have to fetch each word from memory, send it to the I/O interface, and update a counter. In DMA, the I/O device can interface directly to or from the memory. DMA control hardware includes housekeeping tasks such as maintaining the word count, and updating the memory pointer.

DMA can also make use of interrupts. Normally, we load a word count into a register in the DMA controller, and it is counted down as words transfer to or from memory. When the word count reaches zero, an interrupt is triggered to the processor to signal the end of the transfer event.

While the DMA is going on, the processor may be locked out of memory access, depending on the memory architecture. Also, if dynamic memory is being used, the processor is usually in charge of memory refresh. This can be also be handled by the DMA controller, but someone has to do it.

One DMA scheme, used on the IBM pc, toggles between the CPU and the DMA device on a per-word basis. Thus, the processor is never locked out of fetching and executing instructions during a DMA for more than 1 cycle, although the DMA operation is not as fast as it could be.

Also, DMA is not constrained to access memory linearly; that is a function of the DMA controller and its complexity. For example, the DMA controller might be set up to access every fourth word in memory, and data items can be reordered in memory to facilitate processing.

The DMA protocol uses a *Request and Grant mechanism*. The device desiring to use dma send a request to the cpu, and that request is granted when the cpu is able. This is similar to the interrupt request for service mechanism. A dma controller interfaces with the device and the cpu. It may handle multiple dma channels with differing priorities. The controller has to know, for each request, the starting address in memory, and the size of the data movement. For dma data coming in to ram, there may be the additional complication of updating cache.

During the dma transfer, the dma controller takes over certain tasks form the cpu. This includes updating the memory address, and keeping track of the word count. The word count normally goes to zero, and generates an interrupt to signal the cpu that the dma transfer is over. The cpu can continue execution, as long as it has code and data available.

DMA in multicore systems is more exciting. In multicore, dma between the caches can be used as an inter-processor communication mechanism, and cache-cache transfers are supported. There is a cache coherency protocol between the various caches. It is the responsibility of the operating system to enforce this protocol, although hardware mechanisms (like the I/O coherent ARM Cortex A9) are appearing. This is usually implemented with a snooping mechanism, facilitated by hardware. A common cache coherency protocol is termed MESI, standing for Modified, Exclusive, Shared, and Invalid, referring to the possible states of each cache line.

DMA support is the responsibility of the operating system, and modern operating systems handle the complexities of multi-dma in multicore systems.

Busses

The *data bus* allows the CPU, memory, and I/O devices to communicate. It can also provide communications between computers. It is a shared communication medium. A bus is a set of wires or data paths, and an associated communications protocol. It can be serial or parallel. Usually an internal bus refers to one within the computer, and an external bus goes outside the boundaries of the computer. The distinction is a bit fuzzy in a multicore system, with multiple cpu's on the same silicon.

The cpu and memory tend to be tightly coupled, and between the cpu and I/O devices, or I/O devices and memory, more loosely coupled. Ideally, memory operates at cpu speed. I/O devices rarely do.

There are many bus standards, and they define the protocols and implementation of the bus, sometimes down to the physical layer of connectors and wires.

The bus protocol determines how devices communicate. Devices on the bus go through a sequence of states. Protocols are specified by state machines, one state machine per actor in the protocol. They may contain asynchronous logic behavior.

By default, the CPU is *bus master* and initiates transfers. A DMA device must become bus master before a transfer can be started by requesting control from the cpu. The cpu will grant this when it is able. The CPU generally can't use the bus while DMA operates, so it has no access to memory. The bus mastership protocol includes a Bus request and a Bus grant signal.

The CPU sets DMA registers for start address in memory and length of transfer. The DMA status register controls the unit. Once the DMA device is bus master, it transfers data automatically. It may run continuously until complete, or use every n-th bus cycle.

Multiple busses allow parallelism. We may put slow devices on one bus, and fast devices on a separate bus. A bridge is a device that connects two busses, either the same, or different. The bridge circuitry takes care of signal translation, where needed, and issues of timing, drive, and termination. Multiple devices on a slow bus can be connected to a single fast bus node.

The modes of operation of a bus or serial communication scheme are many and diverse. In a point-to-point system, we have two devices, connected by a communications channel. That channel has defined capabilities, including a capacity. The point-to-point connection can be hardware, or switchable. In a master-slave system, one device, usually the cpu, is in charge at all times. In a multi-master system, the cpu is the default master, but there is an arbitration protocol to hand over bus ownership to a device for a temporary period. This is the scheme used for direct memory transfer. Multi-master also works for multiple cpu's on a communication channel. In a peer-peer system, all devices are equal. This is the approach used in Ethernet. A mechanism for self-arbitration must be provided. In a multipoint architecture, there are multiple transceivers (transmitter-receiver) units that may be master-slave, or multi-master.

A bus *architecture* is used as a short-distance communications pathway between functional elements, such as the cpu and memory. Busses can be serial or parallel. The length of parallel signal lines is severely restricted by bit skew, where all the bits don't necessarily get to a particular point at the same time. This is due in some part by the differing characteristics of the parallel wires or traces implementing the bus. Each path must be treated as a transmission line at the frequencies involved, must have balanced characteristics with all the other lines, and be properly terminated. An early parallel bus scheme for transmitting information was the 1807 Francisco Salva Campillo electrochemical telegraph, with up to 35 wires. It had significant length and data rate issues.

A bus can have as many lines as we have signals, or can be a single, serial link. If the number of signals is greater than the number of wires or channels on the bus, we need to multiplex the signals. By this, we mean time-division multiplexing. If we have eight parallel wires, some of the time these can carry address information, and some of the time data, determined by the state of a control line. The multiplexed approach is more complicated, but results in a smaller bus. This has the side effect of less cross-talk between signal lines. Here we trade space for time.

Bus arbitration

Generally, the cpu is in control of the bus. During a dma operation, another device can request bus control, which will be passed to it from the cpu when it can. The dma device is the temporary bus master, and passes control back to the cpu so additional instructions can be accessed and executed. Bus mastership can be passed to co-processors for data fetches, which appear to the cpu as dma.

In multiple cpu systems, there is always a default bus master that takes over at reset. It can grant bus access to its peer cpu's. Usually two signals, bus request and bus grant handle the transfer of control. In Ethernet, which is a serial bus, There is no default mater. Any unit wanting to transmit must listen for the channel to be clear, and then transmit. It can happen that two units transmit at the same time, producing gibberish. In this case, the Ethernet protocol says that each waits a random time, and tries again. This works marvelously well, and gives a very high channel utilization. The Ethernet approach was derived from the previous Aloha net, an RF data network between the Hawaiian Islands. Some parallel bus architectures, both multiplexed and non-multiplexed, are discussed below:

Standard parallel busses

We'll take a look at some of the standard parallel busses available.

VMEbus

The VME bus was originally developed by Motorola in 1981 for the 68000 series of cpu's, and is now the ANSI/IEEE 1014-1987 Standard. It defines electrical, mechanical, and data transfer characteristics. The predecessor 1970's design was termed Versabus. It was a 16-bit architecture, that evolved to 32-bit, and to 64-bit. The 64-bit version achieves a data transfer performance of up to 320 megabytes/second, and uses multiplexing. Being originally designed for the Motorola 68000, the bus has many features specific to supporting that architecture. One example is the support of the seven interrupts levels of the original 68000. Bus mastership can be passed to requesting devices by a round-robin or prioritized scheme. The bus supports a block data transfer mode.

Multibus

The Multibus architecture was developed by Intel in the early 1970's for industrial automation, and became an IEEE Standard, IEEE-796. It supports cpu, memory, and I/O boards. It is an asynchronous bus with 20 address lines, and allows for multimasters. Multibus-I supported 8- and 16-bit data, and Multibus-II (IEEE-1296) supported 32-bits. The London subway system ("Underground") ran on a Multibus–based system.

SCSI

The Small Computer System Interface (SCSI) bus was intended as a host to disk controller interface in 1986. It supported eight devices. It is multi-master, and an ANSI standard, among others. The original SCSI design was an 8-bit wide data path plus parity, expanding later to 16- and 32-bits. It can operate at up to 320

MHz. There are at least a hundred varieties of SCSI, following a loose set of standards. SCSI comes in Wide, Narrow, and Fast varieties.

The connector is not specified, leading to the development of a large variety of adapters. There are several different electrical specifications. Both ends of the SCSI bus, which uses a cable and not a backplane, must be properly terminated, either actively of passively. This is usually a 110 ohm resistor to 3.3 volts for each line. Each device on a SCSI bus (with the cabling scheme, these are "daisy chained") has a unique ID usually set by a switch on the device.

IDE/ATA/PATA

The Integrated Drive Electronics (IDE) interface was developed by Western Digital Corporation as a way to connect hard disks to the cpu. This was a follow-on to their ST-506 hard drive interface. The term IDE refers to the definition of the connector and interface. The controller is built into the disk drive. Before we go any further, we should explain that this interface could be generalized, with a data transfer device serving in place of the disk drive. IDE is a 16-bit wide bus. It became ANSI standard X3.221 in 1994. CDROMS did not fit well into the scheme, and a new standard for Enhanced IDE (EIDE) was developed, along with the ATAPI (ATA Package interface) standard. IDE is a simpler and cheaper alternative to using SCSI for disk connection. ATAPI supports tape drives in addition to disks and CD/DVD, and handled high capacity removable media devices such as the Zip drives. Most of these devices are now attached serially (see, SATA), and the parallel version is now considered obsolete. PATA reached a performance limit at 133 MHz.

The ATA cable had 40 conductors. Later versions added a corresponding number of grounds to reach 80 conductors, for noise and crosstalk abatement reasons. The maximum length of the bus is under a meter. Up to two devices per cable are allowed, one jumpered as master, and the other as slave. Later, a cable-select option was introduced. A version of ATA is used to connect compact flash memory modules to a system.

PCI

The peripheral component interconnect (PCI) is a local computer bus to connect peripherals to a computer system. It was introduced in desktop pc's in 1993, and can handle 132 Mbytes per second transfers between the cpu on the motherboard, and peripheral controllers on I/O cards. The associated AGP (Advanced Graphics Processor) bus is used for high-speed video data, and does not share the channel with other peripherals.

The pci bus accepts circuit cards, and provides external connection to I/O interfaces. The bus standard defines the electrical and physical characteristics of the cards and connectors, as well as electrical, timing, and protocols. As systems have evolved, most of the functions that used pci bus interface have become integrated onto motherboards. PCI was derived from work done at Intel in 1990's. It mirrors the architecture of the x86 series of cpu's and support peripherals. All devices on the bus have a configuration rom that is queried during start-up to enumerate the characteristics of connected devices. A mini-pci bus is defined for use in laptops. PCI has been extended to 64-bit data width with the PCI-X.

PC/104

The PC/104 bus defines a standard approach for an embedded systems bus, and card form factors. It was originally developed by Ampro in 1987, specifically for embedded. It was proposed as an IEEE standard, but was not approved. The PC/104 approach does not use a backplane and connectors, but rather allows the standard sized cards to be stacked. The cpu card and memory are the same form factor as the I/O cards. The "104" comes from the use of 104 pins. The PC/104 is derived from the ISA bus, used in the original pc's. The PC/104-Plus adds support for the pci bus. The bus carries both power and data.

PCI Express

PCI Express is a serial bus that replaced standard pci and the specialized AGP. The PCI special Interest group (PCI-SIG) is an industry group of some 900 companies. It is the bus architecture of choice for current desktops, laptops, and servers. It is a point-point system that uses packets used for data. Besides its use on motherboards, it can be extended with cabling.

IEEE-488

The General Purpose Instrumentation Bus (GPIB) was developed by Hewlett Packard in the 1960's to connect automated test equipment. It became an IEEE standard, IEEE-488, in 1975.

It is a short range (20 meter), cable-based parallel bus with a defined protocol. Devices on the bus can be a talker, listener, controller, or some combination of the three. There are eight bidirectional data lines, three handshakes, five control lines, and eight grounds. The bus operates at ttl levels, and can handle high current loads. It supports fifteen devices with unique 5-bit addresses, transferring data at about a megabyte per second.

The bus uses a unique 24-pin Amphenol connector. Although designed with instrumentation in mind, the bus usage spread to computers and HP calculators, as well as test equipment from manufacturers other than HP.

Software bus

The term software bus refers to a mechanism that allows modules or processes to exchange information without worrying about the details of the underlying hardware. It is a virtual bus, with the functionality implemented in software.

Serial Communication

Serial communication can take place at gigabit or higher rates, and does not suffer from bit skew. In addition, it can take be used over arbitrary distances, and with various carrier modulation schemes. At this moment, the Voyager spacecraft is sending data back to Earth over a serial radio frequency link, even though the spacecraft is outside the solar system, at a nominal 40 bits per second.

A *UART*, Universal Asynchronous Receiver Transmitter, implements industry standard functionality for serial asynchronous communication. An example of the hardware part is Intel's 8251 chip. The architecture of the 8251 UART is include with many cpu's as well as standard cells, and may also be implemented in software. The functionality includes support for all of the standard formats (bits, parity, and overhead).

Serial communication of multiple bits utilizes time domain multiplexing of the communication channel, as bits are transmitted one at a time.

The serial communication parameters of interest include:
- Baud rate. (Symbol rate)
- Number of bits per character.
- endian – MSB or LSB transmitted first
- Parity/no parity.
- If parity, even or odd.
- Length of a stop bit (1, 1.5, 2 bits)

The baud rate gives the speed of transmission of data characters. The bit rate is the speed of individual bits making up the information and the overhead. For example, if we have 8 data bits and 3 overhead bits, and we transfer characters at 1000 baud, we are using a bit rate of 11000 bits or 1375 bytes per second.

What is the length of a bit? That is the time period of a bit, the reciprocal of the frequency. At 1000 Hertz, a bit is 1/1000 second, 1 millisecond long.

In *synchronous communication*, a shared clock is used between the transmitter and receiver. This clock can be transmitted on a second channel, or be a shared resource, such as GPS-derived time. In synchronous systems, characters are transmitted continuously. If there is no data to transmit, a special SYN character is used to fill in.

In asynchronous communication, the transmitter and receiver have their own local clocks, and the receiver must synchronize to the transmitter clock. The receiver and transmitter clocks are usually very accurate, being derived from crystal oscillators. Clock drift between the units is less of a problem than phase – the receiver does not know when a transmission (and thus a bit edge) begins. This is accomplished by a protocol.

When characters are not being transmitted in an asynchronous scheme, the communications channel is kept at a known idle state, known as a "Mark", from the old time telegraph days. Morse code is binary, and the manual telegraphs used the presence or absence of a voltage (current through the line to represent one state, and the absence to indicate the other state. Initially, the key press or "1" state was " voltage is applied", and the resting state was no voltage. Since these early systems used acid-filled batteries, there was a desire among operators to extend the battery life, without having to continuously refill the batteries. The problem is, if the wire was cut (maliciously or accidentally), there was no indication. The scheme was changed to where the resting state was a powered state. Thus, if the line voltage dropped to zero, there was a problem on the channel, probably a cut wire, or a dead battery.

Digital circuitry currently uses 3.3 or 5 volts, and the RS-232 standard for serial communication specifies a plus/minus voltage. Usually 12 volts works fine. In any case, interface circuitry at each end of the line convert line voltage to +5/0 volts for the computer circuitry. One state is called "marking" and the other state is called "spacing". This again goes back to early (1837) Morse recording telegraphs, where one state of the line made a mark on a piece of paper tape, and the opposite state made no mark, or a space. In serial asynchronous communications, the receiver does bit retiming. This is not required for the telegraph. Telegraphs and teletypes were essentially point-to-point or bussed systems. The voice telephone introduced the concept of circuit switching, first by manual switchboards, and later by automatic machinery. This systems required control information, in addition to the data. Sending data over analog lines was used, with the limitation of the voice-bandwidth of the lines. With clever encodings, up to 56-kilobyte data rates were achieved. Further improvement required the abandonment of analog lines for digital lines, and brought about the Internet era. Actually, we can send analog or digital information over the same lines (copper wire, for example). The difference is in the encoding, and the details of the transmitter and receiver units.

At idle, which is an arbitrary length period in asynchronous communication, the input assumes one known state. When it changes to another state, the receiver knows this is the start of a transmission, and the beginning or leading edge of a "start" bit. Since the receiver knows the baud rate a priori, because of a previously negotiated agreement with the transmitter, it waits one bit period to get to the first data bit leading edge, and then an additional one-half bit period to get to the middle of the bit. This is the ideal point (in communications theory terms) to sample the input bit. After, that, the receiver waits one additional bit period to sample the second bit in the center, etc., for the agreed-upon number of bits in a word. Then the receiver samples the parity bit (if the agreement allows for one), and then waits one, one and a half, or two bit periods for the "stop bits". After that, any change in the sensed bit state is the start bit of a new transmission. If the receiver and transmitter use different baud clocks, the received data will not be sensed at the right time, and will be incorrect. If the format is incorrect, if, for example, the receiver expects 8 data bits, and the transmitter sends 7 bits, the received word will be incorrect. This may or may not be caught by the parity bit.

Can the receiver derive clock information from the data stream, without prior knowledge of the baud rate? Yes, if special characters (sync words) are sent first. The format has to be agree-upon. When the receiver sees a state transition on the line, it takes this as the leading edge of the start bit. It starts a local timer, and stops the timer when the line state changes. This means the first data bit has to have the opposite state from a start bit. The receiver now knows the width of a bit, and divides this by two and start sampling the data bits in the middle, as this is the optimum position to do so.

If special characters are used, the receiver can guess the format of the data format to a good degree of accuracy. Given the initial guess, the receiver can transmit a request byte back to the original transmitter for a specific character, which then nails down the format. Note that this is not implemented in hardware UARTs, but can be accomplished in software.

In *full duplex systems*, data can be sent and received simultaneously over the link. This means the communications link has to have twice the capacity of a half-duplex link, which only allows the transmission of data in one direction at a time. Each link has a practical maximum rate of transmission, which is called the communication channel capacity. It is the upper bound to the amount of information that can be successfully transferred on the channel. That depends on noise, which corrupts the received information. Claude Shannon derived the concept of channel capacity, and provided an equation to calculate it. It is related to the signal to noise ratio of the channel.

In a *Master/Slave system*, one device is master and others are slaves. The master can initiate messages to individual slave units. This scheme is typically used in buss systems. The master can also broadcast a message to all units. In a *Multi-Master* scheme there is more than one master, and an arbitration scheme is necessary. This usually is implemented with a protocol for other devices than the current master to request bus mastership, which is then granted when feasible or convenient.

In a *Peer-Peer* scheme, on the other hand, There is no master, everyone is equal. This is the scheme used for Ethernet. If two units transmit at the same time, the transmission is garbled, and each unit retries after a random wait. If the randomness scheme works, this scheme is highly effective.

A crystal oscillator handles baud rate generation locally at a transmitter or receiver. It is usually 16 times the bit rate, to provide adequate sampling of the incoming signal for receivers. It can be selected to one of several values. The sample clock can be different on the receiver and transmitter, but the baud rate must be the same.

Parity is a simple error control mechanism for communications and storage. We add an extra bit to the word, so we can adjust parity. Parity is based on the mathematical concept of even (evenly divisible by two) or odd. In binary, a number is even if its least-significant (rightmost) digit is zero (0).

For example, in ASCII,

$A = 41_{16} = 0100\ 0001 \quad 2\ (1's) = even$
$B = 42_{16} = 0100\ 0010 \quad 2\ (1's) = even$
$C = 43_{16} = 0100\ 0011 \quad 3\ (1's) = odd$

If we want to always have even parity, we would make the extra bit = 0 for A & B, 1 for C, etc.

Here is an algorithm for parity calculation: Count the number of "1" bits in a word. If the count is odd, the word has odd parity. If the count is even, the word has (you guessed it) even parity. If we're going to communicate or store the word, we agree ahead of time it has a certain parity. If we see a different parity, there is an error. If we see the correct parity, the word is good, or has multiple errors. Multiple errors are usually less likely than single errors, so the mechanism works somewhat well. The overhead is one extra bit. If we want to get fancy, there are other encoding schemes that use multiple bits to allow detection, and even correction, of multiple bit errors.

American Standard Code for Information Interchange (ASCII) was devised for communication of symbols for teletypes from the 1960's. It is a 7-bit code with 128 combinations. This gives us four groups of 32: control, lower case, upper case, numbers and punctuation characters. An ASCII character fits in an 8-bit byte, with one bit to spare. This is sometimes used as a parity bit, for error control. At the time, paper tape systems supported 8 bits. Later, support was included in 9-track, reel-to-reel tape and punch cards.

Although a 7-bit code can handle the Roman alphabet, upper and lower case, numbers, punctuation, and control characters, it is not useful for character systems (such as Amharic) that have a large number of letter combinations, or logo-syllabic systems such as Chinese. ASCII extensions address variations in Latin alphabets, such as found in Italian, Spanish, Portuguese, French, and other languages, and regional uses, such as the British Pound sign (for currency), represented on US keyboards as "#".

Earlier codes, such as the 5-bit Baudot code (1870), used a shift mechanism to allow additional codes. The term "baud," referring to the symbol rate of transmission of information, is named for Emile Baudot, the originator of the code. Baud rate is not necessarily the same as bit rate; it depends on how many bits it takes to represent a symbol (such as a Baudot or ASCII character). Baudot code was used well into the 20th century for teleprinter equipment, particularly on the AT&T TWX network. One of the earliest coding schemes, used in Gauss's 1833 electromagnetic telegraph, was simple binary.

An Escape sequence is initiated by a special code, the Escape character (ESC). This defines the following characters to be control characters, not encoded numbers or digits, until a second ESC is received. This is contrasted with the use of control characters that have defined functions, such as tab or carriage return (which is a typewriter term). The ESC key is still included on keyboards. Control characters usually have no displayed equivalent.

ASCII's heritage in teletype machines sometimes causes confusion in modern data communications. For example, teletypes needed both a carriage return (CR) and a line feed (LF) at the end of a line. Non-mechanical systems can do both operations with just a CR. The Bell character, designed to ring the teletype's bell at the receiving end for attention (or annoyance) has no parallels. The Backspace character was used to back up paper tape to overwrite errors. ASCII is defined to be transmitted least significant bit first.

Serial I/O schemes, standards, and protocols

This section presents a quick overview of some industry standard serial communications schemes. All have an associated hardware and software specification. They may operate over different media of transmission. Their common feature is that they provide ways and means of getting bits of information from one point to another.

SPI/Microwire

The *Serial Peripheral Interface* (SPI) bus is a full-duplex synchronous serial communication system. It is a master/slave architecture. It uses four wires for the serial clock, the Master-in/slave-out, the master-out/slave-in, and a slave-select. It is the basis for the *JTAG* (Joint Test Action Group)'s diagnostic interface, and has found application in general I/O device interfacing as well. Microwire is a SPI predecessor, that is half-duplex.

I^2C

The *Inter-Integrated Circuit* (I^2C) bus is designed for short-range communication between chips on a board. It is a 2-wire interface that is multi-master, and bidirectional. There are 7-bit slave addresses, so 128 unique devices can be addressed from the current master. It was developed by Philips Semiconductor in the 1980's. It is widely used in embedded systems.

IrDA

The *Infrared Data Association* defined this standard for short-range communication by infrared carrier in free space. Don't Panic, infrared is just like microwave, but a higher frequency. Range is limited by attenuation in air. It is also a line-of-sight system, limited to about a meter. It can handle up to 1 gigabit/second, and is widely used for remote controls.

Bluetooth

Bluetooth is a short-range, low-power radio networking scheme. It uses a 2400-2480 MHz carrier. It is viewed as a wireless alternative to RS-232 short range wired serial communication. It does use frequency-hopping spread spectrum techniques. It has 79 1-MHz bands defined. It is a master-slave system, and is packet-based. Bluetooth has been widely adopted as the communication mechanism in mobile phone to headset and microphone devices. Two devices can transfer data files via Bluetooth.

Ethernet

Ethernet is the circa-1973 standard for local area networking technology, widely used for inter-computer data communication. It is defined in standard IEEE 802.3. It is packet-based, and routable, because the packets contain a destination and source address. It can be used over twisted-pair, coax cable, RF, or optical fiber. It makes use of repeaters, hubs, switches, and bridges to extend the network. The Ethernet design was developed at Xerox-PARC, based on the earlier Alohanet protocols.

USB

The *Universal Serial Bus* has a simple 4-wire configuration, 2 wires for power, and two for data. It was developed in 1995. The latest specification, USB-3, provides for up to 5 gigabits per second communication speed. USB is hub-based. There is always a master hub in the system. USB has become the interface of choice for peripherals such as the keyboard and mouse, printers, external hard drives and flash drives, scanners, digital cameras, cell phones, and many others.

The system is designed to support 127 peripherals, but is practically limited to much less than this. USB also supplies power, up to 0.5 amp per port. In many devices, only the power leads are used, to recharge the batteries in the device from the host.

CAN

The *Controller Area Network* (CAN) dates from 1983, and has its origins in industrial control and automation. It was developed by Robert Bosch GmbH in 1986, has been widely used in the automotive industry. It has a message-based protocol, and is a multi-master broadcast serial bus. The theoretical limit for devices on the bus is over 2,000, but a practical limit is about 100. It is a two-wire, half-duplex arrangement. It operates at a conservative 1 mbps, and has error detection and containment features. It is widely used in embedded systems.

RS-232

RS-232 is an electrical and functional telecomm standard dating from 1962. It has an associated EIA standard for the electrical, interface, and timing, but does not specify a connector. The 25-pin D-connector, and the 9-pin D are widely associated with RS-232.

The RS-232 scheme defines a *DTE* (data terminal device) which is a data generator/recipient and a *DCE* (data communication device) which is a channel interface device. This works well for telecomm, where we have a DTE and a DCE at each end, but if a computer is talking to a terminal, which is the DCE? This is handled by having the concept of back-to-back modems, called a *null-modem*, essentially a wire-crossover.

RS-232 runs in a minimum 3-wire scheme for full duplex, but includes a group of control signals to facilitate interface between a device and a modem. The modem translates digital signals into analog signals compatible with the telephone system (i.e., tones in the voice band). RS-232 also has a current loop option.

The early printing teletypewriter was developed to automate the process of sending messages by teletype, which involved a skilled operator at both the transmit and receive side. The earliest teletype systems used 5-bit Baudot code, and many of the signaling or control codes in RS-232 derive from the mechanical idiosyncratic characteristics of mechanical printing teletypes, using punched paper tape as the offline storage media.

Early data communication systems included Western Union's Telex network, using shared lines with the Bell Phone system, and the Teletypewriter exchange (TWX) by Bell. Electronic data interchange between the two systems was possible. The TWX systems used special area codes ("addresses"), and the Bell 101 Dataset (modem), a DCE.

RS-422/423

These are ANSI and international standards. They use a balanced voltage, or differential scheme. They can be implemented in a multi-drop or point-point architecture. The standards are for the electrical signaling only. RS-423 uses unbalanced signaling at 4 Mbps, over twisted pair.

These communication schemes use differential drivers over a 2-wire link. Common ground reduces the effect of external noise and cable effects. Voltage swings can be minimized, (faster transmission and less cross-talk) and less susceptible to voltage differences between grounds of transmitter and receiver.

RS-485 is an enhanced RS-422. There can be 32 drivers and 32 receivers on a bi-directional bus. The line typically terminated at the ends by resistors. Addressing uses a polled master/slave protocol.

Firewire

Firewire was invented by Apple Computer in the 1990's and implemented by Texas Instruments. IEEE standard 1394 defines it. It is intended for high-speed data, such as digital video. It has a serial bus architecture for bidirectional data transfer. It allows a master to address up to 63 peripherals in a tree architecture, or a chain. It can operate in peer-peer or multi-master mode, currently up to 3.2 gigabits per second.

Spacewire

Spacewire is IEEE standard 1355. It was developed at the European Space Agency (ESA), and represents a full-duplex, point-to-point routable protocol. It operates to 400 megabits per second. Spacewire has found application in the aerospace industry, and space-rated radiation tolerant parts are available, as are IP cores.

ARINC

Aeronautical Radio, Inc. of Annapolis, Maryland, develops and maintains a series of standards for aircraft systems. ARINC-429 is a digital avionics transfer system specification. It defines a self-clocking, self-synchronizing bus that uses 32-bit words. It is implemented as balanced differential signals over shielded twisted pair. It uses a bipolar differential return-to-zero waveform. It supports only one-way transferal of information, with one transmitter and up to 20 receivers. It is used on Airbus and Boeing aircraft, starting in the early 1980's. More than 150 separate busses can be found in these units. A follow-on standard, ARINC-629 bus supports large data transfers on newer digital aircraft.

MIL-STD-1553

MIL-STD-1553 is a digital time division multiplexed command/response multiplex avionics bus, used in aircraft and spacecraft, and dating from 1973. It uses a coax cable medium, and Manchester bi-phase encoding for code and data transmission. There is a bus controller (BC) and remote terminals (RT's). RT-RT data transmission is allowed, under control for the Bus Controller master. 1553 uses 16-bit words, at a rate of 1 megabit per second. A follow-on standard, 1773, extends the data transmission rate, and uses optical fiber media.

Video

There are various schemes to handle video (high-speed data) over serial transmissions. DVI, or *Digital Visual Interface*, is a source-to-display technique, operating with a 165 MHz pixel clock. It is not analog compatible. HDMI, *High-Definition Multimedia Interface*, allows for the transmission of video and audio. It is covered by the EIA/CEA-861 standard. It uses a 340 MHz pixel clock, and can handle standard high-resolution video data. Beyond this is Sony's Gigabit video interface, GVIF, which is currently distance-limited to some 20 meters.

OBD-II

This is the *on-board diagnostics* system for automobiles, based on a Volkswagen self-diagnostics and reporting scheme from 1969. It reports diagnostic trouble codes. It's use was made mandatory by the California Air Resources Board in 1991 for emissions control systems. It is now required for cars sold in all U. S. States, and most European countries. Take a look under the steering wheel in your car, to the left. Here is the mating connector:

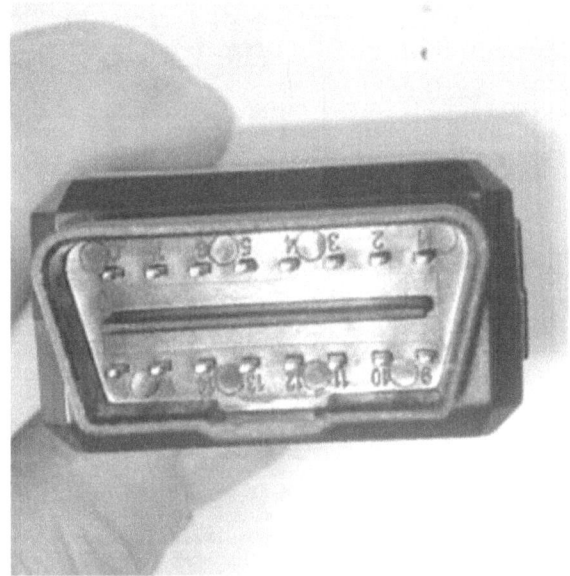

OBD-II uses the J1962 connector, the car end being located under the steering wheel in the passenger compartment. Diagnostic equipment can be linked by cable or a short-range system such as Bluetooth. Over the interface, the CAN protocol is popular.

Serial ATA

SATA is the upgrade of the earlier parallel bus interface for hard drives. The Serial ATA International Organization (www.sata-io.org) manages the standards for interoperability. The first revision was released in 2003, and supported transfers at up to 15 Gbits/second. Hard disk transfer speeds rapidly exceeded this limit, and this was addressed by SATA-2 at 3 Gigi-bits per second. SATA-3 doubled this. SATA can be used for video streaming. The SATA transfer protocol over the PCI Express bus instead of the serial link is also supported.

There is a de facto standard for the host controller, based on an Intel design. The SATA cables are also specified. The data cable has 2 data pairs and 3 grounds, a total of 7 wires.
Data is sent over differential pairs of wires to reduce noise and crosstalk interference. SATA also specified a power connector for the storage device. An external SATA interface, eSATA, can use up to a 2-meter cable. SATA supports hot-plugging.

The SATA protocol has three layers, physical, link and transport. The physical layer supports device detection. The link layer handles the details of data transmission, using packets. SATA physical connections are point-to-point.

Near-Field Communications

NFC uses an establish set of standards to enable distance-limited communications (centimeters) between devices. Applications include SmartPosters, and transaction devices such as Google Wallet. An NFC device can also read a passive RFID tag. Communication protocols include ISO 14443. Communications is encrypted. NFC is similar in function and usage to Bluetooth, with the latter having a larger range and bit rate. NFC is a lower power technology.

RFC-1149

On April 1, 1990, The Internet Advisory Committee issued RFC-1149 for IP data transmission. IP here stands for *internet pigeon*. Carrying messages with pigeons exhibits poor latency, and has a high packet loss, mostly due to hawks and power lines. It does have a high throughput, now that pigeons can carry high-density flash memory devices. The actual capacity of IP, as measure in field trials, has increased 3x over the bandwidth of the internet over the last 20 years. It is always good to have an alternative backup system.

CTAM

Chevy Truck Access Method was a favored scheme in the mainframe ear of computers to move large volumes of tapes and disk packs from storage to data centers. As with IP, the latency is large, but the data transmission rate is high. It is probably not applicable to modern embedded systems, but is presented here as an example to the student.

It is left to the student to compare and contrast the latency and bandwidth of a transcontinental optical fiber versus a 747 freighter filled with DVD's travelling from LaGuardia in New York to LAX airport.

Protocol

In terms of protocol over serial lines, the *Open Systems Interconnect* (OSI) 7-layer model serves as a standard. This is implemented in most operating systems. At the lowest level, we have the details of the physical interconnect, then the protocols for moving bits, bytes, and messages. Further up the hierarchy, we have standard methods of access, for example, ways for programs to request web pages, music, or video files. *IP* is the Internet protocol. Later, we'll also use the term IP to talk about Intellectual Property. It's usually obvious from context. Of course, we can have IP ip.

At the message level, we have two major definitions. *TCP* is the transmission control protocol. It is a connection-oriented protocol, which requires a connection be established before communication begins, just like a phone call. There is an addressing mechanism, similar to a phone number. Once the connection is established, the data movement is stream oriented, and delivery and ordering are guaranteed. In essence, we have established an exclusive and temporary (ad-hoc) channel between a transmitter and receiver. In the UDP, or User datagram protocol, we use a connectionless model, like the post office. This is generally used for text messages, pages, and email. The transmitter broadcasts the messages. There is no guarantee of delivery, and no guarantee of order of reception for multiple messages. The checksum protects data integrity. Both schemes have their uses.

The Internet was derived from the *Arpanet*, a project of the Advanced Research Projects Agency in 1965. It was an attempt to remove data transmission from the Bell System's analog low speed voice lines, for Department of Defense use. The ARPAnet evolved into a packet-switched network, which is very resilient to failure of links and nodes. ARPA net allowed for the exchange of e-mail between different computers at different locations, beginning in 1971. The ARPAnet was built by contractor BBN Technologies, based on local gateway computers known as *Interface Message Processors* (IMP's), which served the same function as DCE's – i.e., network interfaces. IMP's talked to local computers over a standard serial interface, and to each other over 50 kilobit per second leased voice-grade lines. The IMP's were store-and-forward devices, now commonly called routers. The initial IMP's were built from embedded Honeywell DDP-516 minicomputers, with 24 kilobytes of core memory. Each IMP could support up to four local computers. There were four IMP nodes in the network by December of 1969. This grew to over 200 by 1981. By 1970, the network speed was up to 230 kbits/second. The TCP protocol was implemented in 1983.

To date, even though all dedicated telegraph lines and teletype systems have faded into obscurity, dedicated telegraph operators still communicate in various dialects of Morse code, over the Internet.

Memory-mapped I/O versus specific I/O space and instructions

The implementation of I/O-specific instructions does not preclude *memory-mapped* I/O. If there are I/O instructions, the architecture defines two address spaces. The hardware can distinguish between these with specific read-I/O versus read (memory) and write-I/O versus write (memory). I/O devices mapped into the (memory) space are read and written with the memory access instructions. The only real difference is that I/O devices are usually slower than memory, and this is handled in the hardware by adding wait cycles.

Embedded Peripherals

Early in the implementation of microprocessors, it was hard to fit even the 8-bit cpu on a single piece of silicon. As the technology became more advanced, it was common to incorporate more and more functionality onto the same chip. Functions such as interrupt control, dma control, dynamic memory refresh, and floating point operations, that had originally required separate chips, were now merged with the cpu. This reduced the system chip count, speeded up operations, and reduced cost. This was an ideal situation for embedded processors, as it enabled single-chip solutions in many cases. This section discusses the peripheral functionality brought onto the same chip as the cpu. In addition, both ROM and RAM (and now, flash) are incorporated on the same device, in varying combinations.

Counter/Timer

This multipurpose peripheral is invaluable in embedded systems. In timer mode, the input clock is the system or cpu clock. The counter is preloaded with a value, and counts down. When the count reaches zero, an interrupt is generated, and the counter register is reloaded. For example, with an 8-bit counter, if it is preloaded with 128, it generates a square wave at system clock/256 rate. This allows periodic interrupts at sub-multiples of the system clock, and synchronous with it. We can also increment a second counter upon each interrupt to handle longer periods of elapsed time.

In counter mode, the clock comes from an external source, and is asynchronous to the system clock. For example, we might use the output stream of pulses from an optical encoder. Another application might be as the Baud rate clock for a serial I/O line.

Since the counter/timer usually has multiple channels, we might use one channel to generate a known time base, and other units for counting.

Examples of legacy stand-alone counter/timer chips are the Intel 8253 and 8254. These were used along with the 8088/8086 cpu's in the IBM pc architecture in 1981. The functionality is now incorporated in motherboard hardware ("southbridge"). These chips have three 16-bit independent counters. Their outputs are usually connected to system interrupts. In the pc architecture, counter 1 is used for real-time keeping, timer 2 handles dram refresh, and timer 3 generates tones on the system speaker. The counters are handled like standard peripherals for sending command words, and reading status. In the pc architecture, this means they are mapped into the I/O space.

Several modes of operation are supported. In mode 0, the counter generates an interrupt at the terminal count. In mode 1, the timer functions as a programmable one-shot generator. In mode 2, the device is a divide-by-n counter, to generate real-time clock ticks. In mode 3, it functions as a square wave generator. In mode 4 the output remains in a high state until the count is reached, drops low for one clock cycle, then returns to the high state. In mode 5, the count is initiated by an external control signal.

A special-purpose timer essential for embedded applications is the Watchdog. This is a free-running timer that generates a cpu reset unless it is reset by the software. This helps to ensure that the system doesn't lock up during certain critical time periods, and the software is meeting its deadlines. This approach has saved many a system.

If the watchdog is not reset, it generates an interrupt to reset the host. This should take the system back to a baseline state, and restart it. Hopefully, normal operations will resume. The embedded system can't rely on a human operator to notice a fault in the operations or a "hung" system, and press the reset button. Many *very remote* systems, such as those in deep water or on the surface of other planets have successfully recovered from faults with a watchdog.

The watchdog timer is implemented in hardware, and does it's jobs without direct software intervention. If the software fails to reset the timer, the system reboots. This might simply reset operations and restart, or may include diagnostics before the system is restarted.

Time permitting, it is useful to checkpoint the state of the system before the reset is made, to assist in diagnostics.

In some architectures, a second system runs in parallel with the primary, and compares results. If the second system detects a difference, both systems are reset. What happens when the diagnostic hardware/software makes a mistake? This has happened, where the backup system thinks the primary system has made a mistake, and takes over, erroneously. This has resulted in the loss of launch vehicles.

A preferred approach, which is hardware-intensive, is to use three identical systems, with voting logic. The majority wins. The approach is based on the fact that double errors are less likely than single errors. Who watches the watchdogs, the watchcat?

Sometimes the system cannot be shut down, even in the case of an error. A simple hardwired fail-safe backup system may be activated, or other corrective actions can be taken. In the case where the system has to operate through a failure, the term melt-before-fail is sometimes used.

Priority Interrupt Controller

The priority interrupt controller is the manager of multiple, prioritized interrupts in a system. At design time, the interrupts strategy is defined, showing who can interrupt whom. The interrupt controller enforces this.

An example of an early stand-alone interrupt chip is the Intel 8259. This was used in the original IBM pc, and the functionality was moved into the later versions of the motherboard support hardware ("southbridge"). It was originally designed for Intel's 8-bit 8085 processor in 1976.

Each 8259 can support 8 external devices, and uses a single line to signal the processor that one of these interrupts has been asserted. Interrupt prioritization is achieved by connecting devices to specific line of the chip. The chip also provides the interrupt acknowledge to the device.

Up to 8 slave controllers can be connected to a master unit, using one of the master's input lines, connected to the slaves interrupt line, normally connected to the cpu. In this cascade scheme, nine chips support 64 interrupts.

The chip has an interrupt mask register, an interrupt request register, and an in-service register. The interrupt request register keeps track of pending interrupts that need acknowledgment. The interrupt mask register keeps track of interrupts that will not be acknowledged.

The hardware supports both edge-triggered and level-triggered interrupts. It implements both fixed priority interrupts, and rotating priority.

DMA Controller

The DMA controller offloads the details of handling and prioritizing multichannel DMA operations from the cpu. Originally a separate chip, the DMA controller is now typically incorporated along with the cpu. The dma controller interfaces with the external device, and handles control signals and addresses for the memory.

A typical legacy device is the Intel 8237, which handles four channels, but is cascadable. It supports several modes of operation, including single word transfer, block transfer, and on-demand. In auto-initialize mode, address and count values are restored when the transfer ends, allowing for repeated transfers. Typically, a word count for the transfer is loaded to the device, and is counted down. The word count = 0 interrupt signals the end of the process.

A device needing dma access supplies a request, and holds it active until acknowledged. The timing is critical for devices such as rotating magnetic memory and LAN connections. Due to limited buffer size, the acknowledgment must be prompt.

JTAG support

Joint Test Action Group (JTAG) is the name for the IEEE-1149.1 standard for a test access point and a boundary scan architecture for integrated circuit level debug. The JTAG effort began in 1985 as a test and fault isolation methodology for board level products. It is particularly valuable for embedded systems, with limited human interfaces for visibility. It is used in cpu-based systems, FPGA's, and SoC architectures. With the proper application software, the JTAG can access and control test instrumentation included within the chip. JTAG can also be used to load data into internal flash memory. JTAG is used a portal to the chips built-in self test (BIST).

JTAG uses a 4-wire interface (data in, data out, clock, mode select), sometimes with a 5th line, test reset. The data transfer mode is serial, using a short cable. The host side for the JTAG system can be connected via USB or even Ethernet. There are numerous commercial JTAG tool vendors providing multi-platform support, and Open Source tools also exist. Almost all modern embedded architectures provide JTAG support. A 2-wire alternative is Serial Wire Debug, that has the JTAG protocol implemented,

A/D, D/A

Embedded systems typically include analog to digital and digital to analog conversion. Rather than separate hardware, the converters are built onto the same chips as the cpu. The conversion process will be discussed later, but these devices are typically connected with a parallel interface. We will also discuss analog device interfacing later.

Sensors and sensor interfacing

A *sensor* is a device that measures a physical quantity by changing state in response to the stimulation, and producing a signal. It is an analog world. It is rare that we get to interface directly to a digital source. Some sensors may indicate one of two states (presence/absence) with a simple digital signal that may only require voltage level shifting. Other signals, such as a switch closure, may appear digital, but require *debouncing* due to the physics of the actual contact, which actually closes and opens hundreds of times on activation. This is a form of signal conditioning for the sensor. We haven't yet considered voltage levels, current requirements, timing, and all those other real-world interfacing issues. We tend to view sensors as a "black-box" function, where the output is a valid representation of the applied signal. The ugly truth is, sensors are real-world devices that have their own non-linearity, parametric shifts, and they tend to respond to a lot more than the parameter we are interested in.

Some sensors output a digital value that could be sign-magnitude format, 1's complement, 2's complement, Grey code, or some other scheme. The data format might be BCD or binary (signed or unsigned) or something else. The word length may be unique to the sensor, and the data may not come out all at the same time – it might be serial by bit, serial by byte, MSB first, LSB first, etc.

Passive sensors simply collect energy from the sensed phenomena; active sensors require power, or an excitation signal. A *transducer* is a device that converts one form of energy to another; a solar cell is an example. The Grand Coulee dam is another. In the literature, the terms sensor and transducer are often used interchangeably.

All sensors are built to operate within a specified environment that corresponds to the temperature limits and other environmental conditions of its applied surroundings. Even if other sensors exist, they may not satisfy all essential conditions to operate within the system, including operating life, sensing range, accuracy, redundancy, low energy consumption, environments, mounting mechanism, reliability, sensing rate with response time, volume, and mass.

It is expected that the software in the embedded processor will sort this all out. With Smart Sensors with integrated processing, more common interface standards between the sensor and the main processor can be applied.

Signal conditioning refers to processing the sensed signal into a form from which the digital processor can then extract useful information. This may involve amplification or attenuation, analog to digital conversion, filtering, format conversion, electrical isolation, and other techniques. Noise filtering is a commonly applied technique. Sensors exhibit lag and hysteresis, which is a difference in offset from one measurement direction to another. Bias refers to the situation when the output is not zero when the measured quantity is. There can be dynamic errors, caused by rapid change in the input. *Drift* refers to the fact that, over time, the sensor may change output while the input remains steady.

The physics of the sensor must be considered. A relative humidity sensor measures relative humidity, but also temperature. A digital compass also reacts to magnetic fields produced by nearby wiring. Sensors are inherently non-linear. All of these characteristics must be understood and compensated for in software or hardware. With smart sensors, this compensation and processing would be accomplished within the sensor unit itself. For a simple sensor unit, some processing and conditioning must be done within the main embedded processor. Consider issues of operating life, range, maximum and minimum, accuracy, redundancy, energy consumption, heat generation, electromagnetic interference generation, electromagnetic interference susceptibility, mounting, reliability, sense rate, transient and steady-state response time, mass and volume, aging, and mean time to failure when choosing sensors.

As an example, the output signal may not vary linearly with the sensed value, and may depend on other ambient conditions as well.

A polynomial function in software may need to be applied to the sensed input to generate the correct output. This can be implemented by calculation, or a table look-up.

Between the sensor and the processor, we may need a level of isolation, to protect either or both sides. This might be optical, capacitive, or magnetic in nature. Common grounding is also a concern.

We will examine some real sensors and their physics to see the different characteristics.

Types of Measurement

This section will discuss the types of measurement domains that are typically encountered, and the approaches to sensing and detecting in each.

Voltage

Voltage sensing can involve simple analog to digital circuits, with pre-scaling appropriate to the expected range. The issues of accuracy (8, 12, 16 bits) and conversion time (sample time) apply. The voltage sensor can be operated continuously or on demand. If a simple presence or absence of a specific voltage is desired (is the 3.3 volts present?) a Zener diode circuit can be used. Negative voltages may require the use of op amps to shift the ground to a more convenient place.

Current

Current sensors find application as electronic fuses and circuit breakers. They are also used for current limiting and control in power supplies and motors. Besides the Hall effect magnetic sensor discussed below, resistive current sensors are also used. If the current to be sensed is not direct, but alternating, other methods need to be employed.

Capacitance

Capacitive sensing relies on an external physical parameter changing either the spacing or the dielectric constant between the two plates of a capacitor or affecting the capacitor's salient characteristics. The advantages of capacitive sensing are very low power consumption and relatively good stability of the measurement with temperature.

In a "good" capacitor, a dielectric constant K and the element geometry must be stable throughout the operating environments such as temperature, barometric pressure, humidity, and solvents. These "good capacitors" are essential circuit components in electrical circuits, but if their parameters shift during circuit operation the performance is unacceptable. Conversely, if you want to make a good sensor you need to use a "bad" capacitor, whose parameters varies with the stimuli to be sensed and measured. By the proper choice of materials the capacitive sensor's parameters vary with the environmental stimuli to be differentiated in a predictable and repeatable manner.

Inductive Sensing

The basic principle is related to the inductance change by the position change of the moving element that holds either a ferromagnetic material or an electromagnet. Semiconductor devices such as Hall Effect sensors can detect the inductance change. The measurement method enables the integration of numerous applications including flow sensing, position detection (for example Linear Variable Differential Transformer (LVDT) and Rotational Variable Differential Transformer (RVDT)), position rate, angular velocity, and force and torque measurements.

Magnetic field sensing

Magnetic sensing makes use of induction effects, as we move a coil in a magnetic field, or fundamental atomic properties such as Zeeman splitting or nuclear magnetic resonance.

Resistive sensors

These devices have variable resistance in response to particular phenomena. Generally, resistive materials are temperature sensitive, and are also sensitive to moisture.

Temperature and relative humidity sensing

In the simplest case, a precision resistor or semiconductor junction is used, where the current flow is proportional to the ambient temperature. Thermistors are special resistors whose resistance varies with temperature. These devices have to be compensated for self-heating. They are only good over limited ranges. If actual degrees (F or C) are required, the equation is usually a 2nd order polynomial. Relative humidity is usually measured with a capacitive sensor, although conductive polymers with variable resistance are also used. Thermocouples are passive devices, using two dissimilar materials to generate a voltage proportional to the junction temperature. RTD's, resistance temperature detectors, are mostly made of a pure metal or a bulk silicon material.

Sensing at cryogenic temperatures (-150 degrees C or below) is done mostly with resistive sensors. They are very stable once they are temperature stabilized.

Distance, velocity, and acceleration sensing

Distance can be measured with a variety of methods. We can measure direct mechanical motion with a linearly variable resistor or inductor. Velocity is a time difference of distances, and acceleration is a time difference of velocities. The angular distances, velocities, and accelerations are handled just as easily.

Radiant energy sensing and measurement

This includes the spectrum of radio frequency, infrared, optical, ultraviolet, gamma rays, and beyond. The particular sensor technology used depends on the frequency, but the principles are the same.

Thermal detector devices transform a radiant, infrared or thermal transfer energy stimulus into an electrical signal. Most often, the absorbed energy stimuli causes a change in the detectors temperature, and this change in temperature manifests itself as a change in electrical resistance or electrostatic polarization. The sensitivity is limited by the fluctuation in energy of the absorbed energy.

The measurement of radiant energy has many applications. The choice of the measuring device depends on the frequency range of the energy and the particular application location or structure. Thermal detectors include thermocouples, bolometers, thermal imaging devices, resistance-temperature devices such as doped germanium and silicon cells, optical pyrometers, photoconductive cells and photoelectric cells, voltage-current devices such as a thermistor, Seebeck Effect devices or RTD. Some of these radiant energy detectors require special operating temperatures.

Photodetectors are semiconductor devices that can detect optical signals through electronic processes. Quantum photodetectors are nonequlibrium devices. A minimum amount of photon energy is required to create a quantum excitation; this is referred to as a photo-absorption threshold. The photodetector output signal depends on the non-equlibrium between excitation and recombination in the semiconductor crystal lattice. The signal amplitude is directly dependent on the photo-excitation lifetime and the number of absorbed photons.

Physics of Sensors

Basic fundamental physical properties are used to sense real-world phenomena. Some of these are discussed below.

Seebeck effect

The *Seebeck effect* is the conversion of temperature differences directly into electricity and is named for the German physicist Thomas Johann Seebeck. The Seebeck effect is used in thermocouples to measure a temperature difference; absolute temperature may be found by setting one end of the thermocouple to a known temperature. Also, a metal of unknown composition can be classified by its thermoelectric effect if a metallic probe of known composition, kept at a constant temperature, is held in contact with it. Industrial quality control instruments use this method of thermoelectric alloy sorting to identify metal alloys.

Balanced bridge, and difference measurement

The *Wheatstone bridge* illustrates the concept of a difference measurement, which can be extremely accurate. Variations on the Wheatstone bridge can be used to measure capacitance, inductance, impedance and other quantities. The advantage of the bridge circuit is that it is sensitive to small differences in the current flow in the two paths. The bridge circuit uses three known elements, and one element to be measured.

Piezoelectric effect

The *piezoelectric effect* is the linear electromechanical interaction between the mechanical and the electrical state in crystalline materials. The piezoelectric effect is a reversible process in that materials exhibiting the direct piezoelectric effect (the internal generation of electrical charge resulting from an applied mechanical force) also exhibit the reverse piezoelectric effect (the internal generation of a mechanical strain resulting from an applied electrical field). For example, certain crystals will generate measurable piezoelectricity when their static structure is deformed by about 0.1% of the original dimension. Conversely, those same crystals will change about 0.1% of their static dimension when an external electric field is applied to the material. The inverse piezoelectric effect is used in production of ultrasonic sound waves. The first practical application for piezoelectric devices was sonar.

Silicon has significant piezoelectric characteristics. Quartz can generate potential differences of thousands of volts. A piezoelectric sensor can measure pressure, acceleration, strain, or force by converting these to an electrical charge.

Hall effect

Due to a transverse magnetic field, electrons charges migrate toward one side of the sense material strip, which subsequently becomes more negative than the other side of the strip, creating a *Hall effect* voltage. The sign and amplitude of the potential difference depends on both the magnitude and direction of the magnetic field. Depending on the material's crystalline structure, charges may be either negative or positive.

Hall Effect devices operate on fluctuations in the magnetic field created by current flow. When a metal or semiconductor is placed in a magnetic field, the electrons in the material respond by moving in one direction in the material and holes (or absence of electrons) in the opposite direction, accumulating a charge at the edge and thus a potential difference. This assumes no thermal gradient, and thus no Seebeck effect. A zero magnetic field yields zero Hall Effect.

It is the small number of carriers and high mobility in semiconductors that gives a small Hall field and a large Hall angle, which makes them useful for the construction of probes to measure magnetic fields. A Hall effect sensor, then, is a transducer that varies its output voltage in response to a magnetic field.

Types of sensors

This section will discuss the application of the laws of physics and materials properties to real-world sensors.

MEMS accelerometer

The *MEMS*, or micro electro mechanical system, uses a chip-level integrated circuit technology to provide measurement devices. The advantage is that the sensors are made in processes developed for semiconductor manufacturer, and are inexpensive to mass-produce.

A typical accelerometer sensor has a small gas-filled chamber with a center heating element, and four temperature sensors around the edge. A static sensor results in all four temperature elements reading the same value. As the sensor is tilted, the higher sensor will read hotter. The sensor itself translates temperature differences into pulse widths. Some trigonometric calculations are needed to resolve angles. It also does not work in zero G.

These sensors can be used to determine acceleration, tilt, rotation, vibration, and other derived values.

Piezo Accelerometer

In a piezo-electric accelerometer, a mass exerts force on a piezo-electric element, which generates a charge proportional to the force. The charge is amplified at the sensor. These devices have a characteristic resonant frequency, which is typically much higher than what is expected to be measured. These sensors can operate in compression or shear mode.

Tilt switch – mechanical and electrochemical

Mercury switches are out of favor due to toxicity; the mechanical replacements are less satisfactory, due to hysteresis and bouncing. A new class of electrochemical tilt switch provides an output that varies with the tilt angle. This requires an analog-to-digital conversion, or a comparison to a set point.

Ultrasonic rangefinder

An ultrasonic rangefinder is an active sensor that uses a burst of ultrasonic energy to measure the distance to objects, or to detect them. Sonar works in any fluid, particularly air and water. It can be used in tanks of liquid to determine level. An inexpensive ultrasonic rangefinder was developed by the Polaroid Corporation for their series of instant cameras, and found wide general application.

In the rangefinder, a pulse is sent out, and a clock is started. When the return pulse is detected, the counter is stopped, and ½ time corresponds to the distance. This is because we measure the time of the pulse going out and coming back. Ultrasonic signals in air are affected by the relative humidity and temperature, and corrections for these may be required. The timing of the pulse can be done in hardware or software.

The sonar equation for air is: $C = 331.5 + (0.6 \times Tc)$ meters/sec.

The speed of sound in air is 331.5 meters/second at 0 degrees C. At 72 degrees F, the speed is 344.8 meters/second. We can measure air temperature by sending out a sonar pulse to a known distance target and measuring the round trip time.

We can measure velocity from sequential distance measurements, and acceleration form successive velocity measurements. If we can measure the frequency of the returned pulse, we can use the Doppler shift to indicate relative velocity.

The ultrasonic device may provide two pulses, one for the transmitted and one for the received signal. These are then used to control a timer in the embedded processor. A more sophisticated sensor might return a 16-bit word corresponding to the travel time.

Light sensing – intensity

A simple photodiode can be used to distinguish between dark and light. Different spectral sensitivities, perhaps used with filers, can provide color discrimination in the measurement as well. Photodetectors can function as variable resistors, or generators of electricity.

Laser rangefinder/lidar

The *lidar* unit is a light-based analog to radar. With sophisticated processing, it can be used to build a range-map of its surroundings. Depending on the environment and the nature of the sensed object, the lidar can operate in the infrared, visible, or ultraviolet spectrum. Lessons learned from radar can be applied to lidar signal processing. A narrow beam width gives enhanced spatial discrimination. Lidars use a series of movable mirrors to provide 3-dimensional scans in the side-side and up-down directions.

Solid-state laser modules are cheap and mass produced. Lidar units are usually smart sensors, including their own internal processing, and produce large volumes of data.

Thermocouple

A *thermocouple* is a thermoelectric contact sensor. Two dissimilar conductors convert the thermal energy directly into electrical energy and two junctions of these conductors are necessary (refer to Seebeck effect). When different segments of the thermocouple are at different temperatures, creating a thermal gradient, from each other an electrical voltage proportional to the temperature difference is maintained in the thermocouple circuit. A thermocouple is a passive sensor meaning it generates voltage in response to temperature differences, and does not require any external electrical excitation power. The voltage produced depends on the temperature gradient between the two thermocouple junctions, regardless of the absolute temperature of each junction. Therefore, if an absolute temperature is required for reference purposes, an RTD or thermistor is required. Thermocouples are capable of being used to directly measure temperatures up to $2600°$ C.

Thermistor

Thermistors are resistors whose resistance varies with temperature. They can have a positive or negative coefficient. The advantage of a thermistor is that their resistance is usually several orders of magnitude greater than the resistance of the remainder of the circuit. The circuit line resistance therefore has no significant effect on the signal accuracy. A Wheatstone bridge architecture can be used. The thermistor is affected by self-heating. The thermistor was developed by Michael Faraday in 1833.

Piezoelectric Temperature Sensors

These are active sensors whose resistance varies with temperature. The temperature sensor function is based upon the variability of the crystal oscillation frequency at different temperatures. Thermal coupling of the object to be sensed with the oscillating plate of the sensor is often difficult. All piezoelectric temperature sensors have a relatively slow response as compared with thermistor and RTD's or PRT's.

Positive Resistance Thermometers (PRT).

Sometimes called Resistance Thermometer Devices (RTD) or Platinum Resistance Thermometers (PRT), these are temperature sensors that use the predictable change in electrical resistance of some materials subsequent to a corresponding change in temperature. The PRT operates on the principle that the material's electrical resistance changes in a predictable way depending on the rise and fall in temperature. A typical RTD consists of a fine platinum wire wrapped around a mandrel and covered with a protective coating. Usually, the mandrel and coating are glass or ceramic. Wire types consist of a coil of wire which provides a compromise between mechanical stability and allows thermal expansion of the wire but at the expense of mechanical rigidity and strength under mechanical shock and vibration. Film types consist of a thin layer of platinum on a substrate. Due to its small size the device can respond quickly to temperature changes. The Seebeck effect can cause erroneous reading in PRT's.

Strain gage sensors

Strain gage sensors have the attributes of a variable resistor under compressive or tensile strain. They are designed for maximum resistance change due to mechanical strain variations but minimum resistance change in response to other properties such as thermal. The strain gage is manufactured with a thin flexible backing; this enhances ease of handling and installing on the structural or mechanical surface to be strain monitored. As the structure is deformed by either compressive or tensile strain, the resistive element is deformed, causing its electrical resistance to change respectively. This resistance change, usually measured using a Wheatstone bridge, is directly proportional to the surface strain on the structure being monitored.

Tachometer

A *tachometer* is used to measure rotation rate. It can be a simple optical or magnetic encoder unit, or a small dc generator. The output voltage is a function of the rotation rate.

Flow Rate Sensor

The flow rate sensor can use a tachometer to measure the rotation of a small impeller in the fluid stream. This measures the flow rate, which can be integrated to give a volume measurement. These find application in gas pumps, and other liquid delivery systems.

Gyros

A *gyroscope* is a device for measuring or maintaining orientation, based on the principles of angular momentum. Mechanically, a gyroscope is a spinning wheel or disk in which the axle is free to assume any orientation. Although this orientation does not remain fixed, it changes in response to an external torque much less and in a different direction than it would without the large angular momentum associated with the disk's high rate of spin and moment of inertia. Since external torque is minimized by mounting the device in gimbals, its orientation remains nearly fixed, regardless of any motion of the platform on which it is mounted. The force at the gimbals can be measured with strain gages. An electric motor, or an air motor maintains the gyroscope's rotation rate.

Gyroscopes can also be electronic, microchip-packaged MEMS devices found in consumer electronic devices such as cell phones and video games, solid-state ring lasers, or fiber optics. These do not use a rotating mass.

Applications of gyroscopes include inertial navigation systems where magnetic compasses would not work or would not be precise enough, and for the stabilization of flying vehicles like radio-controlled helicopters, unmanned aerial vehicles, or drone aircraft.

The problem with gyros is their drift with time. The gyro's advantage is continuous output and they are not constrained by the need for an external reference.

Charge Transfer Devices (CTD)

The *CTD*'s used in imaging and sensing correspond to shift registers where the data in the register are analog samples. This enables the device to process analog data without first translating the signal into the digital domain, reducing component count and eliminates the need for analog-to-digital converters. A CTD is basically an array of closely spaced sensor diodes. The operation of a CTD requires charge signal injection, transfer, and readout, under the application of a proper sequence of clock voltage. This pulses the diode array so the charge can be stored and transferred in a controlled manner. These sensor arrays are commonly found in digital cameras.

Magneto-resistive sensors consist of a magneto-resistive thin film deposited on an insulating substrate. The film is then etched into segments to form the sensor network. The resulting segments are interconnected forming the sensor cells. These magneto-resistive sensors are often used to measure rotational speeds, much like a tachometer, or may be used for either incremental or absolute magnetic encoders.

Optical Incremental encoders consist of a disc divided up into alternate optically opaque and transparent sectors, which is driven by the input shaft. A light source is positioned at one side of the disc and a light detector at the other side. As the disc rotates the output from the detector will switch alternately on and off depending on whether an opaque or transparent sector is between the light source and the detector. A stream of square wave pulses is produced which indicate the angular position of the shaft. Most incremental encoders feature a second light source and detector, the output of which is phased in such a way in relation to the main detector output, that the direction of the input shaft can be determined. Many encoders also feature a third light source and detector which acts as a once per revolution index marker. Usually, a Grey-code pattern is used, giving one and only one bit change per position change.

While this type of encoder may be useful in some applications it has the disadvantage of having the angular information stored in an external counter. If the information in this counter is lost (for example if the power supply was temporarily interrupted), there is no way of knowing the shaft angle. Also at initial turn on, there is no way of determining the absolute shaft angle until it has been rotated through the index marker.

Tachometers are often used to measure the rotational speed of a spinning object. Some tachometers utilize LED's in conjunction with optical encoders. Other tachometer types consist of a wheel mounted magnet and a fixed sensor like a pickoff coil. The pulse train may be converted to a DC voltage for error signals for a command variable speed feedback network or constant speed determination. Another type of tachometer uses the back EMF generated by the motor armature to produce an analog voltage proportional to the rotational speed.

Absolute encoders

The loss of angular position information in optical encoders can be overcome by the absolute optical encoder. In this device, the disc is divided up into N sectors, each sector also being divided up along its length into opaque and transparent sections forming a digital word with a maximum count of N. The sectors are arranged such that the digital word formed by each set of opaque and transparent sections, increments in value from one sector to the next. A set of N light sources are arranged radially on one side of the disc and corresponding detectors are positioned on the other side such that a parallel word representing the input shaft angle can be obtained at any one of N angular positions.

Pyroelectric detectors consist of a thin slab of crystal, such as triglycine sulfate, sandwiched between two electrodes. Impinging radiation raises the temperature of the crystal, causes spontaneous charge polarization of the crystal material and yields a measurable potential difference across the electrodes.

Chemfet

A *ChemFET*, or chemical field-effect transistor, is a type of field-effect transistor acting as a chemical sensor. It is a structural analog of a MOSFET transistor, where the charge on the gate electrode is applied by a chemical process. It may be used to detect specific atoms, molecules, and ions in liquids and gases. It uses a gas-sensitive coating on the gate of the semiconductor.

An *ISFET*, an ion-sensitive field-effect transistor, is a subtype of ChemFET devices. It is used to detect specific ions in electrolytes.

An *ENFET* is a CHEMFET specialized for detection of specific biomolecules using enzyme reaction.

Compass module

A compass sensor measures the direction of a prevailing magnetic field. If you are on a planet with a good magnetic field (such as Earth), you can use this sensor to determine bearing with respect to magnetic north. This gives a heading reading, the angle with respect to magnetic north. A change in this reading can be used for rotation rate. Trigonometric functions are required in these calculations. Hall effect electronic sensors can also detect and measure magnetic fields. Fluxgate sensors use a set of coils on a core, with associated excitation circuitry. They have a resolution in the milli-gauss range. They are low cost, but have a slow response time. Magneto-restrictive sensors can be mass-produced as an integrated circuit, and have response times on the order of milliseconds, making them more applicable to moving systems.

The Earth's field is about 0.5 gauss. In the case of Earth, the magnetic field is approximately a dipole field. The components of the field parallel to the local surface are used to determine compass direction. The angle of the field relative to the surface is called the inclination, and varies across the surface. True north and magnetic north vary by up to 25 degrees, true north being the rotational axis of the Earth.

Optical incremental encoder (quadrature encoder)

An incremental rotary encoder provides information about the instantaneous position of a rotating shaft. It does this by producing one square wave cycle per increment of shaft movement. This increment is referred to as the resolution of the encoder and is built directly into the internal hardware of the device. A resolution of 360 means that 360 square wave cycles will be produced in one complete rotation of the shaft. By counting the number of cycles, one can tell the position of the shaft, relative to its starting position. For example, 90 cycles means that the shaft is now at a position 90 degrees from where it started. By adding a quadrature signal, we can measure the direction of the rotation, by reading which signal (A or B) we saw first. By starting a counter with the rising edge of one signal, and stopping it with the trailing edge, we can get very accurate position measurements. Often a Zero signal is added so that the baseline zero position can be known. Commercial (i.e., volume control knob) and industrial (conveyor belt control, motor feedback) uses for optical encoders are plentiful.

Strain gages

Strain gages are passive sensors that exhibit a change in resistance due to an applied compressive or tensile strain. The effect is small, and these devices are usually used in a bridge configuration, where a small change in one element unbalances the bridge, and the voltage difference is proportional to the applied phenomena.

Resolvers and synchros

Resolvers and synchros are sometimes called differential transformers. Conventional speed sensors are based on the principle of electromagnetic induction and use a rotating gear tooth to interrupt a magnetic path, inducing an alternating output voltage. The frequency of the output is proportional to the rotating speed. The conventional coil is simple but requires a large number of turns to generate a reasonable output voltage.

A *resolver* is a form of rotary magnetic device similar to a transformer on a shaft. The magnitude of the energy through the magnetic windings varies sinusoidally as the shaft of the resolver rotates. The windings consist of a reference winding on the rotor with two input stator windings. Rotor windings are an enlargement of the shaft and act one set of transformer windings. The two-stator windings are respectively, sine and cosine out of phase or offset mechanically at 90° to each other. The ratio of the induced SIN and COS voltage vectors provides a rotor shaft angle reference zero position with reference to the fixed stator winding. Exciting one input of a resolver with voltage A produces outputs of $A \sin \theta$ and $A \cos \theta$. Exciting the other input with voltage B produces outputs of $B \sin (\theta + 90)$ or $B \cos \theta$ and $B \cos (\theta + 90)$ or $-B \sin \theta$. Energizing both windings at once results in two outputs. Note that the output voltage is constant with rotor position. However, the time-phase shift in electrical degrees between the output and the input is equal to the rotor position angle in mechanical degrees.

Since they are electro-magnetic devices, synchros and resolvers have a very long life expectancy. The nature of a transformer permits the isolation of the input and the output circuits.

Star Sensors

Star sensors measure star coordinates in a spacecraft frame of reference and provide attitude information when these observed coordinates are compared with known star directions obtained from a star catalog. Star sensors can achieve accuracies in the arc-second range. Most star sensors consist of a Sunshade, an optical system, an image definition device which defines the region of the field of view that is visible to the detector, the detector and an electronic assembly. The detector such as a photomultiplier transforms the optical signal into an electrical signal. Solid-state detectors may be noisier than photomultipliers. The electronics assembly amplifies and filters the electrical signal from the detector. If the amplified optical signal from the detector is above a fixed signal intensity, an output is generated signifying the star's presence.

A charge transfer device star sensor is an optical system consisting of a digitally scanned array of photosensitive elements whose output is fed to an embedded microprocessor. A charge pattern corresponding to the received image of the star field viewed is produced. The charge pattern is then read out serially line-by-line to an analog to digital converter and this subsequent signal is stored in memory.

Smart sensors.

Smart sensors include embedded processing. The IEEE Standard 1451 covers functions, communication protocols, and formats for smart sensors. Networked and wireless sensors are also covered. Moving the processing closer to the sensor offloads this task from the main computer, freeing up resources for other tasks.

Sensor Network

A group of sensors working together can be organized into a network. These can be an array of similar or identical sensors, or a group of sensors using different technologies to gather a more complete perspective of the sensed item of interest. The sensor network can be wired or wireless. The detection devices monitor the local conditions and perform a small local area surveillance, collect data, and translate the acquired raw data to usable information. The network can be rigidly preplanned, or ad-hoc and self-organizing. This latter approach involves swarms of sensors, not all of which need to be the same.

Actuator and Mechanism Interfacing

It is an analog world. Until recently, a digital interface to a motor or actuator was not common. Digital to analog conversion circuits were required. The other issue is power amplification. The actuators usually operate beyond the available range of voltages of computer components, and may require orders of magnitude more current. An actuator as we use it here means an electrical to mechanical transducer. This includes motors and solenoids. Actuators can be electrical, pneumatic, or hydraulic. Pneumatic units use a compressible fluid, and hydraulic actuators use a non-compressible fluid. Electromechanical actuators are also used. Chemical actuators are also possible.

Piezoelectric actuators are inherently linear, as solenoids. Standard mechanical mechanisms can be used to convert linear to rotary motion, or vice versa. An actuator may also be used to clamp an object to prevent motion. Actuators are usually classified by their efficiency.

Analog and power interfacing

In a direct current motor, dc is applied to both stator and rotor, or the rotor is a permanent magnet. If there are rotor connections, these must be by slip ring and brushes to allow rotation. Electric motors have gained interest in the field of electric and hybrid automobiles, although their use in railroad locomotives goes back a hundred years. Modern diesel-electric locomotives operate with 6,000 horsepower diesels driving alternators, and six AC traction motors, each independently slip-controlled. Electric traction (Metro, trolley) operates with third-rail or overhead power.

Pulse width modulation control is typically used for motor speed control. In this scheme, the width of a pulse determines the duty cycle of the motor, from 0 to 100%. The pulse repetition rate must be greater than the motor's inertia will allow it to respond to. Typically, this works well with 1 kilohertz, although systems up to 100 KHz are used. During the period of time when the pulse is not active, the back-emf (electro-magnetic force) of the motor can be measured as an indicator of load, and the next pulse adjusted accordingly.

Electrically commutated motors

Electrically commutated, or brushless direct current motors, are the latest variation on a technology that is more than a hundred years old. DC motors with brushes have been in commercial use since the 1880's, with demonstrations of the technology around 1840. They can produce large amounts of torque, but are inefficient, and high-maintenance because of the brush wear.

Brushless motors are a type of stepper motor, a configuration usually used for precise positioning. These are used to maintain specific rotation increments or rotary positions.

Brushless motors develop maximum torque at start, and have linearly decreasing torque at speed. They have permanent magnet rotors, and the armature windings are fixed. Electronics, an embedded controller, switches the phase of the motor windings to start and maintain the rotor rotation. This configuration leads to increased efficiency (more torque per watt, and more torque per weight), lack of brush wear and sparking, and less susceptibility to dirt and contamination.

Brushless motors require a position feedback, usually with a Hall effect or rotary encoder. The back-EMF induced in the un-driven coils may also be used to estimate position.

These motors find application in cooling fans for electronics and are popular for small model aircraft, helicopters, and racing cars.

Alternating current motors, or *induction motors*, require a sinusoidal-varying voltage or varying frequency alternating current for operation. They exhibit a high efficiency, and can use multiphase power.

Servos

By definition, a *servomechanism* is an automatic device with feedback. The first may have been James Watt's steam engine speed governor. Earlier, windmills had mechanical speed regulators and wind direction adjusters. Feedback is used to reduce system error. A modern example would be an automotive cruise control system.

The servo system may control position, velocity, acceleration, and angular variations for these quantities, temperature, or other physical parameters.

Today, small servo systems developed for model aircraft and cars are cheap and plentiful. These normally use radio links as a control mechanism. The system consists of an electric motor and a variable resistor for position feedback. The radio link sends a PWM signal, where the width of the pulse indicates a position command. The feedback allows the servo to hold the commanded point. The standard servos used in radio controlled models use a 50-Hertz frame rate. Each pulse has a 20-millisecond width.

The actual mechanism may be capable of 90, 180, or possibly 360-degree rotation. The system was originally developed as analog (continuous), but is now digital (discrete). Interfaces between servo systems and standard computer interfaces such as USB are available.

Solenoids

Solenoids are linear motion devices using a coil and magnet. They are used for actuating valves, for example. They require a simple application of voltage for operation. Working against a spring, a fairly accurate position can be maintained, at the cost of continuously applied current.

Smart Actuators

Actuators can have built-in embedded computers. These are referred to as smart actuators. They may incorporate a local feedback and monitoring loop. IEEE-1451 is a set of standards for interfacing smart sensors and smart actuators. The standards cover functions, communication protocols, and formats.

Software

"Software gets slower faster than hardware gets faster," Nicholas Wirth, 1995.

Instruction Set Architecture

The *Instruction Set Architecture* (ISA) defines the data types, the instructions, the internal architecture of the cpu, addressing modes, interrupt handling, and input/output. The ISA is defined before implementation of the hardware. It may be legacy, as is the case with the Intel 16-bit ISA, now extended to 64 bits, or the ARM ISA. Many other examples can be found in the computer field.

The ISA defines what the processor does, not how it does it. There are different implementations of the ISA that produce the same results with different methods. Numerous examples of this are found in the x86 world.

The ISA can be emulated or simulated on another machine. Specific hardware does not need to exist to run an ISA. The *Java Virtual Machine* (JVM) came before the hardware, and was not intended to be instantiated in hardware. It was later implemented in hardware as an exercise, after many software implementations of the JVM on diverse platforms.

Data type definitions are part of the ISA. The available data types might include bits, 4-bit nibbles, BCD, 8-bit bytes, 16- 32- and 64-bit words, complex number pairs, floating point, double-precision floating point, pixels, etc. Now, the choice of binary over decimal is clear, as binary has the edge in implementation with current state-of-the-art microelectronics. When Charles Babbage designed his difference engine in the 1840's, decimal seemed the better choice. This was partially due to the fact that Boole had not yet formulated his algebra, to show how logic functions could implemented in arithmetic.

Instruction types in an ISA define data movement and operations on data. Data movement includes operations to input and output data from external devices, move data to and from internal registers, and to and from memory. Operations on data include the standard mathematical and logical operations. Control flow instructions provide a mechanism for the independent and data-dependent transfer of control. This group includes branches, jumps, loops, subroutine calls and returns, interrupt vectoring, and operating system calls.

The instructions can provide additional features, such as block moves of data, stack operations, or an atomic test and set. This latter instruction helps implementing coordination among multiple processes, using a mutual exclusion property.

Instruction sets can also have complex entities to implement digital signal processing functions on data, or SIMD (single instruction – multiple data) constructs for vector data processing.

Instructions can have fixed or variable length. Fixed length instructions are easier to pipeline. We can specify multiple operations within one instruction word, allowing more instructions to be fetched at one time. This is the basis for the very long instruction word (VLIW) method. VLIW computer architectures take advantage of instruction-level parallelism. Within the long instruction word are instructions that can be executed simultaneously. These instructions are discovered by the compiler, and grouped together into the VLIW's. Thus, some of the inherent complexity of the problem is removed from the hardware, and placed on the software. The term and the concept of VLIW are attributed to computer architect Josh Fisher at Yale in the 1980's. The first microprocessor to use VLIW techniques was Intel's i860.

The instruction set can be rich and redundant (*complex instruction set computer*- CISC) or reduced (*reduced instruction set* computer

(RISC). In the limit, we might have a *one instruction set computer* (OISC), a *zero instruction set computer* (ZISC), or a *no instruction set computer* (NISC), which are interesting academic abstractions. In a sense, a specific implementation of a problem in read-only memory becomes a One-instruction set computer, as the hardwired unit does its job when it's turned on. The particular job can consist of thousands of instructions. This is a fast and simple approach that is not necessarily easy to change.

An instruction consists of several parts, the operation (op) code, and the operands. The *op code* is usually the leftmost part of the instruction, the first to be fetched, allowing the decoding process to begin as the *operands* (data) are fetched. There may be zero, one, two, three, or more operands. The standard logical or mathematical operation is usually a function of two (input) variables, and produces a single output.

$$\text{Output} = \text{function}\,(\,\text{input1},\,\text{input2}\,)$$

A standard number of operands, then, would be three. We can reduce this to two, if one of the input operands is destroyed by the operation, and used as the output. If our data structures allow, we might have *implied, or zero, operands*. This would be the case in a *stack architecture*, where all the action takes place at the top of the stack. The stack data structure is instantiated in memory. When we say "ADD", the operand at the top of the stack is added to the next operand on the stack, and the result is put on the top of the stack. We don't need to mention the operands, they are implied. In a VLIW architecture, we may have multiple sets of op codes and operands in a single instruction word.

Implementation of the instruction set can take many forms. The instruction decoding can be hardwired, or table-driven. *Hardwired instruction decoding* is fast, but not flexible or changeable. *Table-driven instruction decoding* allows for the possibility of additions to the instruction set. An ISA can also be implemented in a software emulator, which is a computer program that lets one computer pretend to be another.

Semaphore

Semaphores are structures used for signaling between tasks or processes. The semaphore was invented in 1974 by Edsger W. Djikstra, a Computer Scientist who received the Turing award in 1972 for fundamental contributions to programming languages. Semaphores allow for task synchronization and signaling for more than two tasks.

Open Source versus Proprietary

This is a topic we need to discuss before we get very far into software. It is not a technical topic, but concerns your right to use (and/or own, modify) software. It's those software licenses you click to agree with, and never read. That's what the intellectual property lawyers are betting on.

Software and software tools are available in proprietary and open source versions. Open source software is free and widely available, and may be incorporated into your system. It is available under license, which generally says that you can use it, but derivative products must be made available under the same license. This presents a problem if it is mixed with purchased, licensed commercial software, or a level of exclusivity is required. Major government agencies such as the Department of Defense and NASA have policies related to the use of Open Source software.

Adapting a commercial or open source operating system to a particular problem domain can be tricky. Usually, the commercial operating systems need to be used "as-is" and the source code is not available. The software can usually be configured between well-defined limits, but there will be no visibility of the internal workings. For the open source situation, there will be a multitude of source code modules and libraries that can be configured and customized, but the process is complex. The user can also write new modules in this case.

Large corporations or government agencies sometimes have problems incorporating open source products into their projects. Open Source did not fit the model of how they have done business traditionally. They are issues and lingering doubts. Many Federal agencies have developed Open Source policies. NASA has created an open source license, the NASA Open Source Agreement (NOSA), to address these issues. It has released software under this license, but the Free Software Foundation had some issues with the terms of the license. The Open Source Initiative (www.opensource.org) maintains the definition of Open Source, and certifies licenses such as the NOSA.

The GNU General Public License (GPL) is the most widely used free software license. It guarantees end users the freedoms to use, study, share, copy, and modify the software. Software that ensures that these rights are retained is called free software. The license was originally written by Richard Stallman of the Free Software Foundation (FSF) for the GNU project in 1989. The GPL is a *copyleft* license, which means that derived works can only be distributed under the same license terms. This is in distinction to permissive free software licenses, of which the BSD licenses are the standard examples. Copyleft is in counterpoint to traditional copyright. Proprietary software "poisons" free software, and cannot be included or integrated with it, without abandoned the GPL. The GPL covers the GNU/linux operating systems and most of the GNU/linux-based applications.

A Vendor's software tools and operating system or application code is usually proprietary intellectual property. It is unusual to get the source code to examine, at least without binding legal documents and additional funds. Along with this, you do get the vendor support. An alternative is open source code, which is in the public domain. There are a series of licenses covering open source code usage, including the Creative Commons License, the gnu public license, copyleft, and others. Open Source describes a collaborative environment for development and testing. Use of open source code carries with it an implied responsibility to "pay back" to the community. Open Source is not necessarily free.

The Open source philosophy is sometimes at odds with the rigidized procedures evolved to ensure software performance and reliability. Offsetting this is the increased visibility into the internals of the software packages, and control over the entire software package. Besides application code, operating systems such as GNU/linux and bsd can be open source. The programming language Python is open source. The popular web server Apache is also open source.

Operating system

An *operating system* (OS) is a software program that manages computer hardware and software resources, and provides common services for execution of various application programs. Without an operating system, a user cannot run an application program on their computer, unless the application program is itself self-booting.

For hardware functions such as input, output, and memory allocation, the operating system acts as an intermediary between application programs and the computer hardware, although the application code is usually executed directly by the hardware and will frequently call the OS or be interrupted by it. Operating systems are found on almost any device that contains a computer. The operating system functions need to be addressed by software (or possibly hardware), even if there is no entity that we can point to, called the Operating System. In simple, usually single-task programs, there might not be an operating system per se, but the functionality is still part of the overall software.

An operating system manages computer resources, including:

- Memory.
- I/O.
- Interrupts.
- Tasks/processes/application programs.

The operating system arbitrates and enforces priorities. If there are not multiple software entities to arbitrate among, the job is simpler. An operating system can be off-the-shelf commercial or open source code, or the application software developer can decide to build his or her own. To avoid unnecessary reinvention of the wheel an available product is usually chosen. Operating systems are usually large and complex pieces of software. This is because they have to be generic in function, as the originator does not know what application space it will be used in. Operating systems for desktop/network/server application are usually not applicable for embedded applications. Mostly they are too large, having many components that will not be needed (such as the human interface), and they do not address the real-time requirements of the embedded domain.

Adapting a commercial or open source operating system to a particular embedded domain can be tricky. Usually, the commercial operating systems need to be used "as-is" and the source code is not available. The software can usually be configured between well-defined limits, but there will be no visibility of the internal workings. For the open source situation, there will be a multitude of source code modules and libraries that can be configured and customized, but the process is complex. The user can also write new modules in this case.

Operating Systems designed for the desktop are not necessarily suited to the embedded space. There were developed under the assumption that whatever memory is required will be available, and real-time operation with hard deadlines is not required.

Real-time operating systems, as opposed to those addressing desktop, tablet, and server applications, emphasize predictability and consistency rather than throughput and low latencies. Determinism is probably the most important feature in a real-time operating system.

A microkernel operating system is ideally suited to embedded systems. It is slimmed down to include only those features needed, with no additional code. Barebones is the term sometimes used. The microkernel handles memory management, threads, and communication between processes. It has device drivers for only those devices present. The operating systems may have to be recompiled when new devices are added. A file system, if required, is run in user space. MINIX, as an example of a streamlined kernel, with about 6,000 lines of code.

Some example off-the-shelf operating systems include:

Android

The *Android* operating system by Google has found application in numerous smartphone and tablet computers since its introduction in 2008. It is an Open Source product based on Gnu-Linux, although not all of the code is covered by Open Source licenses. It has evolved into versions for set-top boxes, robotics, digital cameras, and digital television applications. Android supports several hardware computing platforms including ARM, POWER, x86, and MIPS.

Like Java, Android provides a virtual machine execution engine for a specific hardware platform. This virtual machine is termed Dalvik. It's strengths are in memory-limited systems, and those with hard real time requirements. Android is targeted to user input from touch, with a screen using icons. In an embedded application, it may have no direct user interface. Android uses the Gnu-Linux kernel, plus middleware, libraries of code, and API's. The user community supports a large library of applications for Android. Android has built-in support for power management.

VxWorks

VxWorks is a commercial real-time embedded operating system and associated Integrated Design Environment from Wind River. It is widely used in the embedded world. VxWorks is not open source. It has a multitasking kernel with preemptive and round-robin scheduling and fast interrupt response. Symmetric multiprocessing is supported. Several file systems are also supported. A wide range of target architectures are available, both chip-level, and board level products. Wind River also has a version of Gnu-Linux, derived from RTLinux, called WindRiver Linux 5. Currently, VxWorks is the operating system of choice for Mars exploration rovers.

GNU/Linux

GNU/Linux is a Unix variation, written originally for the x86 architecture by Linus Torvalds. It is important to keep in mind that standard GNU/Linux is not a real-time system. There are several enhancements to the GNU/Linux kernel that address soft real time and some hard real time issues. Being free and open software, there are many GNU/Linux variations. For embedded systems use, most of these need to be slimmed down, removing the gui and desktop-specific applications. Another approach is the build the system up by including only those modules needed. This requires a good working knowledge of the kernel build process.

Linux from scratch (LFS)
This interesting project allows one to build a custom GNU/Linux system, including the modules that are needed, and leaving out

those that are not. In the end, you will know more about the GNU/Linux operating system that you wanted to know. The advantage of being able to choose what goes into the build is the ability to construct a minimalist system with small footprint. It does require, however, a good understanding of the interrelationships between modules. For real-time embedded use, the appropriate kernel patches need to be applied.

Real Time and embedded Linux

There are several approaches to make GNU/Linux a real-time operating system. One version developed by FSM labs, and used by VxWorks, is a hard real-time RTOS microkernel that runs the entire Gnu-Linux operating system as a fully preemptive process. To address soft real-time, the GNU/Linux kernel can be modified by several available patches to add non-preemption and low latency, with a deterministic scheduler.

The standard GNU/Linux (or BSD) kernel is not pre-emptable. This means kernel code runs to completion. The run time is not bounded, which interferes with responding to time-critical events. It is important to keep in mind that the Gnu-Linux kernel was not designed for non-preemption, as a true real-time operating system would be. Preemption has overhead, and influences throughput, usually adversely. There is a real-time Linux Foundation (.org) that is a good source of information on these topics.

Ubuntu Mobile and Embedded are variations of the Ubuntu Linux distribution for Mobile Phones, and embedded applications in general.

BSD

BSD is a desktop/server open source operating system, and is not intended for embedded use. However, very small builds of BSD can be used provided real-time and determinism is not an issue.

BSD, the Berkeley Software Distribution, is a licensed derivative of Unix, from Bell labs, dating from 1977. There are multiple variations of BSD, targeting different problem domains. Some of these include FreeBSD, OpenBSD, DesktopBSD, PC-BSD, and NetBSD. BSD influenced SunOS, Windows, and Apple OS X. BSD code is available under very permissive license terms. Device drivers in BSD are part of the kernel, and run in privileged mode. Symmetric multiprocessing is supported.

Embedded BSD

The same approaches to make GNU/Linux real-time at the kernel level are generally applicable to BSD as well. FreeBSD has real time extensions per POSIX 1003.4.

LynxOS

The LynxOS RTOS is a Unix-like real-time operating system from LynuxWorks It is a real-time POSIX operating system for embedded applications. LynxOS components are designed for absolute determinism (hard real-time performance), which means that they respond within a known period of time. Predictable response times are ensured even in the presence of heavy I/O due to the kernel's unique threading model, which allows interrupt routines to be extremely short and fast. LynuxWorks has a specialized version of LynxOS called LynxOS-178, especially for use in avionics applications that require certification to industry standards such as DO-178B.

QNX

QNX is a real-time operating system based on Unix. QNX Neutrino RTOS is SMP capable, and supports POSIX APIs. It is not open source.

The QNX microkernel contains only CPU scheduling, inter-process communication, interrupt redirection, and timers. Everything else runs as a user process, including a special process known as *proc,* which performs process creation, and memory management by operating in conjunction with the microkernel. There are no device drivers in the kernel. The network stack is based on NetBSD code.

RTEMS

RTEMS is the Real-Time Executive for Multiprocessor Systems, designed for embedded use, and free and open source. It is POSIX compliant. The TCP/IP stack from FreeBSD is included. RTEMS does not provide memory management, but is single process, multithreaded. Numerous file systems are supported. RTEMS is available for the ARM, Atmel AVR, and a wide variety of other popular embedded cpu's and DSP's. An RTEMS system is currently in orbit around Mars.

Microsoft Windows

The Microsoft Windows offerings for desktop and server use are not intended for real-time application. Microsoft has special variations of their operating system for embedded use (WIN-CE, XP-embedded, Win-8 embedded), and in specific domains, such as automotive. Windows is a proprietary operating system. Source code is available for purchase under non-disclosure licensing. Security in Windows-based systems, particularly those connected to the Internet, is problematic, as Windows systems are major targets of viruses and malware. This has happened in medical equipment that is Windows-based.

BSP

The *Board Support Package* (BSP) is the set of specific software that customizes a generic operating system to a particular hardware architecture. Think of it as a collection of definitions and device drivers, with a bootloader. A software toolkit may also be included with the BSP. The BSP may be supplied by the hardware vendor, or the OS vendor.

BIOS

The *basic input output subsystem* is a small, tightly written piece of code that is invoked after a hard reset. It resides at a defined area of memory, usually read-only, and runs to completion. Most bios allow for extension code that is entered after the main BIOS is completed. The functions of the bios include: initial hardware configuration, hardware functional checking, implementation of rudimentary I/O control, and hand-off of control to the rest of the operating system, which may be located on secondary storage.

Process

In multi-rate systems, tasks may be synchronous or asynchronous. Synchronous tasks may recur at different rates. Processes run at different rates based on computational needs of the tasks.

A *process* is a software entity managed by the operating system. Processes can be in one of three states, executing, ready, or waiting. The process is one instance of a program; multiple processes, including multiple instances of a single process, may be involved. A process includes the resources (context) it needs to execute. A program may result in multiple processes. Multitasking allows multiple processes to share resources, managed by the operating system. Time-sharing is a common form of multitasking. This is an improvement over the scenario where each program has to run to completing before the next can start. Task switching occurs depending on various criteria. A fair task switching scenario allocates equal time to each process. Another scheme is to allow processes to run until a resource they require is not yet available.

There is a major distinction in process scheduling between conventional computers, and those intended for real-time systems.

Processes are commonly called tasks in embedded systems. Workstations and servers allow equal access to cpu cycles. This is a fairness approach. Real-time embedded systems have hard deadlines. This means that lower priority tasks may be locked out for long periods. Real-time systems are not fair. Hard deadlines are not fair.

A *thread of execution* is the smallest unit of processing that can be scheduled by the operating system. Multiple threads can exist in the same process, and share resources with other process threads. A process or task is an independent entity, but a thread is a part or subset of a process. Processes need more state information than threads. Context switching between threads is thus quicker. Threads are managed by the operating systems, as are tasks. Threads are supported in most modern higher-level languages.

Thrashing refers to areas of resource contention in the system. It is usually an operating system problem. A shared resource in contention will result in thrashing. Unrestrained processes share resources like kids share a candy bar on a playground – not well, without adult intervention.

The IBM 2321 Data Cell was a circa-1964 secondary storage device faster than tape, not as fast as disk. The storage capacity of the refrigerator-sized device was 400 Megabytes. Data were stored on removable strips of magnetic material, arranged in bins in a drum configuration. When data was accessed, the assembly rotated to the correct bin, and the correct magnetic strip was removed and read. This was accomplished by a mechanism using Mobil DTE hydraulic fluid at 1,500 psi. Where are we going with this? Stay with me here.

Each magnetic strip held about 200k bytes. If one were to write a program to multiply two matrices, one of which was on a particular strip, and the other was on a strip 180 degrees away, a large of amount of time would be consumed by thrashing, and the drum rotated back and forth to access the next data item. The hydraulic system kept this going until the bearings burned out. Not that I would have tried this.

Communication between processes is handled by the operating system. This can take the form of message passing, or a shared mailbox area. Inter-process communication can take the form of blocking or non-blocking, With blocking, the sending processes waits for and requires a response. In non-blocking, the data is just broadcast, and we hope the receiver gets it.

A *shared memory approach* has some memory in common between processes. A race condition, or contention for access is possible. This is addressed by a hardware feature, the atomic test and set mechanism, which assures exclusive access to a data item or other resource.

A *message passing approach* uses real or virtual channels between processes to send messages, with the operating systems as the postmaster. This is sometimes called the software bus.

In a single processor system, only one process can be executing at a time. In a multicore system, one can be executing on each core. On a single processor, we can implement multithreading as time-division multiplexing of threads. Multiple CPU cores can be multithreaded as well.

A real-time operating system is a multitasking operating system that aims at executing real-time applications. Real-time operating systems use specialized scheduling algorithms so that they can achieve deterministic behavior. The main objective of real-time operating systems is their quick and predictable response to events.

They have an event-driven or time-sharing design and often aspects of both. An event-driven system switches between tasks based on their priorities or external events while time-sharing operating systems switch tasks based on clock interrupts.

Certain software elements facilitate inter-process communication and coordination. Coordination mechanisms in real time operating systems provide for protecting critical resources with mutual exclusion. Implementation includes mutexes and semaphores. These rely on the underlying architectural support of an atomic test-and-set function.

A test-and-set is an operation defined to write to a memory location and return the old value as a single non-interruptible action. This may be implemented as a cpu instruction, in memory devices such as dual-port memory, etc. Test-and-set is used to implement mutual exclusion, and is the basis of semaphores

A mutex is a binary flag used to protect a shared resource with exclusivity. With two tasks at different priorities and co-ordination via a mutex create the possibility of a priority inversion.

Embedded operating systems are designed to be used in embedded computer systems. They are designed to operate on small machines like cell phones or tablets with less autonomy. They are able to operate with a limited number of resources. They are very compact and extremely efficient by design.

The operating system provides an interface between an application program and the computer hardware, so that an application program can interact with the hardware only by obeying rules and procedures programmed into the operating system. The operating system is also a set of services which simplify development and execution of application programs. Executing an application program involves the creation of a process by the operating system kernel which assigns memory space and other resources, establishes a priority for the process in multi-tasking systems, loads program binary code into memory, and initiates execution of the application program which then interacts with the user and with hardware devices.

The bootstrap ("boot") process

How does the processor get started? In a process equivalent to pulling yourself up by your own bootstraps, the computer executes a specific sequence at start-up. At power on, a simple circuit generates a RESET signal to the processor. Reset is a special interrupt. The RESET signal takes the processor to a known predefined state.

In a typical boot process, registers are forced to fixed values, and the processor starts executing code from a fixed physical address (which assumes there's code there). The next step is to test and initialize the hardware. After that, the Master boot record is read from a non-volatile storage device, or possibly a communications link. This gets the operating system into memory.

Power-On-Self-Test, or POST, executes a rudimentary series of tests of the system components. This is a difficult task conceptually, because the computer hardware and software tests itself. Assumptions must be made about minimal functionality.

The boot software is considered part of the operating system, but can support different operating systems in dual-boot or multi-boot systems. Boot code can be put in ROM, or flash.

File system

There are several popular file systems, usually defined as part of a specific operating system. A file system provides a way to organized your data, and file systems management services are part of the operating system. The operating systems may support several file formats. A file system organizes data. It presents a data-centric view of a digital storage system. (Early computer data storage systems were analog, such as the mercury delay line and the Williams tube.)

A file is a container of information, usually stored as a one-dimensional array of bytes. Historically, the file format and the nature of the file system were driven by the mechanism of data storage. On early computer tape units for mainframes, the access mechanism was serial, leading to long access times. With disk and solid-state storage, the access time is vastly improved, as the device is random access – the same access time applies for any data item.

Metadata includes information about the data in a file. This consists of the file name and type, and other parameters such as the size, date and time of creation, the data and time of last access, the owner and read/write/access permissions, when a backup was last made, and other related information.

A directory, like the manila file folder, is a special file that points to ("contains") other files. This allows files to be organized. This implements a hierarchical file system.

There are many file system standards. The Microsoft operating systems support the FAT and NTFS file systems among others. The FAT (File Allocation System) format originated with early support of 8-bit microprocessor systems with MS-DOS. Fat-12 and FAT-16 had restrictions on the number of files in the root file system, but this has largely been removed with the introduction of FAT-32. File names are restricted to 8 characters, with a 3-character type specifier, the 8.3 format for file names. NTFS is the extended file system developed for the Windows-NT and subsequent operating systems from Microsoft.

Linux supports a variety of file formats, including .ext2, ext3, and ext4. Apple Computer uses the HFS Plus, derived from the earlier Mac OS, and it's Unix heritage.

Opsys in hardware

The operating functions can be implemented in hardware, with tables of parameters. This provides a faster implementation. We can have a Real Time kernel in hardware (for FPGA & ASIC). This will be deterministic and secure. The associated data structures will be in memory. The scheduler would be implemented in hardware. This is currently a research concept. The concept was implemented in the Intel 80130 chips, circa 1981.

The 80130 was a ROM plus a programmable interrupt controller, several timers, and a baud rate generator. In the ROM was a rudimentary operating system; basically, software in silicon. The firmware contained 35 operating system primitives, including task management, interrupt management, message passing via mailboxes, synchronization, and memory allocation. Tasks had 256 possible priority levels, and 5 possible states, asleep, suspended, asleep/suspended, ready, and running.

IP Cores

An *intellectual property (IP)* core is a reusable logic unit that can be licensed, owned, and included in a design. IP cores can be used as building blocks for ASIC's, FPGA's, and Soc's. The discussion in the software section regarding proprietary versus open source applies. IP cores can also be proprietary or open source. Cores as a product are available in hardware description language form, essentially, source code for hardware. Proprietary cores may or may not be modifiable, and may or may not be supported by the vendor. Cores may also be available as netlist files, which are a Boolean algebra representation that has to be instantiated in a specific technology. A gate level netlist is seen as analogous to assembly language, and is portable to any process (implementation) technology.

The cores can contain digital and analog components, but the analog components require specific transistor layout formats. Complete embedded processors such as the 8-bit Intel 8051 series and various members of the ARM family are available as cores. Besides entire cpu's, IP cores are available for various interfaces and I/O devices. Individual developers can produce cores, and include them in libraries.

The intellectual property owner, the developer of the core, sees a return on his NRE cost of developing the hardware, and can have the design used in a large number of application areas, perhaps leading to an industry standard or industry-preferred approach.
Core vendors are wary of reverse engineering of their core, just as software suppliers are concerned with the same process in their domain.

Hard cores are defined at a physical layer, and provide a predictable performance. They are supplied as transistor-level layout format. This is subject to using a particular target chip foundry. Generally, a hard core cannot be changed. It represents a plug-in function. Soft cores, on the other hand, are specified in the RTL language, or as a netlist, and are "compiled" into a design. They can be easily changed by industry-standard toolsets. The design is portable, with respect to a fabrication technology.

CPU cores are readily available for popular CPU architectures. A PCIexpress bus core is available, as well as Ethernet, CAN bus, usb, and other standards. Various cores to address specific application areas such as DSP are also available.

Real-Time Embedded

In a real-time system, the timing of the result is as important as the logical correctness. Embedded systems find themselves in these situations a lot. There are two types of deadlines, hard and soft, and various scheduling policies to address these. A scheduling policy should have the ability to meet all deadlines. The scheduling overhead should be minimal.

In soft real time, the average performance or response time is emphasized. Desktops and servers can meet soft real time requirements. Missing a deadline is not necessarily catastrophic. Embedded examples include an elevator controller, vending machines, gas pumps, cash registers and POS, thermostats, mobile phones, and a bike computer. Missing a deadline may result in a degradation of service, but not a failure.

In hard real time, on the other hand, critical sections of code have absolute deadlines, regardless of how busy the system is. Missing a deadline means system failure. Response times must be deterministic. Examples of hard real time systems include avionics fly-by-wire system, antilock brakes, stability control in automotive applications, and nuclear power plant safety systems.

Interestingly, meeting a deadline early may be just as bad as meeting it late. There are constraint requirements on the response time for the systems.

We can have systems with the characteristics of both; these multi-rate systems handle operations and deadlines at varying rates.

Non-Real Time (NRT) systems are fair; they provide resources (time, I/O) to all users or programs on an equal, or pre-determined priority basis. They can arbitrate resource allocation to maximize the number of deadlines met, or minimize lateness, or some combination. Everyone gets a turn. NRT systems have high throughput and fast average response.

Multiple approaches to scheduling have evolved.

In Round Robin scheduling, we can bound maximum CPU load, but may leave unused CPU cycles. The scheduling can be adapted to handle an unexpected load. We want to use all the available time slots by the end of period. We will schedule tasks that are ready, and use equal time intervals. Of course, if a ready low priority task can lock out a not-yet-ready high priority task, we have a problem. This is not a good approach for hard real time.

Not all CPU time is available for processes, some is used for operating system overhead. The scheduling process itself consumes CPU time. Scheduling overhead must be taken into account for the exact schedule.

In the case of scheduling for general-purpose computers, we seek to optimize the average case, even though we may not know what that is. In real time systems, we need to optimize the worst case. We can determine the worst case from the relative priorities that the embedded system has to accomplish. This is part of the requirements. We need to meet the deadline of the worst case all the time. The correct result at the wrong time is a system failure. Being late is a failure. Being early is no help.

To evaluate and define the worst case, we need to examine the requirements, and the implementation design in terms of the cpu, the program that is running, the specific task that is addressing the worst case, and the context of the operating system and other software activities. We can ensure meeting deadlines by hardware or software, or both. We can develop faster or smarter software, or choose faster hardware.

One approach is the use of a cyclic executive. Here, a timer triggers a task every frame. This is a periodic interrupt. Timers are on-chip peripherals that can be used by the scheduler.

When using event driven programming, some events are asynchronous to the system, and the embedded system must react to them. We would determine our latency requirements and program our system accordingly. However, many events need to be tightly synchronized to a specific clock.

Timers allow us to perform event-driven operations on an accurate time-scale without tying up our processor, providing deterministic performance. Timers give us greater time resolution than we could accomplish (easily at least) using sequential programming techniques.

We need to generate a predefined list of tasks that the systems will accomplish, based on the system requirements. If we need concurrency, we will require a synchronization mechanism. We are trying to achieve a predictive response under all conditions. We also need to know data dependencies between processes. We need to profile the software to define the execution times, average and worst case.

There are multiple *real time scheduling policies*, which are tailored to the application domain and its requirements. Each task has an associated priority. The resources are allocated to the highest priority task that is ready. Priorities determine the scheduling process. Priorities can be fixed or time-varying. The problem becomes whether the system can meet all required deadlines. One solution is to increase the cpu speed. You do this by waiting for the next generation of hardware. But, faster systems can also consume more power, and dissipate more heat.

We also may have *aperiodic processes*, which execute on demand, controlled by asynchronous external processes.

In the *Fixed Priority Preemptive scheme*, a higher priority task can preempt a lower priority task. In the *Rate Monotonic* scheme, the higher the frequency of a task, the higher its priority.

We always need to keep in mind the context switch overhead; there is a finite amount of time and resources required to switch tasks (or threads of execution). This is the task switch overhead.

Real-time tasks share resources for which they contend, and they may be forced to wait.

Priority inheritance protocols bound priority inversion. Real time operating systems generally use a priority based preemptive scheduler. Each task has a unique priority based on system requirements. Tasks have an associated state, running, ready, or waiting. A scheduler program ensures that of the list of ready tasks, the highest priority one is running. A lower priority task may be preempted. A problem may occur because of shared resources. In *priority inversion*, the highest priority task fails to run when it should due to a shared resource conflict.

Priority inversion was demonstrated on the surface of Mars in July 1977 during the Pathfinder Mission. A higher priority task was forced to wait for a lower priority task, due to shared resource contention. A lower priority task had control of a resource that it needed to access until completion. This locked out the critical higher resource task.

In unbounded priority inversion, we have multiple medium priority tasks. The tasks are periodic. If we have a lower priority task holding a critical resource, and a medium priority tasks preempt the lower priority task, which can't complete, we have a problem. And, since the tasks are periodic, they keep getting rescheduled.

In a priority inheritance protocol, a task runs at its original priority, unless it is blocking a higher priority task. Then, it runs at the priority of the higher level task it is blocking. Mutual deadlocks are possible; this is the deadly embrace scenario. Here, neither task can proceed until the other allows it.

In the *Priority ceiling* protocol, no task can be blocked for longer than the duration of the longest critical section of a lower priority task, instead of for the entire duration of the lower priority task. Aperiodic tasks are non-periodic events with no fixed deadlines, but they interfere with periodic tasks.

Embedded Systems Standards

There are many Standards applicable to embedded systems. These range from general computer standards to embedded-specific standards. Why should we be interested in standards? Standards represent an established approach, based on best practices. Standards are not created to stifle creativity or direct an implementation approach, but rather to give the benefit of previous experience. Adherence to standards implies that different parts will work together. Standards are often developed by a single company, and then adopted by the relevant industry. Other Standards are imposed by large customer organizations such as the Department of Defense, or the automobile industry. Many standards organizations exist to develop, review, and maintain standards.

Standards exist in many areas, including hardware, software, interfaces, protocols, testing, system safety, security, and certification. Standards can be open or closed (proprietary). Sometimes, the embedded systems customer will require an adherence to specified standards.

Hardware standards include the form factor and packaging of chips, the electrical interface, the bus interface, the power interface, and others. The JTAG standard specifies an interface for debugging.

In computer architecture, the ISA specifies the instruction set and the operations. It does not specify the implementation. Popular ISA's are x86 (Intel) and ARM (ARM Holdings, LTD). These are proprietary, and licensed by the Intellectual Property holder.

In software, an API (applications program interface) specifies the interface between a user program, and the operating system. To run properly, the program must adhere to the API.

There are numerous Quality standards, such as those from ISO, and Carnegie-Mellon's CMM (Capability Maturity Model). CMM defines five levels of organizational maturity in a company or institution, and is independently audited. Language standards also exist, such as those for the ANSI c and Java languages. Networking standards include TCP/IP for Ethernet, the CAN bus from Bosch, and IEEE-1553 for avionics.

The ISO-9000 standard was developed by the International Standards Organization, and applies to a broad range of industries. It concentrates on process. It's validation is based on extensive documentation of organization's process in a particular area, such as software development, system build, system integration, and test and certification.

It is always good to review what standards are available and could be applied to an embedded system, as it ensures the application of best practices from experience, and interoperability with other systems.

The Portable Operating System Interface for Unix (POSIX) is an IEEE standard, IEEE 1003.1-1988. The standard spans some 17 documents. POSIX provides a Unix-like environment and API. Various operating systems are certified to POSIX compliance, including BSD, LynxOS, QNX, VxWorks, and others.

ARINC 653 is a software specification (API) for space and time partitioning in safety critical real-time operating systems. Each piece of application software has its own memory and dedicated time slot. The specification dates from 1996.

Embedded Systems Security

All embedded systems have aspects of security. Even a billing transaction from a gas pump has to have the credit card numbers protected. Controllers for electrical grid switching and nuclear power plant control need to be protected. A user's personal data on cell phones and ATM's is vulnerable. A denial-of-service attack on a 9-1-1 emergency system is going to cost lives.

Embedded systems operate in an unfriendly world. They are available to attacks from hacking, viruses and malware, theft, damage, spoofing, and other nasty techniques from the desktop/server world. But here, they can result in disruption of infrastructure (such as the electric grid or aircraft safety), denial of service, such as bank networked-ATM's, and as an entry point to larger systems and databases. Traffic light systems, although rather simple, can disrupt traffic flow over a wide area. ATM networks can be used not only as theft targets, but also as entry points to a bank's database. 9-1-1 (emergency) systems can be disrupted, slowing response to emergencies. GPS systems can be hacked to provide incorrect location or critical time information. Guess what controls elevators? The automobile, trucking, aircraft, maritime, and rail industries are increasingly dependent of networked embedded controllers. Gas pumps are controlled by embedded devices, that communicate your bankcard information over a network to a database. Cell phones and tablets are connected wirelessly to large networks. Health care is increasingly dependent on embedded medical devices that can be hacked, and embedded processor controlled diagnostic and treatment equipment. The key cards used for access control in secure facilities and simple hotel rooms have been hacked to provide the master code. The smart grid, with smart meters, has been attacked to provide residency information. A clever hacker can convince an ATM machine to provide free money. A bored teenage hacker in Europe took over the city Tram system as his private full-scale railroad, using a TV remote. Just because the crossing gate is up, does that mean a train is NOT coming? Just because your traffic light is green, does that mean the other is red? What about the teenager in an internet café is a third-world country. Can he raise and lower your garage door, turn off your security system, start your car? Sleep well.

Some of these issues are addressed by existing protocols and standards for access and communications security. Security may also imply system stability and availability. Standard security measures such as security reviews and audits, threat analyses, target and threat assessments, countermeasures deployment, and extensive testing apply to the embedded domain.
A security assessment of a system involves threat analysis, target assessment, risk assessment, countermeasures assessment, and testing. This is above and beyond basic system functionality.

The completed functional system may need additional security features, such as intrusion detection, data encryption, and perhaps a self-destruct capability. Is that self-destruct capability secure, so not just anyone can activate it? All of these additional features use time, space, and other resources that are usually scarce in embedded systems.

Virus and malware attacks on desktops and servers are common, and an entire industry related to detection, prevention, and correction has been spawned. These issues are not as well addressed in the embedded world. Attacks on new technology such as cell phones, tablets, and GPS systems are emerging. Not all of the threats come from individuals. Some are large government-funded efforts or commercial entities seeking proprietary information or market position. Security breaches can be inspired by ideology, money, or fame considerations. The *CERT* (Computer Emergency Response Team) organization at Carnegie Mellon University, and the *SANS Institute* (SysAdmin, Audit, Networking, and Security) track security incidents.

Techniques such as hard checksums and serial numbers are one approach to device protection. Access to the system needs to be controlled. If unused ports exist, the corresponding device drivers should be disabled, or not included. Mechanisms built into the cpu hardware can provide protection of system resources such as memory.

Security has to be designed in from the very beginning; it can't just be added on. Memorize this.

Even the most innocuous embedded platform can be used as a springboard to penetrate other systems. It is essential to consider security of all embedded systems, be aware of industry best practices and lessons learned, and use professional help in this specialized area.

Systems that provide "satellite control software" are included under the *International Trafficking in Arms* (ITAR) regulation, as the software is defined as "munitions" subject to export control. The Department of State interprets and enforces ITAR regulations. It applies to items that might go to non-US citizens, even citizens of friendly nations or NATO Partners. Even items received from Allies may not necessarily be provided back to them. Software and embedded systems related to launch vehicles and satellites are given particular scrutiny. The ITAR regulations date from the period of the Cold War with the Soviet Union. Increased enforcement of ITAR regulations recently have resulted in American market share in satellite technology declining. A license is required to export controlled technology. This includes passing technical information to a foreign national within the United States. Penalties of up to $100 million have been imposed for violations of the ITAR Regulations, and imprisonment is also possible. Something as simple as carrying ITAR information on a laptop or storage medium outside the US is considered a violation. ITAR regulations are complex, and need to be understood when working in areas of possible application. ITAR regulations apply to the hardware, software, and Intellectual Property assets, as well as test data and documentation. It is a complex topic.

The first detection of *backdoor code* in a military grade FPGA came in May of 2012. This was detected in an Actel ProASIC3 chip. It was built into the silicon and was activated by a secret key code. This caused much distress worldwide in the FPGA/ASIC world, and for their military customers. Although this was the first detected instance of this security breach, it was probably not the first instance. The story of how it was discovered is of interest. We can expect more of this type of behavior in the future of embedded systems. See:

http://www.cl.cam.ac.uk/~sps32/Silicon_scan_draft.pdf

Virtualization of Embedded Systems

Virtualization in embedded systems is enabled by multicore technology. This allows us to assign applications to processor cores, with proper regard for determinism. One approach is to have a "real-time" core and a non-real-time core. Utilization of processors and load-leveling is secondary to determinism. Virtualization is a key tool for embedded, enabled by multicore architectures.

Virtualization has been successfully applied in servers for some time, but there are unique problems in the real-time embedded world. Determinism and consistency are important, with resource balancing nice, but not essential. A mechanism for scaling real-time processes across multiple cores is required. This mechanism is provided in software. Threads have to have direct control over I/O interfaces.

Different cores can be running different OS's. Communication between cores can be via shared memory (or cache) and/or specific message-passing interfaces. Inter-core communication does not need to leave the chip boundary. Core can be connected in various network topology's, such as bus, ring, mesh, or torus. If part of the embedded system involves a human-machine interface, this can be hosted on its own core, so as to minimize impact on the hard real-time part of the system.

With multicore, we have the option of segregating real-time and non-real time tasks, hard real time from soft real time. An embedded virtualization manager (VM) controls the entire process. With hardware virtualization assist built into the cores, the VM can be invisible to the underlying operating systems. The VM is, essentially, an operating system for operating systems, managing and orchestrating resources such as I/O, memory, and time. Actual hardware resources are virtualized, but virtualized models of non-existent interface and hardware may also be provided. This provides a mechanism for support of legacy interfaces.

The resources that are present in the virtual machine can be mapped from the real machine, or defined in terms of the basic I/O resources available. We can define and use virtual resources by modeling these in software, even if they don't actually exist.

Hypervisor – the operating system's operating system

A hypervisor is a virtual machine manager. It manages virtual resources, including operating systems. It presents to a guest operating system a standard platform interface. Examples include XEN, VmWare, and QEMU. Hypervisors are top-level software supervisors that control the allocation of resources to multiple operating systems. Embedded hypervisors support real-time operations. The Hypervisor runs on the host machine, and support one or more guest environments. The name dates from 1965, in its use on an IBM S/360 mainframe. The System 360 model 67 introduced dynamic address translation, which enabled virtualization.

Hypervisors are characterized as Type 1 (runs directly on the hardware) or Type 2 (runs on an operating system).

In addition, we can have VM's defined in high-level languages. Java is the prime example. Hypervisors are top-level software supervisors that control the allocation of resources to multiple operating systems. Embedded hypervisors support real-time operations.

Hardware assisted virtualization is an example of platform virtualization. It uses assistance from the hardware to provide full virtualization, so unmodified guest operating systems can be supported.

Virtualization is done with a second stage of address translation with its own page tables. The Hypervisor runs in a unique new privilege mode. The mode is entered with a Hypervisor Call, instead of the previous Hypervisor Trap. The Virtualization privilege mode is a new third privilege level. There is the user code level, the operating system level, the Hypervisor level, and a TrustZone Privilege level, at the top. The Embedded Xen product supports virtualization on the ARM architecture.

In the ARM scheme, before virtualization, the Operating System controlled the memory resource. Now, there is a second level of address translation. Where virtual addresses used to map to physical addresses, they now map to Intermediate addresses, which are then mapped to physical addresses by the Hypervisor.

Prof. Daniel Rossier introduced embedded XEN in a white paper in June 2012. XEN is available for the ARM architecture, and can run on ARM-based mobile devices. It uses Android as the host, and addresses real-time systems support and multiprocessing. Like all XEN products, it is free and open source software. Support for hardware assist to virtualization in ARM, and for the ARM 64-bit architecture, are being incorporated into XEN. I/O can also be virtualized. Running RS-232 protocols over USB is an example.

Architecture of some embedded systems and chips

This section presents and discusses some "real-world" embedded systems, at both the chip and system-level.

Arduino

The Arduino is a simple open-source single-board microcontroller. The hardware consists of a simple open hardware design for the Arduino board with an Atmel processor and on-board I/O support. The software support includes a standard compiler and a boot loader that runs on the board, along with numerous libraries of code.

Arduino hardware is programmed using a language similar to C++ with some simplifications and modifications, and an IDE.

The project began in Italy in 2005 to produce a device for implementing student-built design projects less expensively. By mid-2011, more than 300,000 Arduino boards had been shipped.

An Arduino board consists of an 8-bit Atmel AVR microcontroller or an Atmel 32-bit ARM. An important aspect of the Arduino is the standard way that connectors are arranged, allowing the CPU board to be connected to a variety of interchangeable add-on modules called *shields*. Shields allow for interfacing with sensors and actuators, as well as general I/O. Most boards include a 5-volt linear regulator and a 16 MHz crystal oscillator although some designs dispense with the on-board voltage regulator. An Arduino's microcontroller comes with a boot loader that simplifies uploading of programs to the on-chip flash memory.

Boards are programmed over an RS-232 serial connection. Serial Arduino boards contain a simple inverter circuit to convert between RS-232-level and TTL-level signals. Newer Arduino boards are programmed via RS-232 protocol over USB.

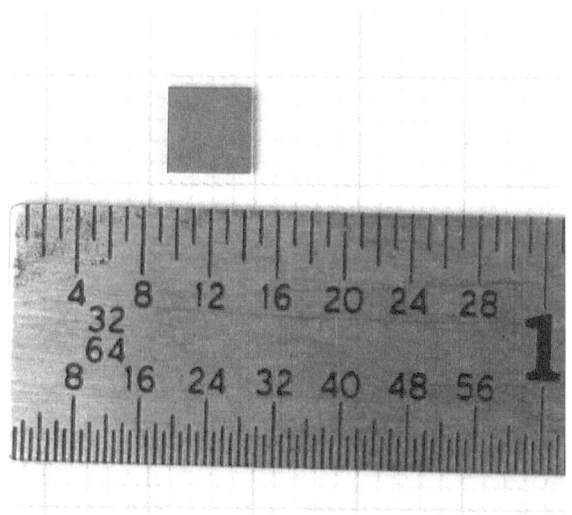

The Arduino board brings out the microcontroller's I/O pins for use by external circuits.

The Arduino IDE is a cross-platform application implemented in Java. It is designed to introduce programming to newcomers unfamiliar with traditional software development. It includes a code editor with features such as syntax highlighting, parenthesis matching, automatic indentation, and is also capable of compiling and uploading programs to the board with a single click. There is no need to edit makefiles or run programs on the command line.

The Arduino IDE comes with a C/C++ library called "Wiring", which makes many common input/output operations much easier. It uses the gnu toolchain and AVR libraries. The Atmel development Studio can also be used. Arduino programs are written in a variant of c/c++.

The Arduino hardware reference designs are distributed under an Open Source Creative Commons Attribution Share-Alike 2.5 license and are available on the Arduino Web site. Layout and production files for some versions of the Arduino hardware are also available. The source code for the IDE and the on-board library are available and released under the GPLv2 license. The Arduino design has influenced many other similar devices.

ARM

The ARM processor has come a long way from being an obscure British microprocessor of the 1980's to being the dominant basis for the current generation of smart phones, pda's, and tablet computers. They are also used extensively in television set-top boxes, routers and other embedded applications. The ARM parts represent the highest volume of 32-bit processors shipped, as of this writing.

ARM architecture is discussed in more detail in the author's ARM-specific book, see ASIN B00BAFF40Q.

In 2010, over 6 billion ARM chips were sold, mostly in the smartphone market. ARM is the target architecture for the gnu/Linux-based Android operating system, and the ARM has ports of OpenSolaris, BSD, and various Linux variations, including Gentoo, Debian, Slackware, and Ubuntu.

ARM is an Instruction Set Architecture (ISA) specification. It is instantiated in silicon by numerous companies under license. ARM Holdings plc, a British Multinational company, is the inheritor of the intellectual property (IP) of the 32-bit CPU design, and licenses its use worldwide. The products include the intellectual property for the ARM7, ARM9, ARM11, and the Cortex series.

The ARM architecture today accounts for around 75% of all 32-bit embedded processors. ARM code can be developed in Java or variants of most languages, and many off-the-shelf operating systems are available. The ARM architecture reached critical mass in the embedded market niche. ARM separates the Intellectual Property of the design and the Instruction Set Architecture from the implementation. The ARM architecture has over 900 licenses, and it grows by about 100 per year. More than 4 ARM billion chips are produced every year.

The Thumb Instruction set state is a 16-bit subset of the ARM7 architecture. This reduces functionality but provides a greater code density. Sections of code that are computer-intensive can be hand-optimized for the Thumb mode. Most Thumb instructions map directly to ARM opcodes. Thumb-2 mode includes some 32-bit instructions.

The ARM Cortex processors are the latest in the 32-bit series, and expand into multicore and 64-bit models for higher performance. There are three basic models of the Cortex processors, targeting different applications areas. These chips allow a multicore implementation. The Cortex-A8 is a superscalar architecture, with dual instruction issue. The NEON SIMD unit is optional, as is floating point support.

The Cortex-A9 can have multiple cores that are multi-issue superscalar and support out-of-order and speculative execution using register renaming. It has an 8-stage pipeline. Two instructions per cycle can be decoded. There are up to 64k of 4-way set associative Level-1 cache, with up to 512k of Level 2. A 64-bit Harvard architecture memory access allows for maximum bandwidth. Up to four double word writes per five machine cycles are possible. Floating point units and/or a media processing engine are available for each core. A9 architecture includes loop unrolling in hardware, and uses four pipelines with out-of-order execution. There are extensions to the floating-point unit as well as extensions for SIMD and media processing for audio and video data. A quad multiply-accumulate is provided to accelerate digital filters. A9 has both 64- and 128-bit registers.

SIMD includes 43 MMX instructions derived from Intel's SSD for the x86 architecture. Operations include multiply-accumulate, vector floating-point instructions, support for 2D and 3D transforms and digital filters.

The ARM Cortex-R has specific features to address performance in real-time applications. These include an instruction cache and a data cache, a floating-point coprocessor, and an extended 8-stage pipeline. Cortex-R supports the Thumb and Thumb-2 instructions as well as ARM. Up to 64-bit data structures are supported.

Cortex M addresses microcontroller applications, as are likely to be found in embedded systems. The STM 32F103 is a typical 32-bit MCU in the ARM Cortex line. It has the M3 core, and runs at a maximum frequency of 72 MHz. It includes 20 kbytes of SRAM, and up to 128 kbytes of flash memory. The SRAM operates at the cpu clock speed. It has power-on reset, which loads the program counter with the value in the reset vector, which is at memory address 4. A 32 KHz oscillator is included for the real-time clock. The clock maintains time and date, and can provide an alarm interrupt or periodic interrupt. Three low power modes are implemented: sleep, stop, and standby. In sleep mode, the cpu clock is stopped but the peripherals are awake, and can awaken the CPU. Stop mode has all of clocks stopped. Content of the SRAM and registers are maintained. The chip can be awakened with the EXTI line, a non-maskable external interrupt. Standby mode has the lowest power consumption. Memory and register contents are lost. Standby mode is exited with a WKUP external signal or a NRST. The real time clock can also force an exit from Standby; its clock is not stopped in that mode.

The chip includes dual 12-bit analog to digital converters, with up to 16 channels available by multiplexing. There are seven channels of DMA available with timers, USARTS, and SPI and I2C support on I/O channels. There are a maximum of 80 map-able I/O ports that can be configured, and 16 vectored external interrupts. At reset, the vector table is at address 0. The chip runs on 3.3 volts, but the inputs are mostly 5 volt tolerant. A JTAG debugging port is available. There are three 16-bit timers that can be used for quadrature encoder input, or PWM output, and two watchdog timers. The 16-bit general-purpose timers can count up or down, and have a capture/compare feature. The watchdog timer is independent of the main clock.

Standard communication interfaces that are supported include I^2C, USART, SPI at 18 mbps), CAN, and USB 2.0. One or two I2C buses can be supported in multi-master or slave modes. The USART interface operates up to 4.5 Mbps, and can use DMA. The SPI interface can operate to 18 Mbps in full duplex and master mode. Can bus supports 2.0A and B formats to 1 Mbps, and uses frames with 11- or 29-bit identifiers. The USB interface goes to 12 Mbps. The chip includes a CRC calculation circuit with a 96-bit capacity. The STM32F represents a family chips, with low-, medium-, and high-density models. Higher density models include more memory and I/O devices. The STM 32F103 is considered a medium density device. The chip can be configured to boot from system memory, user flash, or internal SRAM.

Any of the general-purpose I/O pins can be software configured to be an input or an output. The ARM architecture uses memory-mapped I/O. The two built-in analog-digital converters share 16 channels, and include sample and hold. The chip also has an internal temperature sensor with a voltage that varies linearly with temperature. This is connected internally to ADC channel 12, input 16.

TI Evalbot

The LM3S9B92 microcontroller chip from Texas Instruments uses the ARM Cortex-3 core plus the Thumb-2 instruction set. It is a member of TI's STellaris product family. It implements single-cycle hardware multiply and divide, and supports unaligned data access. It has separate buses for instructions and data. Interrupt handling is deterministic, always being 12 cycles. Memory protection is provided. The chip is optimized for single-cycle flash memory. It supports a 80-MHz clock. It has a 24-bit integrated system timer, a vectored interrupt controller with an NMI and dynamically re-prioritizable interrupts.

The microcontroller includes 96 Kbytes of single cycle RAM on chip and 256 kBytes of single cycle flash. Flash blocks of 1-kbyte in size can be marked as read-only or execute-only. The I/O can support 10/100 Ethernet, 2 CAN controllers, USB 2.0, three UART's, dual I2C, and dual synchronous serial. There are four 32-bit timers, eight PWM's, two watchdog timers, and up to 65 general purpose I/O's. Two quadrature encoder inputs are provided for motor feedback. There are two 10-bit A/D's with 16 shared channels. In additional, there are three analog comparators that can generate an interrupt. JTAG is supported.

The Raspberry Pi

The Raspberry Pi is a small, inexpensive, single board computer based on the ARM architecture. It is targeted to the academic market. It uses the Broadcom BCM2835 system-on-a-chip, which has a 700 MHz ARM processor, a video GPU, and currently 512 M of RAM. It uses an SD card for storage. The Raspberry Pi runs the GNU/linux and FreeBSD operating systems. It was first sold in February 2012. Sales reached ½ million units by the Fall. Due to the open source nature of the software, Raspberry Pi applications and drivers can be downloaded from various sites. It requires a single power supply, and dissipates less than 5 watts. It has USB ports, and an Ethernet controller. It does not have a real-time clock, but one can easily be added. It outputs video in HDMI resolution, and supports audio output. I/O includes 8 general purpose I/O lines, UART, I2C bus, and SPI bus.

The Raspberry Pi design belongs to the Raspberry Pi Foundation in the UK, which was formed to promote the study of Computer Science. The Raspberry Pi is seen as the successor to the original BBC Microcomputer by Acorn, which resulted in the ARM processor. The unit has enough resources to host an operating system such as linux.

The Maple board

The Maple board, from LeafLabs is an Arduino-derived ARM architecture using the STM32F103RBT6, a 32-bit ARM Cortex M3 microprocessor. It is implemented on a 2 x 2 inch board, the design of which is open source. It operates at 72 MHz, and has 128 KB of flash and 20 KB of SRAM. There are 43 general digital I/O pins (GPIOs), 15 PWM pins at 16 bit resolution, and 15 analog input (ADC) pins at 12-bit resolution. It includes dual SPI peripherals, dual I^{2}C peripherals, seven channels of DMA, and three USART (serial port) peripherals. There is one advanced and three general-purpose timers, and a dedicated USB port for programming and communications, which also supplies power. JTAG support is included. There is a nested vectored interrupt controller (NVIC). The Maple board is small and inexpensive, yet very capable, and a good learned tool for embedded systems. The associated IDE is hosted on a variety of platforms, including Windows, Linux, and Apple. It is Open Source, and has extensive libraries. The Maple is a good and inexpensive board to play with, and develop hands-on experience with the technology.

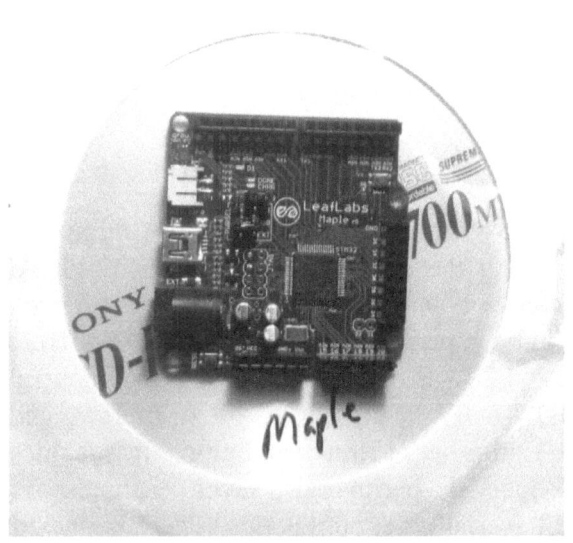

The Intel Microcontrollers

The Intel 8051 8-bit chip was developed as an embedded control processor by Intel in 1980. Embedded processors can operate with fewer external parts, and the 8051 included memory and input/output on the same chip. Even now, many manufacturers offer versions of the 8051, and it is widely used in college-level embedded systems courses. The most recent instantiations of the design include IP core versions, for implementation within FPGA's that need one or more CPU's. Why re-invent the wheel, when the 8051 comes with a development history, loyal following, and support tools? The 8051 has been used on NASA's environmental satellites Aqua and Aura.

The Intel 8051 was developed from the earlier 8048 as an embedded control processor by Intel in 1980. The 8048 had serial I/O plus dual timers, 4k of ROM, and 128 bytes of RAM. They operated up to 16 MHz, and came in ROM-less versions (8031), and in CMOS. The 8044 was an 8051 with a synchronous serial interface to a host machine, and EPROM.

The 8742 was an associated peripheral 8-bit slave microcontroller, meant to be used with the 8051, 8048, and even the general purpose 8080 and 8085. It was a follow-on to the 8741 with twice the memory. It was a peripheral chip, but included a complete 8-bit cpu, with 2k of EPROM, 128 bytes of RAM, a clock/timer, and I/O control lines. It was intended to offload I/O from the main cpu. It supported asynchronous transfer with the main processor.

80186/188

The 80186 was an embedded version of the 16-bit general purpose 8086, incorporating an integral clock generator, dma channels, interrupt controllers, and chip selects. This greatly reduced the number of external chips required in a design. It could address 64k of 8-bit I/O ports, or 32k of 16-bit ports. It supported 256 vectored interrupts.

The 80188 was a 80186, with an 8-bit external bus. This allowed for the use of less expensive 8-bit wide memory, at the cost of time. Each memory word access (16 bits) required two 8-bit wide sequential memory accesses. With the sharply reduced price of memory, this technique was no longer required.

8096/80196 (MCS-96) and i960

The Intel MCS-96 family of embedded microcontrollers was derived from the 8061 chip, which resulted from a project for the Ford Motor Company for a 16-bit engine controller. That unit was called the EEC-IV. The 8061 had 8 pulse measuring inputs, 10 pulse generating outputs, and multichannel 10-bit A/D.

The 809x parts operated at 12 MHz. They included a cpu and a 4-channel, 10-bit A/D, and 8-bit PWM, a watch-dog timer, and four general 16-bit timers. They featured hardware multiply and divide, and 8 kbytes of ROM. The 8095 version came with no internal ROM, but did include high speed I/O plus a serial port. CMOS versions of the chip were available. A later model was the 80196.

The Intel i80960 was a 32-bit RISC embedded processor family dating from 1984. They were not code-compatible with other Intel products. They featured 32, 32-bit register, with a priority interrupt controller, on chip instruction cache (1k to 16k), with data cache (1k to 8k) on some models, a PCI controller, and a memory controller on chip. Some models included dual 32-bit timers and an i2c bus. They were a superscalar architecture with register scoreboarding. Some models had an integral IEEE-754 floating point unit.

The processor is still in use for selected military applications. It's design was influenced by the iAPX432 project at Intel, and the i960 design was a joint effort with Siemens. In order not to compete with its own i860 and i386 products in the general purpose computing market, Intel targeted the i960 to the embedded market.

The i960 followed the Berkeley school of RISC design, with register windows and fast subroutine calls. The memory space was flat.

80130

The 80130 was a ROM plus a programmable interrupt controller, several timers, and a baud rate generator. In the ROM was a rudimentary operating system, basically, software in silicon. The firmware contained 35 operating system primitives, including task management, interrupt management, message passing via mailboxes, synchronization, and memory allocation. Tasks had 256 possible priority levels, and 5 possible states, asleep, suspended, asleep/suspended, ready, and running.

80376 and 80386EX

The 80376 was an embedded variation of 386 architecture introduced in 1989. It did not support Intel's real mode, but booted directly to protected mode. It was replaced by the 80386EX, which was a static design, true 32-bit processor with extensive peripherals on chip. It included power management circuitry, up to 24 I/O lines, 3 channels of 8254- equivalent timer/counters, two 8259- equivalent interrupts controllers, dual full-duplex Async serial (uart) channels, one synchronous five mbps I/O channel with baud rate generator, DRAM refresh, 32-bit watchdog timer, dual channel DMA control, and JTAG debugging support.

Embedded pc

Embedded versions of 8- and 16-bit Intel chips evolved from the general purpose cpu's. For the 32-bit versions, the 80386 family, the embedded chip version was the 80386EX. It included a static core which could run as slowly (and thus, power efficiently) as desired, down to a full halt.

The Intel ISA found its way into embedded variants of the popular 80x86 chip set, used mostly in desktop applications. These included the 80386EX, the 80387, the Vortex 86 SOC, the AMD Geode, and the ZET 80186, an open core for FPGA's. The advantage of this approach is the widespread knowledge base of the 80x86 software architecture, although the hardware architecture was not optimized for embedded applications. Most of the chips included a standard 80x86 processor core, with additional I/O and system features to reduce chip count.

As mainstream cpu's evolved for desktop and server usage, with increased speed and addressing capability, the chips became less well suited to the embedded environment. But, as family chips were developed for the laptop and tablet market, they were generally applicable in a subset of the embedded world, mostly for cost-sensitive systems with soft real time requirements, if any.

The Intel Atom cpu is an x86 architecture optimized for low power (several watts). It was introduced in 2008, and is now available in multicore and hyper-threaded editions, with speeds beyond 2 GHz. It translates x86 instructions into internal RISC instructions on the fly, and can execute two integer instructions per clock. Because the parts are IA-32 compatible, there is a large amount of available legacy software for the part. Atom processors are available on pc-architecture motherboards of a small form factor. System-on-a-chip devices are being phased in.

Nano-ITX is a pc motherboard form factor first proposed by VIA Technologies in March 2003, and implemented in late 2005. Nano-ITX boards measure 120 × 120 mm (4.7 × 4.7 in), and are fully integrated, very low power pc motherboards targeted at smart digital entertainment devices such as PVRs, set-top boxes, media centers, car PCs, and thin devices. PC operating systems such as Windows, Gnu-Linux, and bsd Unix are supported. The following photo shows a nano-ITX system, using a motherboard from Artigo. The system has 1 gigabyte of ram, 250 gigabytes of sata hard drive, 4 usb ports, and support vga and hdmi video. The power input is 12 volts. This system, configured by the author, dual-boots Windows-XP and Ubuntu linux.

Pico-ITX is a PC motherboard form factor announced by VIA Technologies in January 2007 and demonstrated later the same year at CeBIT. The Pico-ITX form factor board is 10 × 7.2 cm (3.9 × 2.8 in), which is half the area of Nano-ITX. The processor can be a VIA C7, a VIA Eden V4, a VIA Nano with speeds up to 1.5 GHz, with 128KB L1 & L2 caches. It uses DDR2 400/533 SO-DIMM memory, with support for up to 1GB. AGP Video is supplied by VIA's UniChrome Pro II GPU with built-in MPEG-2, 4, and WMV9 decoding acceleration.

PC/104 and PC/104+ are examples of standards for ready-made computer boards intended for small, low-volume embedded and ruggedized systems, mostly x86-based. These are physically small compared to a standard PC, although still quite large compared to most simple monolithic embedded systems. They often use MSDOS, Linux, NetBSD, or a true embedded real-time operating system such as MicroC/OS-II, QNX or VxWorks.

In certain applications, where small size or power efficiency are not primary concerns, the components used may be compatible with those used in general purpose x86 personal computers. Boards such as the VIA EPIA range help to bridge the gap by being PC-compatible but highly integrated, physically smaller or have other attributes making them attractive to embedded engineers. The advantage of this approach is that low-cost commodity components may be used along with the same software development tools used for general software development. Systems built in this way are still regarded as embedded since they are integrated into larger devices and fulfill a single role. Examples of devices that may adopt this approach include ATMs and arcade machines, which contain code specific to the application.

A typical board includes the BIOS, an ATA-133 disk interface and a SATA interface, Ethernet port, four USB ports, and power management features.

Texas Instruments

According to the Smithsonian Institution, Texas Instruments engineers Gary Boone and Michael Cochran created the first microcontroller and the first single chip CPU in 1971. The result of their work was the TMS-1000, which went commercial in 1974. It was widely used in embedded applications such as toys (the legendary TI Speak-n-Spell), games, appliances, burglar alarms, copy machines, and more. It was widely used in TI hand-held calculators, starting with the TI-16, and including the TI-35. There was a wide family of TMS-1000 parts with different configurations.

TI was awarded U.S. Patent 3,757,306 for the single-chip microprocessor architecture on September 4, 1973. In 1971 and again in 1976, Intel and TI entered into broad patent cross-licensing agreements, with Intel paying royalties to TI for the microprocessor patent. A history of these events is contained in court documentation from a legal dispute between Cyrix and Intel, with TI as intervener and owner of the microprocessor patent.

A computer-on-a-chip combines the microprocessor core (CPU), memory, and I/O (input/output) lines onto one chip. The computer-on-a-chip patent, called the "microcomputer patent" at the time, U.S. Patent 4,074,351, was awarded to Gary Boone and Michael J. Cochran of TI. Aside from this patent, the standard meaning of microcomputer is a computer using one or more microprocessors as its CPU(s), while the concept defined in the patent is more akin to what is now called a microcontroller.

The PMOS, 300 KHz, TMS-1000 had 8192 bits of ROM, 256 bits of RAM, and a 4-bit ALU in a single package. There was a 4-bit input port, and 19 outputs. The instruction decoder is programmable, so the instruction set is not rigidly defined. There were 43 standard instructions, with the ability to add more via microinstructions. Later versions featured more RAM and ROM, and CMOS versions became available. The PMOS versions operated at 15 volts.

TI is a licensee of the ARM architecture, and produce many variants extending into multicore architectures, and digital signal processing, one of their key strengths.

TI MSP430

The TI MPS430 is a low power 16-bit microcontroller. It can run at 25 MHz, but is a static design, so the clock can be slowed for lower power consumption. They are many different configurations of the device, featuring combinations of features including timers, PWM, serial I/O, analog to digital converters, analog comparators, digital to analog conversion, hardware multiply, and DMA. There is no external memory bus, but the newest models have internal flash, loaded via serial port. Internal memory goes up to 256 kbytes of flash, with 16 kbytes of RAM. The device is currently in its 6th generation.

TMS320

TI's TMS320 series is a family of DSP chips dating from 1983. Some versions use fixed point, and some include floating point capability. The architecture evolved from a coprocessor for general purpose cpu's. The architecture is Harvard, with separate instruction and data memory, but includes the ability to read data from instruction memory. The first generation products were 16-bit. The later C80 product has a 32-bit floating point master processor and four 32-bit fixed point processors for video processing. The C2000 series are DSP's with 32-bit microcontrollers (ARM architecture), with support for I^2C, SPI, CAN, a watchdog timer, external memory interface, and GPIO. The C5000 series is 16-bit fixed point, with a 6-stage pipeline. These find application in mobile phones. Linux has been ported to the C6000 series parts.

OMAP (Open Media Application Platform) is the name of a series of image/video processors from TI. They have an ARM processor and one or more specialized coprocessors in various combinations. One of the coprocessors is a TMS 320 DSP. OMAP is targeted to the embedded realm, although it came from the mobile phone application area. OMAP-1 was used in mobile phones, and included an ARM core and a C55x DSP. OMAP-2 included an ARM and a C64x DSP, and was targeted to tablets and phones. OMAP-3 is a SoC design, with a IVA2 (Image, Video, Audio) accelerator. The OMAP-4 includes a dual core ARM Cortex A9, and two CARM Cortex-M3 cores. Some models include a 2D graphics accelerator core, and all have the IVA3 core. OMAP-5 is a SoC design with a dual core ARM Cortex-A15, dual Cortex M4 cores, dual graphics processing cores, and the graphics accelerator. These chips support full 3D High Definition digital video recording. OMAP-5 supports USB 2.0 and SATA 2.0 interfaces.

Analog Devices

In Digital Signal Processing, we are operating on audio or video data with computationally-intensive digital filters. This is applicable in the embedded domain, and one of the key strengths of Analog Devices.

The key to digital filtering is the Multiply-Accumulate instruction (MAC). Digital filters usually operate on long vectors (single dimensional arrays) of data.

One example is Analog Devices' Blackfin extensive series of embedded DSP's. The Blackfin is 32-bit RISC processor with dual 16-bit multiply/accumulate (MAC) units, and provision for 8-bit video processing in real-time. The Blackfin architecture was developed in cooperation with Intel, and was announced in 2000. These are derivatives of Analog Device's earlier SHARC architecture and Intel's XScale.

In Blackfin, the DSP part has dual 16-bit MAC units, dual 40-bit ALU's, and a 40-bit barrel shifter. The architecture can execute three instructions per clock. The RISC part has single-cycle instructions, and incorporates data and instruction L1 and L2 caches, as well as on-chip peripherals. It has a memory protection unit, not a memory management unit. Operating systems for the chip can't take advantage of virtual memory. User and Supervisor modes are supported, with an additional emulation mode. The instruction set has 16-, 32-, and 64-bit instructions.

Motorola

Motorola has been involved in the development of embedded versions of its architecture since the beginning of microprocessors. The 6802 chip was a general purpose 6800 with 128 bytes of RAM, and a clock oscillator. This reduced the number of additional chips required in simple embedded controller applications. The 6801 had 2 Kbytes of ROM, 128 bytes of RAM, 31 parallel I/O lines, 3 serial lines, and triple 16-bit timers. General Motors used this chip in automotive applications. The 6803 was the 6801, less the ROM. The 68701 had EPROM instead of ROM. The 6808 was used in the Heath Company's Robot, HERO-1, and was a 6800 with integral clock.

The 6811 was a follow-on chip that featured 16 bit registers and a 16-bit multiply. Radiation hardened versions of the 68HC11 are used in communication satellites. Regular versions are found as embedded controllers in bar code readers, hotel electronic locks, and robots. The HC11 model has an additional Y index register. There is an 8x8 multiply, and a 16 by 16 divide. Hitachi's 6309 chip extended the operations to allow four of the 8-bit registers to be used together as a 32-bit register. The 68HC12 is an enhanced version of the HC11. It operates up to 25 MHz, and has 512 kbytes of flash, and 8 kBytes of RAM.

Embedded controller models of the 68000 evolved from the basic architecture, and a fully-static core version became available. When idle, this required only 2 microwatts. The 683xx series is the embedded line. The 68000's found use in Industrial control as programmable logic controllers (PLC's) from Allen-Bradley, Texas Instruments, and Siemens. The 68k embedded processors are found in video games, telecomm switching equipment, the TI-89 and TI-92 calculators, and others. The 68ECxx embedded core version evolved into the Dragonball processors from Freescale.

The Motorola 88000 was a RISC design from the late 1980's, following the MIPS and SPARC designs. It was a 32-bit machine, with a register-register architecture, and supported both little-endian and big-endian data. It had separate instruction and data caches. Some 88k features found their way into the joint Motorola-IBM PowerPC architecture. In embedded use, three 88k's were used to implement the triply modular redundant avionics computer in the F-15 aircraft. Generally, Motorola dropped the 88k line in favor of the PowerPC architecture, a joint project with IBM.

Microwave controller

The author found a modern 4-bit microcontroller lurking in his old microwave oven when he disassembled it to see why it had failed. The Daewoo DMC423008 model is a CMOS 4-bit processor with 8kbytes of ROM and 512 4-bit data words of RAM. Program memory is 10 bits wide. There are eight 4-bit registers, vectored interrupts (4 external, 6 internal), a watchdog timer, an interval timer, an 8-bit counter, PWM, 8-bit serial port, an 8-bit A/D converter, and 31 I/O pins. It looked like the magnetron tube shorted out, negating the effects of the microcontroller.

PIC

PIC is a family of Harvard architecture microcontrollers made by Microchip Technology, derived from the PIC1650 originally developed by General Instrument's Microelectronics Division. The name PIC initially referred to "Peripheral Interface Controller".

PICs are popular with both industrial developers and hobbyists alike due to their low cost, wide availability, large user base, extensive collection of application notes, availability of low cost or free development tools, and serial programming (and re-programming with flash memory) capability. Microchip announced on February 2008 the shipment of its six billionth PIC processor.

The PIC architecture is characterized by its multiple attributes, including separate code and data spaces (Harvard architecture) for devices other than PIC32, which has a Von Neumann architecture. It has a small number of fixed length instructions, with most instructions being single cycle execution (2 clock cycles, or 4 clock cycles in 8 bit models), with one delay cycle on branches and skips. There is One accumulator (W0), the use of which (as source operand) is implied (i.e. is not encoded in the opcode), All RAM locations function as registers as both source and/or destination of math and other functions. A hardware stack is used for storing return addresses. A fairly small amount of addressable data space is provided (typically 256 bytes), which can be extended through memory banking. The program counter is mapped into the data space and writable (this is used to implement indirect jumps).

There is no distinction between memory space and register space because the RAM comprises both memory and registers, and the RAM is usually just referred to as the register file or simply as the registers.

PICs have a set of registers that function as general purpose RAM. Special purpose control registers for on-chip hardware resources are also mapped into the data space. The addressability of memory varies depending on device series, and all PIC devices have some banking mechanism to extend addressing to additional memory. Later series of devices feature move instructions which can cover the whole addressable space, independent of the selected bank. In earlier devices, any register move had to be achieved via the accumulator.

External data memory is not directly addressable except in some high pin count PIC18 devices. The code space is generally implemented as ROM, EPROM or flash ROM. In general, external code memory is not directly addressable due to the lack of an external memory interface. The exceptions are PIC17 and select high pin count PIC18 devices.

All PICs handle (and address) data in 8-bit chunks. However, the unit of addressability of the code space is not generally the same as the data space. For example, PICs in the baseline and mid-range families have program memory addressable in the same word size as the instruction width, i.e. 12 or 14 bits respectively. In contrast, in the PIC18 series, the program memory is addressed in 8-bit increments (bytes), which differs from the instruction width of 16 bits.

PIC's have a hardware call stack, which is used to save return addresses. The hardware stack is not software accessible on earlier devices, but this changed with the 18 series devices.

A PIC's instruction set varies in size from about 35 to 80. The instruction set includes instructions to perform a variety of operations on registers directly, the accumulator and a literal constant or the accumulator and a register, as well as for conditional execution, and program branching.

Some operations, such as bit setting and testing, can be performed on any numbered register, but bi-operand arithmetic operations always involve W (the accumulator), writing the result back to either W or the other operand register. To load a constant, it is necessary to load it into W before it can be moved into another register. On the older cores, all register moves needed to pass through W, but this changed on the "high end" cores.

PIC cores have skip instructions which are used for conditional execution and branching. The skip instructions are 'skip if bit set' and 'skip if bit not set'. Because cores before PIC18 had only unconditional branch instructions, conditional jumps are implemented by a conditional skip (with the opposite condition) followed by an unconditional branch. Skips are also of utility for conditional execution of any immediate single following instruction.

PIC instructions fall into 5 classes:

• Operation on working register (WREG) with 8-bit immediate ("literal") operand.

• Operation with WREG and indexed register.

• Bit operations.

• Control transfers.

• Miscellaneous zero-operand instructions, such as return from subroutine, and sleep to enter low-power mode.

The architectural decisions are directed at the maximization of speed-to-cost ratio. The PIC architecture was among the first scalar CPU designs and is still among the simplest and cheapest. The Harvard architecture—in which instructions and data come from separate sources—simplifies timing and microcircuit design greatly, and this benefits clock speed, price, and power consumption.

The PIC instruction set is suited to implementation of fast lookup tables in the program space. Such lookups take one instruction and two instruction cycles. Many functions can be modeled in this way.

Execution time can be accurately estimated by multiplying the number of instructions by two cycles; this simplifies design of real-time code. Similarly, interrupt latency is constant at three instruction cycles. External interrupts have to be synchronized with the four-clock instruction cycle, otherwise there can be a one instruction cycle jitter. Internal interrupts are already synchronized. The constant interrupt latency allows PICs to achieve interrupt driven low jitter timing sequences. An example of this is a video sync pulse generator. This is no longer true in the newest PIC models, because they have a synchronous interrupt latency of three or four cycles.

The PIC architectures have small, easy to learn instruction set. They are a RISC architecture. They have a built in oscillator with selectable speeds, and feature in-circuit programming plus in circuit debugging. There is a wide range of I/O interfaces including I2C, SPI, USB, USART, A/D, programmable comparators, PWM, LIN, CAN, PSP, and Ethernet.

The PIC architectures do have several limitations, including only a single accumulator. Register-bank switching is required to access the entire RAM of many devices. Operations and registers are not orthogonal; some instructions can address RAM and/or immediate constants, while others can only use the accumulator.

The hardware call stack is not addressable, so preemptive task switching cannot be implemented. Software-implemented stacks are not efficient, so it is difficult to generate reentrant code and support local variables.

In November 2007 Microchip introduced the PIC32MX family of 32-bit microcontrollers. The initial device line-up is based on the industry standard MIPS32 M4K Core. The device can be programmed using the Microchip MPLAB C Compiler for PIC32 MCUs, a variant of the GCC compiler. The first 18 models currently in production (PIC32MX3xx and PIC32MX4xx) are pin to pin compatible and share the same peripherals set with the PIC24FxxGA0xx family of (16-bit) devices allowing the use of common libraries, software and hardware tools. The PIC32 architecture extends the features of the Microchips.

The CADC

Recently, an embedded processor project that predates the Intel 4004 was declassified, a set of 6 custom chips for the fly-by-wire F-14 Tomcat fighter aircraft's Central Air Data Computer (CADC). It was developed by Ray Hold, who was finally able to discuss his work for the Navy after 1998. The work was started in 1968. The previous CADC for the F-4 Phantom aircraft was an electromechanical device. The new design was complete in June of

1970, and flew in December. It was implemented in PMOS technology, and met the full mil-spec temperature range. the chips were fabricated by American Microsystems. The design came in at fewer than 75,000 transistors, most of which were in the rom storage, not the cpu.

The design was totally digital, and dual-redundant, with self-checking. Since what it interfaced to was analog, there were both A/D and D/A converters. It used 10 watts of power. It's job was to compute and display data for the pilot, and control the targeting and launch of the aircraft's missiles. It also controlled the control surfaces on the plane's wings and tail. It used fixed-point 2's complement arithmetic with 20-bit data. It used a 375 KHz clock, and had parallel multiply and divide units. There were 16 data registers and 128 words of memory. Instructions were held in ROM.

Whirlwind

The first embedded real-time computer was Whirlwind. This machine was developed at MIT's Servomechanisms Lab around 1947, and implemented by 1951. It was for coordinating the air defense of the United States during the Cold War. It was purpose-built for this function, as no large scale computer systems were available as a basis. It was influenced by the earlier ENIAC digital architecture. Whirlwind was a 16-bit machine. There was to be 2048 words of memory, and the basis technology was either mercury delay lines, or electrostatic "Williams" tubes. The tube solution was chosen, essentially a CRT, these could hold 1024 bits, with an access time of 30 microseconds. This was too slow, and R&D efforts resulted in the development of core memory (as a Master's thesis project). The main cpu used 5,000 vacuum tubes. The Whirlwind computer was at the center of a complex network. Numerous radar stations transmitted data over standard telephone lines to it. CRT's were used for display, and the computer calculated intercept solutions to incoming enemy aircraft.

Whirlwind is now located in the Computer History Museum in Palo Alto, California.

Embedded Microprocessors in space applications

Soon after their development, general purpose microprocessors were used in embedded roles. Eventually, most chip manufacturers produced special models of embedded chips, allowing the use of their standard software tools, but including lower power models with special capabilities for the embedded world. Many of these found application on spacecraft. The harsh environment of space imposed particular requirements on the chips, in the areas of vibration and shock tolerance for the launch phase, and temperature and radiation tolerance during the operational lifetime.

The Intel 4004 was used on the Pioneer-10 Deep Space Mission launched in 1972. The mission studied the asteroid belt, the solar wind, Jupiter, and the outer reaches of the solar system. The computer was used to hold, decode, and distribute commands transmitted from Earth. The mission lasted until 2003, when communications was lost due to distance, a mission duration of 30 years. As of March 2011, the spacecraft is some 102 Astronomical Units (AU= 93 million miles) from the Sun, and radio (or sunlight) takes 14 hours to get to and from it. It is the farthest man-made object from Earth.

8-bit

The 8-bit 1802 was released by RCA in 1976. It was quite a different architecture than other contemporary cpu's, and was produced in complementary metal oxide semiconductor (CMOS) technology, which is both low-power and radiation resistant, though susceptible to electrostatic discharge. It is also a static logic design, which could operate at a wide range of clock speeds down to zero. The architecture has also been implemented in silicon-on-sapphire technology which greatly improves its radiation hardness.

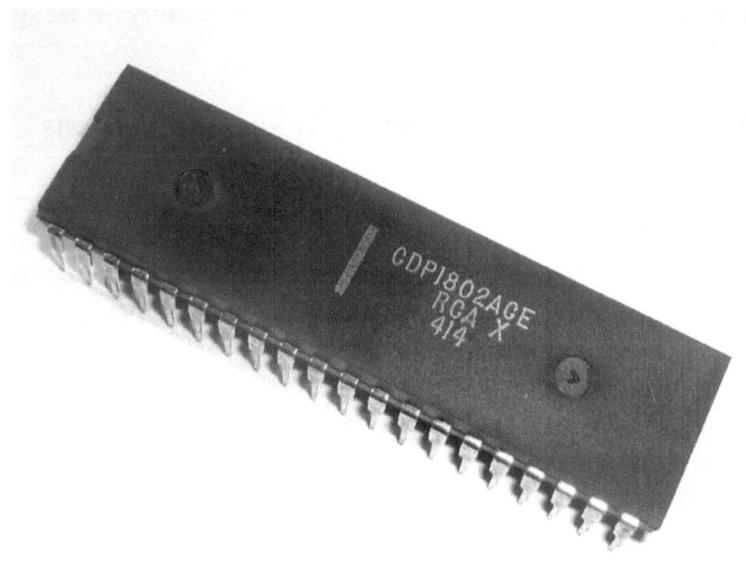

The 1802 had a register file of 16 registers of 16 bits each. Using the SEP instruction, one could select any of the registers to be the program counter or index register.

The RCA 1802 was one of the first RISC chips. The 1802 was used on JPL's Voyager, Viking, and Galileo space probes. Multiple units were used on Galileo. Prior to the Voyager, JPL was using simple flight computers, purpose-built, and not based on a microprocessor architecture. This Command Computer System (CCS) architecture was 18-bit.

The two Voyager spacecraft, previously called the Mars-Jupiter-Saturn-77 project, were launched during a unique opportunity in 1977 to take them past the maximum number of outer planets. They went on to explore Jupiter, Saturn, Neptune, and Uranus before heading off to interstellar space. The Voyager's are now some 13 light-hours beyond the Sun, and still returning data. In 2010, the returned data from Voyager-2 was garbled, leading to an investigation that showed the most likely cause was a flipped memory bit. Adjustments were made to the ground equipment to accommodate this, and the spacecraft continues to still return useful data some 33 years after launch. The 1802 was also quite popular with the builders of the OSCAR series of amateur spacecraft.

16-bit

The MIL-STD-1750 lays out a formal definition of a 16-bit instruction set architecture. It does not specify an implementation. The standard allows for memory mapping, and there are 16 general purpose registers. Some can be used as index registers, some as base registers. Any register can be used as the stack pointer. Both 16 and 32-bit integer arithmetic are supported, as well as 32- and 48-bit floating point.

There are many implementations of the 1750A architecture, including several that are built as radiation-hardened.

The preferred language for the 1750A was Jovial, an Algol language variant; later, ADA and c were used as well. The 1750A is found in many aircraft and missile applications by the United States Armed Forces and their allies. A quick list of examples includes the USAF F-16 and F–18 aircraft, the AH-64D helicopter, and the F-111 aircraft. The architecture is also used by the Indian

Space Research Organisation (ISRO), and the Chinese Aerospace industry. In 1996, the 1750A architecture was declared obsolete for future military projects.

The 1750A found applications in many space projects, including NASA's Earth Observation Satellites (EOS) Aqua, Terra, and Aura. It was used on ESA missions Cluster and Rosetta. JPL used seven of the processors on the Cassini Mission to Saturn, and more units on Mars Observer and Mars Global Surveyor. It was used on the Clementine spacecraft, a NASA-Naval Research Laboratory program to study the Moon. The 1750A was deployed on the Johns Hopkins University Applied Physics Laboratory's MSX – Midcourse Space Experiment spacecraft, which used nine. The 1750A flew on EUVE, MSTI -1, -2, & -3, Landsat-7, NEAR, and is on the GOES-13, GOES-O, and GOES–P NOAA spacecraft. The SPOT-4 mission includes a F9450, a National Semiconductor implementation. GEC-Plessey also manufactures a radiation-hard RH1750A.

RTX2010

The Intersil RTX2010 is a radiation-hardened 16-bit processor organized as a stack machine. The architecture supports direct execution of the Forth language. The Forth environment can be seen as a dual-stack virtual machine. The chip has two stacks, each 256 words deep. Context switches only take a single machine cycle. The interrupt latency is 4 cycles, making the processor ideal in real-time applications.

The initial application came in a gate array in 1983, proceeding to an implementation by Harris Corporation in 1988.

The RTX2010 was used in numerous NASA missions, including the Advanced Composition Explorer (ACE), the NEAR/Shoemaker mission, Timed, IMAGE (2000), instruments on AXAF, EOS, and EUV, MSX, XTE, Cassini, and MagSat.

<u>32-bit</u>

Surrey Space System's MicroSat series, including UoSat-12 used the 80386EX, an embedded version of the 80386. This circa-1994 chip had a static design, meaning the clock could be slowed or stopped without the microprocessor losing state.

The 80386EX model included the memory management features of the baseline 80386, and added an interrupt controller, a watchdog timer, sync/async serial I/O, DMA control, parallel I/O and dynamic memory refresh control. These devices were DOS-compatible in the sense that their I/O addresses, dma and interrupt assignments correspond with an IBM pc board-level architecture. The DMA controller is, however, an enhanced superset of the 8237A DMA controller.

The 80386EX includes two dma channels, three channels of 8254 timer/counter, dual 8259A interrupt controller functionality, a full-duplex synchronous serial I/O channel, two channels of 8250A asynchronous serial I/O, a watchdog timer, 24 lines of parallel I/O, and support for dram refresh.

The LEON project was started by the European Space Agency (ESA) in late 1997 to develop a high-performance processor. It was to be an open, portable, and non-proprietary processor design, capable of meeting future requirements for performance, software compatibility, and low system cost. To maintain correct operation in the presence of single event upsets (SEU's), extensive error detection and error handling functions were needed. The goals were to detect and tolerate one error in any register without software intervention, and to suppress effects from Single Event Transient (SET) errors in combinational logic.

The LEON family includes the LEON1 design that was used in the LEONExpress test chip to validate the fault-tolerance concept. The second LEON2 VHDL design was used in the processor from Atmel and various system-on-chip devices. These two LEON implementations were developed by ESA. Gaisler Research, now Aeroflex Gaisler, developed the third LEON3 design and the fourth generation LEON4 processor.

A LEON processor can be instantiated in programmable logic such as an FPGA or an ASIC. LEON processors are available as soft IP cores.

All processors in the LEON series are based on the SPARC-V8 RISC architecture. LEON2 has a five-stage pipeline while later versions have a seven-stage pipeline. LEON2 and LEON2-FT are distributed as a system-on-chip design. The standard LEON2 includes an interrupt controller, debug support hardware, 24-bit timers, a UART, a 16-bit I/O port, and a memory controller.

The LEON2-FT processor is the single event upset (seu) tolerant version of the LEON2 processor. Flip-flops are protected by triple modular redundancy (TMR) and all internal and external memories are protected by error detection and correction (edac) or parity. The LEON3 is a synthesizable VHDL model of a 32-bit processor compliant with the SPARC V8 architecture. The model is highly configurable, and particularly suitable for system-on-a-chip (SOC) designs. The full source code is available under the GNU GPL license. LEON3 includes SMP support.

The LEON3FT is a fault-tolerant version of the standard LEON3 SPARC V8 Processor. It was designed for operation in the space environment, and includes functionality to detect and correct single event upset (SEU) errors in all on-chip RAM memories. The LEON3FT processor support most of the functionality in the standard LEON3 processor, and adds Register file SEU error-correction of up to 4 errors per 32-bit word, Cache memory error-correction of up to 4 errors per tag or 32-bit word, and Autonomous and software transparent error handling. There is no timing impact due to error detection or correction. It is a static design, using a 2.5 volt supply. It supports the IEEE-754 floating point standard.

In January 2010, the fourth version of the LEON processor was released. It has static branch prediction added to pipeline, optional level-2 cache, 64-bit or 128-bit path to AMBA AHB interface, and higher performance.

The Real Time Operating Systems (RTOS's) that support LEON are RTLinux, PikeOS, eCos, RTEMS, Nucleus, ThreadX, VxWorks, LynxOS, and POK (a free ARINC-653 implementation released under the BSD license).

The Mongoose-V processor was a space-rated derivative of the LR-3000 processor of MIPS heritage. It includes a 4-kbyte instruction cache and a 2-kbyte data cache, as well as floating-point capability. However, the omission of the memory management unit forces the use of a flat memory model and precludes one of the more powerful features of advanced operating systems.

The Mongoose-V processor first flew on NASA's EO-1 spacecraft launched in November, 2000, where it functioned as the main flight computer. A second Mongoose-V controlled the satellite's solid-state data recorder.

The RH-32 was a radiation-hard 32-bit processor chipset developed by the USAF Rome Laboratories for the Ballistic Missile Defense Agency, and produced by Honeywell (later, TRW) for Aerospace applications. It achieves a throughput of 20 MIPS. It was a three-chip set, consisting of Central Processing Unit, Floating Point Unit, and Cache Memory

The Honeywell and TRW RH32 were developed from a MIPS R3000 model, under sponsorship of the USAF Phillips Lab at Kirkland Air Force Base in New Mexico. It features 16 kilobytes of data cache and 16 kilobytes of instruction cache. It includes four serial I/O channels, four timers, a built-in 1553 bus, 40 programmable I/O lines, and DMA capability. At a module level, the Sun M-bus is supported. The module is available in 100 K rad to one mega-rad hardness with no single-event latch-up. It incorporates IEEE-754 floating-point capability, and memory management features. The RH32 processor is an integral part of the Advanced Spaceborne Computer Module (ASCM). The RH32 supports the VxWorks operating system and the gnu-c compiler.

The RAD6000 radiation-hard single board computer based on the IBM risc chip, was manufactured by IBM Federal Systems. Later sold to Loral and by way of acquisition, ended up with Lockheed Martin, and is currently a part of BAE Systems.

The radiation-hardening of the original RSC 1.1 million-transistor chip to make the RAD6000's CPU was done by IBM Federal Systems Division working with the Air Force Research Laboratory. As of June 2008 there were some 200 RAD6000 processors in space on a variety of NASA, DoD, and commercial spacecraft.

FPGA embedded approach - SpaceCube

The Space Cube Processor is a family of reconfigurable architectures, using the Xilinx Virtex FPGA's with four integral PowerPC-405, 450 MHz microprocessor cores. The SpaceCube was developed at NASA's Goddard Space Flight Center. The first SpaceCube into space was on the Hubble Servicing Mission 4, as part of the Relative Navigation Sensors autonomous docking experiment. A subsequent mission (STS-129) carried a SpaceCube that was attached to the outside of the International Space Station, on the Naval Research Laboratory's MISSE7 experiment. SpaceCube is so-called because the packaging is a 4-inch cube. It uses less than 10 watts, and weighs less than four pounds. A unique stacking architecture is used for the mechanical and electrical inter-connection of the boards. This is the prototype:

The original SpaceCube was 4 inches by 4 inches by three inches, and used SpaceWire Ethernet, and RS-422 as I/O interfaces. Each of the four PowerPC's had 128 Mbytes of memory, and they shared 64k of PROM, and 1 gigabyte of Flash memory. There was a JTAG interface, and user I/O lines. The reconfigurable resources of the Virtex-4 FPGA included 56,880 logic cells, and there were DSP resources. The support software was VxWorks, RTEMS, and Linux. Three of the cpu's could be tied together in a voting arrangement, where an Aeroflex rad-hard FPGA was the decision-maker.

The follow-on SpaceCube's use the newer Xilinx Virtex-5 architecture, available in a radiation hardened version. Previous versions used the commercial version, with a "Rad hard by Architecture" approach. The four integral processors provide a quad-redundant system, and a small, inherently radiation-hard processor (LEON) serves as the voting device.

The FPGA in the SpaceCube has four instantiated PowerPC cpu's, and the ability to include more in the "sea of logic" that makes up the bulk of the device. The Xilinx "Microblaze" cpu architecture is popular, and the chip can easily hold 16 of these devices, with an associated interconnect mechanism. The device can be reprogrammed or reconfigured in orbit.

The Xilinx FPGA's in non-radiation hardened versions have also flown on a variety of space missions, including the Australian FEDSAT mission, the Spirit and Opportunity Rovers on Mars, the MARS 2003 Lander and Rover, the Mars Science Laboratory, the Venus Express, TacSat-2, and others. Mitigation techniques for radiation effects include combinations of Triple Modular Redundancy (TMR), Error Detection and Correction (EDAC) circuitry, and memory scrubbing.

NASA/Goddard's SpaceCube is a reconfigurable technology and systems architecture development effort focused on using Xilinx field programmable gate arrays with embedded PowerPC processor technology on NASA missions. The SpaceCube 2.0 design is leveraged off of the knowledge and experience from the design and flight of the SpaceCube 1.0 design. The current design and development efforts are of SpaceCube processor cards which contain Xilinx Virtex 7 processors. The planned processor card is physically sized as either a standard commercial 6U or 3U compact PCI card.

Radiation Hardness Issues for Spacecraft Embedded computers

A complete discussion of the physics of radiation damage to semiconductors is beyond the scope of this book. However, an overview of the subject is presented. The tolerance of semiconductor devices to radiation is in terms of their damage susceptibility. The problems fall into two broad categories, those caused by cumulative dose, and those transient events caused by very energetic particles. These are generated during a period of intense solar flare activity, for example.. The unit of absorbed dose of radiation is the *rad*, representing the absorption of 100 ergs of energy per gram of material. A kilo-rad is one thousand rads. At 10k rad, death in humans is almost instantaneous. One hundred kilo-rad is typical in the vicinity of Jupiter's radiation belts. Ten to twenty kilo-rad is typical for spacecraft in low Earth orbit, but the number depends on how much time the spacecraft spends outside the Van Allen belts, which act as a shield by trapping energetic particles.

Absorbed radiation can cause temporary or permanent changes in the material. Usually, neutrons, being uncharged, do minimal damage, but energetic protons and electrons cause lattice or ionization damage in the material, and resultant parametric changes. For example, the leakage current can increase, or bit states can change. Certain technologies and manufacturing processes are known to produce devices that are less susceptible to damage than others.

Radiation tolerance of 100 kilo-rad is usually more than adequate for low Earth orbit (LEO) missions that spend most of their life below the shielding of the Van Allen belts. For Polar missions, a higher total dose is expected, from 100k to 1 mega-rad per year. For synchronous, equatorial orbits, that are used by many communication satellites, and for some weather satellites, the expected dose is several kilo-rad per year. Finally, for planetary missions to Venus, Mars, Jupiter, Saturn, and beyond, requirements that are even more stringent must be met. For one thing, the missions usually are unique, and the cost of failure is high. For missions towards the sun, the higher fluence of solar radiation must be taken into account. The larger outer planets, such as Jupiter and Saturn, have large radiation belts around them as well.

Cumulative radiation dose causes a charge trapping in the semiconductor's insulating oxide layers, which manifests as a parametric change in the devices. Total dose effects may be a function of the dose rate, and annealing of the device may occur, especially at elevated temperatures. Annealing refers to the self-healing of radiation induced defects. This can take minutes to months, and is not applicable for lattice damage. The internal memory or registers are usually the most susceptible area of the chip. The gross indication of radiation damage is the increased power consumption of the device, with one researcher reporting a doubling of the power consumption at failure. In addition, failed devices could operate at a lower clock rate, leading to speculation that a key timing parameter was being affected in this case.

Single event upsets (seu's) are the response of the device to direct high energy isotropic flux, such as cosmic rays, or the secondary effects of high energy particles colliding with other matter (such as shielding). Large transient currents may result, causing changes in logic state (bit flips), unforeseen operation, device latch-up, or burnout. The transient currents can be monitored as an indicator of the onset of SEU problems. After SEU, the results on the operation of the processor are somewhat unpredictable. Mitigation of problems caused by SEU's involves self-test, memory scrubbing, and forced resets.

The *LET* (linear energy transfer) is a measure of the incoming particles' delivery of ionizing energy to the device. Latch-up refers to the inadvertent operation of a parasitic SCR (silicon control rectifier), triggered by ionizing radiation. In the area of latch-up, the chip can be made inherently hard due to use of the Epitaxial process for fabrication of the base layer (ref. 12). Even the use of an Epitaxial layer does not guarantee complete freedom from latch-up, however. The next step generally involves a silicon on insulator (SOI) or Silicon on Sapphire (SOS) approach, where the substrate is totally insulated, and latch-ups are not possible.

In some cases, shielding is effective, because even a few millimeters of aluminum can stop electrons and protons. However, with highly energetic or massive particles (such as alpha particles, helium nuclei), shielding can be counter-productive. When the atoms in the shielding are hit by an energetic particle, a cascade of lower energy, lower mass particle's results. These can cause as much or more damage than the original source particle.

IBM's PowerPC chips were produced in a rad-hard version for spaceflight applications.

Radiation Mitigation Techniques

The effects of radiation on silicon circuits can be mitigated by redundancy, the use of specifically radiation hardened parts, *Error Detection and Correction* (EDAC) circuitry, and memory scrubbing techniques. Hardened chips are produced on special insulating substrates such as Sapphire. Bipolar technology chips can withstand radiation better than CMOS technology chips, at the cost of greatly increased power consumption. In error detection and correction techniques, special encoding of the stored information provides a protection against flipped bits, at the cost of additional bits to store. Redundancy can also be applied at the device or box level, with the popular *Triple Modular Redundancy* (TMR) technique triplicating everything, and assuming the probability of a double failure is less than that of a single failure. Watchdog timers are used to reset systems unless they are themselves reset by the software. Of course, the watchdog timer circuitry is also susceptible to failure, as is the EDAC circuitry.

Radiation effects are also of interest in Nuclear Power Plant control and monitoring systems, and Medical diagnostic and treatment.

Other Problems in the Space Environment

Besides the high radiation environment, some of the other environmental issues in space present unique problems to embedded system designers.

Thermal problems

With no gravity there is no convection cooling. There is some radiated cooling if there is enough difference in temperature. Most cooling takes place, internal to the spacecraft, by conduction. The heat is transferred to the outside of the spacecraft, where it can be radiated out to free space, which has a temperature of only a few degrees K. Facing the sun is hot, facing space is cold. Next to a planet, the planet itself is a source of heat.

Power constrained

Once they leave the Earth, the systems are on their own as regards to power. Generally, solar power is used. Deep space missions, very far from the sun, may rely on nuclear power.

Remote debugging

Debugging remote systems in orbit and on the surface of other planets present unique challenges. One of these is the significant delay in the communications link over interplanetary distances. Systems should ideally be self-diagnosing, because the cost to "phone home" is high.

Different space environments

The near-Earth environment includes the Van Allen belts and the South Atlantic Anomaly. Spacecraft could be fixed or returned to Earth in the Shuttle era, but this is no longer feasible with the retirement of the fleet. Spacecraft at Synchronous altitude, like the communication satellites, are not reachable for repair at the present time.

As we head towards the sun, it gets hotter, and the solar fluence is greater. This is the realm of the planets Venus, Mercury. Spacecraft have been sent to both, and landed on Venus.

As we go away from the sun, it gets cold, and the solar fluence lessens. This is the realm of Mars, Jupiter, Saturn, Uranus, Neptune and their associated moons. The larger planets have their own trapped radiation belts.

Planetary missions include Lunar rover and surface packages, Mercury and Venus landers (which tend to melt), Mars rovers, Jovian and Saturnine moon probes.

The Embedded controller functions for these space missions include Attitude control and pointing, orbit control and maintenance, navigation, thermal control, energy management, and data management and communications.

Protocols for use in space systems include IP-in-space, a variation of mobile IP. In low Earth orbit, delay is not a problem. By the time we get to the moon, the round trip speed of light delay time becomes an issue. This interferes with standard internetworking protocols that work well on Earth. The CCSDS, Consultive Committee on Space Data Standards, has developed a delay tolerant internet protocol for space use. There is also an Interplanetary Internet, see www.ipnsig.org.

Memory for embedded spacecraft systems has some unique characteristics. Tape, disk, rotating magnetic or optical media is not used, due to the problem with added momentum. Bulk memory , usually dram, is popular. This can be Triple modularly redundant, and use Scrubbing techniques and CRC error correcting codes to address radiation induced errors.

Embedded Case studies

This section presents a series of embedded systems case study's from a cross-section of application domains.

Apollo Guidance Computer

The MIT Instrumentation Lab, headed by Charles Stark Draper, using heritage from the Polaris submarine-launched missile guidance computers, developed the Apollo Guidance Computer (AGC). It was built by Raytheon. The AGC was critical for guidance and navigation of the lunar craft.

There were two Apollo Guidance computers on each mission, one in the Command Module; and one in the Lunar Lander. This proved to be a good idea on Apollo 13, which suffered an explosion that crippled the Command module on the way to the moon. The computer in the Lunar Lander was re-tasked to provide guidance computations to get the astronauts back to Earth, before the Command Module would be re-activated for re-entry.

Later, the AGC design was used as the basis for aircraft fly-by-wire systems and in a Navy Deep Seas Submersible project.

The calculations were done internally in metric, but the astronauts (mostly test pilots) preferred English units for display. (What's the worst that could happen?)

An HP-65 handheld scientific calculator was carried on the Apollo-Soyuz mission, circa 1975, to perform calculations for the rendezvous maneuvers. This was a backup to the Apollo computer onboard the craft.

Architecture, CPU, Memory, I/O

The computer had a complexity of some 5,000 RTL logic gates from Fairchild Semiconductor (a pc has 100's of millions), which represented some 60% of the total US production of microcircuits at the time. The computer was a 16-bit machine, and had a 1.7 microsecond cycle time (current machines are sub-nano-second). It had 2048 bytes of random access memory, and 36k of read-only memory, both implemented in a magnetic core technology. There were four registers, the accumulator, the program counter, the remainder from the DV instruction or the return address after a transfer of control instruction, and the lower product after a multiply instruction. There were five vectored interrupts.

The guidance computers had 152 kilobytes of storage for the entire mission. The size was 6 inches, x 1 foot x 2 feet; they weighed 70 pounds, and used 55 watts of electricity. They were constructed of 5600 3-input nor gates, and featured a cycle time 11.7 microseconds. The clock was 1.024 MHz.

Software

The Apollo computers were programmed in YUL – an assembly language of 40 operations, and there was an Interpretive language for math-intensive calculations. The software was released in January of 1966, with the first flight was in August 1966. The unit was used until 1975. No in-flight errors were ever attributed to software. None. This was after 2,000 person-years of independent verification and validation (IV&V).

Sensors, Actuators

The AGC interfaced with the Inertial Reference Platform and with the astronaut, via a keypad and numeric display.

References

The Apollo Flight Journal, The Apollo On-board Computers, http://history.nasa.gov/afj/compessay.htm

Apollo Guidance Computer emulator, http://www.ibiblio.org/apollo/index.html
Hall, Eldon C. *Journey to the Moon: The History of the Apollo Guidance Computer*, 1996, AIAA Press, ISBN 1-56347-185-X.

O'Brien, Frank *The Apollo Guidance Computer: Architecture and Operation*, Springer Praxis Books, 1st Edition, 2010, ISBN-1441908765

LG Electronics Internet Refrigerator

The Internet Digital DIOS from LG Electronics features a complete Internet "WebPad" in the door that also captures and records still digital images with its built-in digital camera; is capable of Internet shopping, videophone calls and e-mailing. The screen also doubles as a TV, and can be used to get more information on cooking from the Web and to access new recipes.

The refrigerator has its own LAN port for Internet connectivity and can take voice messages

Smart fridges work as a network of distributed fridges, each fitted with control technology that allows them to communicate with each other via a network to share and store the energy provided by renewable-power generators.

"The fridges are designed to talk to each other, negotiating when it's a good time to consume electricity and when it's better not to," according to LG "These scheduling decisions improve the quality of electricity produced by renewables and can help increase renewable uptake in the energy market."

Samsung HomePad Refrigerator

The control unit for this refrigerator includes a x86-class cpu, with 128 MB of sdram, 64 MB flash, running the WindowsCE operating system, a 10.4 inch lcd screen, wireless lan 802.11b, usb, headphone, microphone, digital display and a control panel.

The unit provides a video messaging feature as well as schedule management and timer/alarm functions. Refrigerator management functions include temperature of the refrigerator and freezer sections, ice cube production, crushed ice production, and also a melting function for frozen foods. The control and monitoring portion of the refrigerator is accessible over the Internet.

CSIRO's Intelligent Energy team developed a fridge capable of maintaining its average temperature while regulating its power consumption from renewable-energy generators, such as solar panels (photovoltaic) or wind turbines.

Smart Washing machine

LG's washing machine has a communication cable that links to a PC with an Internet connection. You can then connect to the washing machine's website, download washing programs suitable to the different types of clothes you want to wash, and store them in the washing machine.

LG prepared a technology, codenamed Thinq, which allows the user to manage and operate the fridge, oven, or washing machine from an LG phone.

The washing machine cycles can send an alert message when it is finished. The fridge can alert you if the door has been left ajar.

At the center of Thinq is the concept of an intelligent WiFi grid built around a smart meter enabling home owners to schedule the oven cook time, washing machine cycle, and refrigerator defrost at the most cost-effective or convenient times. Smart Access allows homeowners to control and monitor appliances from outside of the home and, better yet, control LG's HOM-BOT robotic vacuum cleaner to clean or remotely view the house. LG's smart refrigerators can count and display the number of times the door has been opened and alert home owners when the door is ajar. Alerts can also be scheduled when the ice-maker is switched off or the washing machine is off balance or a load is finished. LCD displays on LG's Thinq appliances show daily, weekly, or monthly reports detailing each appliance's energy consumption. You can access daily totals from your smartphone or tablet. New Smart Diagnosis features include downloadable diagnostic information and the ability to hit a few buttons on the appliance to emit a series of tones to assist LG technicians troubleshooting problems over the phone. The food management feature works by dragging and dropping food icons around the LCD display or by using built-in voice recognition. Unfortunately, the inventory must be managed manually making this feature pretty useless for all but the most obsessive of home owners. All the appliances are software upgradeable with the ability to download new features like pre-programmed recipes and advanced wash cycles.

LG smartphones and tablets of that brand will be able to interface with the home appliances.

Athena Missile Guidance Computer

In the 1960's, missile guidance computers were developed that could adjust the trajectory after launch, but only during power flight. These included the Univac Athena computer for the Air Force's Titan missile system, and the Burroughs Mod 1 for the Atlas missile system. The Smithsonian has one of each computer.

These units were not for flight; they exceeded weight budget by 9 tons. The idea of putting the computer onboard the vehicle was just a dream at this point.

The Univac Athena requires 370 square feet of floor space underground in a hardened bunker. Using radar data input, it calculated course corrections during engine burn. It only had to work for two minutes. It was programmed in assembly language, and was a Harvard architecture, meaning the instructions and data were kept in different stores. In the case of the Athena, the instructions were kept on a magnetic drum, and the data was kept in core.

The Athena cost about $1,800,000. when new, and weighed over 18,000 lbs. The machine was built by Sperry Rand Univac in 1957, with Seymour Cray was the chief designer. It had 256 words of 24-bit core memory for data and a 8192-word drum for program and constants. Once in service, it was found to have a mean time to failure of 48 days, twenty times better than the original specifications.

The Titan launch complex was located underground, and a single Athena could be used with multiple missiles, launched one at a time. There were eighteen missile complexes, each capable of launching multiple missiles. The liquid-fueled Titan's were considered to be only a stop-gap measure pending the deployment of the solid fuel Minuteman Missile, and none of the complexes were operational for more than four years.

The computers, when declared surplus by the Federal Government, went to various US universities. The one at Carnegie was used as an undergrad project until 1971, when the former EE undergrad students (Athena Systems Development Group) orchestrated its donation to the Smithsonian. It joined a sister unit, the Atlas Mod I Guidance Computer, at the Smithsonian.

The computer had a Harvard architecture design; separate data and instruction memories were used.

A Frieden printing terminal with paper tape equipment was used with the Athena, as well as an operating console. An interesting feature is the mode "battleshort". In this mode, referred to as "melt-before-fail", the power to the machine could NOT be shut off by a failsafe.

The Athena used a massive motor-generator set with 440 volt 3 phase AC input. I hooked this up from the lab mains, and got the generator set going initially. When the generator was started, the building lights dimmed, and there was no question that the machine was on. The motor generator control unit (seen behind the console) weighed a ton, and the motor/generator itself weighed more than two tons.

The last launch supported by an Athena computer was a Thor-Agena missile launched in 1972 from Vandenberg AFB in California. It was used on over 400 missile flights. In its operational life, it never launched a missile in anger.

Ford Sync Telematics System

The Ford Sync is a vehicle *info-tainment* system based on the ARM processor. It is a factory installed feature, first available on 2008 model year vehicles.

The system allows the driver to use Bluetooth-enabled devices such as phones and media players in the vehicle, and operate these with voice command or steering wheel based controls. The steering wheel has, for example, a push-to-talk button for the connected phone. The SYNC system also provides a text-to-voice feature for reading messages aloud.

Integration of digital music players can be via Bluetooth or USB connection. A voice recognition feature is implemented in the SYNC system, and it supports English, French, Spanish, and Brazilian Portuguese. Direct calling to 911 in case of emergency is supported.

The operating system is Microsoft's Windows Embedded Automotive. The SYNC system uses proprietary software. Certain BlackBerry, Android, or iPhone apps can be triggered by the steering wheel buttons, or voice command.

The computer hosting SYNC is the Accessory Protocol Interface Module (APIM), which interfaces with vehicle systems over the CAN bus. The initial implementation of SYNC used a 400 MHz Freescale ARM-11 processor, with 256 Mbytes of SDRAM, and 2 Gbytes of flash. As mentioned, USB and Bluetooth I/O are provided.

When Sync is included in work trucks, such as the F-150, an in-dash computer supports applications such as real-time vehicle location, vehicle maintenance monitoring, and diagnostic monitoring. A specific Bluetooth keyboard and printer, plus the ability to remotely access an office computer, provides data and application support in the vehicle. Another application inventories equipment and supplies in the truck by reading RFID tags.

Implantable medical devices

These devices present unique challenges, as there failures can result in death or injury. Such devices are used to treat irregular heart rhythms, sleep apnea, pain, Parkinson's disease, autoimmune diseases, and OCD. They can also deliver precise dosages of drugs on demand or on a regular basis. Many implantable devices are life-sustaining.

The key parameters for these devices are size, weight, and power. Of course, reliability is a key issue. The lifetime of the device is a consideration, due to the need for replacement in the patient. The implantable device usually consists of an analog front end for sensing, possibly an analog output for stimulation, the cpu, memory, I/O, and power management. Communication is via wireless, and can use the same antenna for device charging. Standards exist in the area of Medical Implantable Communication Service. Also, one does not want one's implantable device to be hacked.

Mars Science Laboratory Curiosity

The Mars Science Laboratory's lander, named *Curiosity*, landed successfully on the Martian surface on August 6, 2012. It had been launched on November 26, 2011. It's location on Mars is the Gale crater, and was a project of NASA's Jet Propulsion Laboratory. The project cost was around $2.5 billion. It is designed to operate for two Martian years (sols). The mission is primarily to determine if Mars could have supported life.

The Rover vehicle weights just about 1 ton (2,000 lbs.) and is 10 feet long. It has autonomous navigation over the surface, and is expected to cover about 12 miles over the life of the mission. It uses six wheels

The Rover Compute Elements are based on the BAE Systems' RAD-750 cpu, rated at 400 mips. Each computer has 256k of EEprom, 256 Mbytes of DRAM, and 2 Gbytes of flash memory.

The power source for the rover is a radioisotope power system providing both electricity and heat. It is rated at 125 electrical watts, and 2,000 thermal watts, at the beginning of the mission.

The operating system is WindRiver's VxWorks real-time operating system.

The computers interface with an inertial measurement unit (IMU) to provide navigation updates. The computers also monitor and control the system temperature. All of the instrument control, camera systems, and driving operations are under control of the onboard computers.

Communication with Earth uses a direct X-band link, and a UHF link to relay spacecraft in Mars orbit. At landing, the one-way communications time to Earth is 13 minutes, 46 seconds.

The science payload includes a series of cameras, including one on a robotic arm, a laser-induced laser spectroscopy instrument, an X-ray spectrometer, and x-ray diffraction/fluorescence instrument, a mass spectrometer, a gas chromotograph, and a laser spectrometer. In addition, the rover hosts a weather station, and radiation detectors.

References

http://www.nasa.gov/mars

www.nasa.gov/msl/

http://en.wikipedia.org/wiki/Mars_Science_Laboratory

www.space.com/16385-curiosity-rover-mars-science-laboratory.html

http://www.windriver.com/announces/curiosity/Wind-River_NASA_0812.pdf

Nikon Exspeed

The Nikon Expeed is an embedded image processing system for Nikon digital cameras.

The Exspeed is implemented in an ASIC by Fujitsu. It is a multiprocessor design, with a multicore cpu, a DSP, and a controller. The image processor is the ARM-based Milbeaut design from Fujitsu. The image is processed as 16-bit pixels by the 32-bit Fujitsu FR RISC processor, which is 256 bit VLIW. The video codec engine also uses an FR core. The DSP is 16-bit. The controller is based on a dual core ARM.

Interface is made to the image sensors with a mixed analog-digital circuit, with integral 14-bit a/d conversion.

NASA Standard Spacecraft Computer -1

The NSSC-1 was developed as a standard component for the Multi Mission Modular Spacecraft at GSFC in 1974. The basic spacecraft was built of standardized components and modules, for cost reduction. The computer had 18 bits of non-volatile core or plated wire memory; up to 64 k. 18 bits was chosen because it gave more accuracy (x4) for data over a 16 bit machine. Floating point was not supported.

The NSSC-1 was used on the Solar Maximum Mission (SMM), Space Telescope, and Landsat-D, among others. The hardware was developed by Westinghouse and NASA/GSFC. The machine used DTL (diode-transistor logic), the lowest power parts available at the time on the Preferred Parts List; Initially fabricated from 1700 SSI (nor-gate) packages, it was later updated to 69 MSI (medium scale integration) chips.

The NSSC-1 had an Assembler/loader/simulator toolset hosted on Xerox XDS 930 (24- bit) mainframe. An associated simulator ran at 1/1000 of real time. The Xerox computer was interfaced to a breadboard OBP in a rack, which operated at room temperature ambient conditions. Later, the Software Development and Validation Facility (SDVF) added a flight dynamics simulator hosted on a PDP-11/70 minicomputer.

A purpose-built NSSC-1 Flight Executive was developed and used on the SMM and subsequent flights. It time-sliced tasks at 25 ms. It included a stored command processor that handled both absolute time and relative time commands. It included a status buffer that could be telemetered back to the ground. It required a lot of memory, typically more than half of that available, leaving the rest for applications and spare.

The Space Telescope used a more advanced flight computer called the DF-224 from Rockwell Autonetics for spacecraft control.. The DF-224 was a 24-bit fixed point machine. It operated a 1.25 MHz, with 64 kilowords of memory. It was programmed in assembly language. There were three redundant CPU's, and 6 memory modules, using plated wire memory, a non-volatile technology similar to core. The computer weighed 110 pounds.

At the first servicing mission of the telescope by the Space Shuttle in 1993, a 16- MHz, dual redundant 80386/80387-based computer with 1 megabyte of ram designed at the Goddard Space Flight Center was added to the DF-224 to augment its capabilities. It interfaced by shared memory. The upgrade was possible because the DF-224 had accessible external electrical connectors. The upgrade by accomplished by astronaut extra-vehicular activity (EVA) operations.

The Third Servicing Mission in 2008 replaced the augmented DF-224 with a 50 MHz 80486-based computer that was radiation-hard.

References

NSSC-1 Onboard Flexibility for Space Missions, IBM Federal systems Division, Feb. 1978, 78-67K-001.

Trevathan, Charles E., Taylor, Thomas D., Hartenstein, Raymond G., Merwarth, Ann C., and Stewart, William N. "Development and Application of NASA's First Standard Spacecraft Computer," CACM V27 n9, Sept 1984, pp. 902-913.

Styles, F., Taylor, T., Tharpe, M. and Trevathan, C. "A General-Purpose On-Board Processor for Scientific Spacecraft," NASA/GSFC, X-562-67-202, July 1967.

Stakem, Patrick H. The History of Spacecraft Computers from the V-2 to the Space Station, 2009, PRB Publishing, ASIN B04L626U6.

IBM pc keyboard and mouse

The keyboard for the standard desktop pc includes an 8-bit embedded processor, the Intel 8042. The keys are scanned as an X:Y matrix, and a scan code is derived. This is then sent to the computer over a serial line. The protocol is 2 start bits, 8 data bits, 1 stop bit. There is a "keypressed" code. The keyboard can also be made to reset the pc. Because the keyboard is seen as an X:Y array of switches, the computer can distinguish between left shift and right shift. The standard ps/2 connector has 5 pins. Power is supplied from the computer.

Pin configuration:

1 CLK

2 DATA

3 -RESET

4 GND

5 +5V

On the computer side, the keyboard data port is at I/O address 60h, with the status port at I/O address 64h. The status port is read-only. The command port is at I/O address 64h, and is write-only. The keyboard can send the data over an IR port, short range radio such as Bluetooth, or over USB.

The mouse is a two-dimension pointing device which allows interface with a graphical user interface. It is widely attributed to development efforts at Stanford University in the early 1960's. Generally, a mouse has a ball with two freely rotating rollers, connected to quadrature encoders that measure distance and speed. Mice also include switches activated by the user's fingers. A small embedded controller inputs these values, formats the data, and sends it to the computer in a serial format. The ps/2 mouse uses a 3-byte packet protocol. Mice without moving parts use photodiodes to detect motion. They can also use accelerometers. A trackball is, for all practical purposes, an upside-down mouse.

QES-III Locomotive computer

This embedded computer product from Q-tron includes a 15 slot rack, which houses the computer, memory, and I/O boards. The system is designed to operate from the standard 74 volts dc power found in modern diesel locomotives. Memory includes up to 2 megabytes of battery backed RAM, up to 1 megabyte of scratchpad ram, and up to 1 megabyte of flash memory for program. It communicates with a laptop over an RS-232 line, and with locomotive control and monitoring modules using RS-422.

The computer system replaces older relay-based control equipment. It monitors and controls battery charging, the blower motors for cooling, dynamic braking, the main generator field current, and the traction motor current. It samples water temperature, air temperature, and air brake pressure. It keeps track of hours of use, mileage, and horsepower-hours, which is a billable quantity.

The associated High Voltage module measures 0-1400 volts from the main generator. The Traction Motor Current module measures 0-1500 Amps. The Dynamic Brake current module measures 0-1500 amps for the dynamic brakes. Many other interface modules to locomotive equipment are available.

The functions implemented include main generator excitation control in power and dynamic braking modes, wheel slip control, control of engine cooling, sensor tests, and diagnostic monitoring. It also includes an event recorder function, and logs anomalies and tracks required maintenance by hours of use.

The computer is responsible for the operation of the 6,000 horsepower diesel, the associated a/c alternator, and the 6 traction motors, which are controlled independently. Active traction control is used to prevent wheel spin. The computer also does monitoring and diagnostics, and can "phone home" to report impending problems or maintenance issues.

Smart Meter/Smart Grid

Smart meters at residential and industrial customer locations allow the electric company to access the energy consumption without a human meter-reader visit. In addition, the meter can store time-of-day usage information. In addition, the meter reports power outages promptly. The smart meter is accessed electronically. Although typically applied to electrical meters, smart gas and water meters are also in production. Smart meters can also be set up to communicate and control large energy consumers such as air conditioners. There are also significant security concerns with the implementation technology, the least of which is determining whether a building is occupied based on usage. The possibility of disruption of the electrical grid by hacking is also of concern to agencies such as the FBI, which issued an alert in 2010. There have also been instances where the meter was hacked to report less than the actual energy usage.

References

Smartgrid.ieee.org

www.smartmeters.com

Embedded System Failures Case studies

"Anything that can go wrong, will" attributed to Murphy.

"…at the worst possible time, when you least expect it…" Anon.

"Murphy was an optimist." Anon.

Unfortunately, we learn more from failures than from successes. This section discusses some significant embedded systems failures, and analyzes them to define the lessons-learned.

This section will present a series of computer failures, most related to embedded systems, in a standardized format. Each study includes specific references and a root cause of the failure. Let's learn from someone else's mistakes. Don't have your embedded project highlighted in the next edition of the book.

Ariane 5 Launch Vehicle

Ariane 5's first test flight (Ariane 5 Flight 501) on 4 June 1996 failed, with the rocket self-destructing 37 seconds after launch because of a malfunction in the control software. A data conversion from 64-bit floating point value to 16-bit signed integer value to be stored in a variable representing horizontal bias caused a processor trap (operand error) because the floating point value was too large to be represented by a 16-bit signed integer. The software was originally written for the Ariane 4 where efficiency considerations (the computer running the software had an 80% maximum workload requirement) led to 4 variables being protected with a handler while 3 others, including the horizontal bias variable, were left unprotected because it was thought that they were "physically limited or that there was a large margin of error". The software, written in Ada, was included in the Ariane 5 through the reuse of an entire Ariane 4 subsystem despite the fact that the particular software containing the bug, which was just a part of the subsystem, was not required by the Ariane 5 because it has a different preparation sequence than the Ariane 4. The incident resulted in a loss of over $500 million.

Architecture, CPU, Memory, I/O

Thales Avionics

Software

Programmed in ADA; essentially the same as Ariane 4.

Sensors, Actuators

Input: Inertial reference system (IRS); output: nozzle vector control, via servo actuators

Root Cause

Flight control system failure. A diagnostic code from failed IRS-2 was interpreted as data. IRS-1 had failed earlier. The diagnostic data was sent because of a software error. The software module was only supposed to be used for alignment, not during flight. The diagnostic code was considered a 64-bit floating point number, and converted to a 16-bit signed integer, but the value was too large. This caused the rocket nozzles to steer hard-over to the side, causing the vehicle to veer and crash into a Mangrove swamp.

References

De Dalmau, J. and Gigou J. "Ariane-5: Learning from flight 501 and Preparing for 502, http://esapub.esrin.esa.it/billetin/bullet89/dalma89.html
Lions, Prof, J. L. (Chairman) ARIANE 5 flight 501 Failure, Report by the Inquiry Board, 19 July 1996,

http://www.esrin.esa.it/tidc/htdocs/Press/Press96/ariane5rep.html

Jezequel, Jean-marc and Meyer, Bertrand "Design by Contract: The Lessons of Ariane," IEEE computer, Jan. 1997, vol. 30, n. 2, pp129-130.

"Inquiry Board Traces Ariane 5 Failure to Overflow Error,"

http://siam.org/siamnews/general/ariance.html

Baber, Robert L. "The Ariane 5 explosion as seen by a software engineer," http://www.cs.wits.ac.za/~bob/ariane5.htm

Big Bay Boom

This was an incident at the Independence Day fireworks display in San Diego, California, July 4, 2012. Seven thousand fireworks, on 4 barges and a pier went off simultaneously, instead of being sequenced by a computer over 17 minutes. There were ½ million viewers. The event lead to no injuries, but did result in over four million YouTube views of the video.

Root Cause

"The company's statement included an explanation of how fireworks shows are produced through code, with a primary launch file and a secondary back-up. The two files are merged to create a new launch file, and sent to each of the five fireworks locations.

Somehow, an "unintentional procedural step" happened in that process, causing an "anomaly" that doubled the primary firing sequence, the report said."

"The command code was initiated, and the 'new' file did exactly what it 'thought' it was supposed to do," the report says. "It executed all sequences simultaneously because the new primary file contained two sets of instructions. It executed the file we designed as well as the file that was created in the back-up downloading process."

References

http://www.bigbayboom.com/
http://www.utsandiego.com/news/2012/jul/12/july-4-fireworks-fiasco-solved-technically/

Mars Climate Orbiter

The spacecraft was lost on Mars in September 1999. The system-level requirements did not specify units, so JPL used SI units and the contractor Lockheed Martin used English units. This was not caught in the review process, and led to the loss of the $125 million mission. The spacecraft crashed due to a navigation error.

Architecture, CPU, Memory, I/O

Single RAD6000 cpu, 128 meg ram, 18 meg flash.

Software

VxWorks operating system with flight software developed at Lockheed Martin Corp.

Sensors, Actuators

Dual 3-axis gyros, star tracker, dual sun sensors, 8 thrusters, 4 reaction wheels.

Root Cause

The primary cause of this discrepancy was human error. Specifically, the flight system software on the Mars Climate Orbiter was written to calculate thruster performance using the metric unit Newtons (N), while the ground crew was entering course correction and thruster data using the Imperial measure Pound-force (lbf). This error has since been known as the *metric mixup* and has been carefully avoided in all missions since by NASA.

"The root cause of the loss of the spacecraft was the failed translation of English units into metric units in a segment of ground-based, navigation-related mission software, as NASA has previously announced," said Arthur Stephenson, chairman of the Mars Climate Orbiter Mission Failure Investigation Board. "The failure review board has identified other significant factors that allowed this error to be born, and then let it linger and propagate to the point where it resulted in a major error in our understanding of the spacecraft's path as it approached Mars."

Reference

http://mars.jpl.nasa.gov/msp98/orbiter/

Mars Rover Pathfinder

The computer in the Mars Rover *Pathfinder* suffered a series of resets while on the Martian surface, but was later recovered.

Architecture, CPU, Memory, I/O

Single RS-6000 cpu, 1553- and VMEbus.

Software

VxWorks, with application code in c.

Sensors, Actuators

Sun sensors, star tracker, radar altimeter, accelerometers, wheel drive.

Root Cause

Priority inversion in the operating system. Pre-emptive priority thread scheduling was used. The watchdog timer caught the failure of a task to run to completion, and caused the reset. This was a sequence of tasks not exercised during testing. The problem was debugged from Earth, and a software correction uploaded.

The failure was identified by the spacecraft as a failure of one task to complete its execution before the other task started. The reaction to this by the spacecraft was to reset the computer. This reset reinitializes all of the hardware and software. It also terminates the execution of the current ground commanded activities.

The failure was a classic case of priority inversion (The details of how this was discovered and corrected is a fascinating story – see refs.) The higher priority task was blocked by the much lower priority task that was holding a shared resource. The lower priority task had acquired this resource and then been preempted by several of the medium priority tasks. When the higher priority task was activated, to setup the transactions for the next 1553 bus cycle, it detected that the lower priority task had not completed its execution. The resource that caused this problem was a mutual exclusion semaphore used to control access to the list of file descriptors that the select() mechanism was to wait on.

The select mechanism created a mutual exclusion semaphore to protect the "wait list" of file descriptors for those devices which support select. The VxWorks pipe() mechanism is such a device and the IPC mechanism used is based on pipes. The lower priority task had called select, which had called other tasks, which were in the process of giving the mutex semaphore. The lower priority task was preempted and the operation was not completed. Several medium priority tasks ran until the higher priority task was activated. The low priority task attempted to send the newest high priority data via the IPC mechanism which called a write routine. The write routine blocked, taking the mutex semaphore. More of the medium priority tasks ran, still not allowing the high priority task to run, until the low priority task was awakened. At that point, the scheduling task determined that the low priority task had not completed its cycle (a hard deadline in the system) and declared the error that initiated the reset.

References

http://www.nasa.gov/mission_pages/mars-pathfinder/

http://research.microsoft.com/en-us/um/people/mbj/Mars_Pathfinder/

Montgomery County (MD) traffic light system

The traffic signal system in Montgomery County, MD, erred on November 5, 2009 when it did not enter "rush hour mode." This meant that rush hour optimizations for traffic flow did not occur, inconveniencing 10's or 100's of thousands of commuters. This lasted for four rush-hours. This made some students to my Embedded Systems class late. Simultaneously, but not related, a software glitch in the Metro train system occurred that blocked usage of debit cards for fare payment. This provides yet more empirical evidence for the existence of Murphy's law.

Architecture, CPU, Memory, I/O

Data General minicomputer, 16-bit, 29 years old at the time.

Software

custom

Sensors, Actuators

Road traffic sensors, traffic lights (750 units).

Root Cause

The central computer failed to distribute timing information over the network to the individual intersection controllers. The clocks in the remote units drifted.

References

Green, J. J. "CyberChaos: Commuters get a glimpse of the future, http://www.wtop.com/?nid=778&sid=1803720

NSW Rail Outage

In April of 2011, a signal problem on the New South Wales Railroad System (Australia) caused all signals to turn red. This was the safest approach, of course, but resulted in over 100,000 passengers to be stranded for several hours. There were 847 trains delayed, and 240 had to be cancelled.

Architecture, CPU, Memory, I/O

LAN and WAN for distributing control information.

Software

Custom, ATRICS

Sensors, Actuators

Train sensors, switch controls, signal lamp controls.

Root Cause

Two failed capacitors plus a software design problem. The capacitors in the network interface hardware put the network into a partially failed state that the software couldn't handle. The system had previously operated correctly for 8 years.

References

http://spectrum.ieee.org/riskfactor/computing/it/

Charette, Robert "Two Capacitors and Poor Software Design Cause of Major NSW Rail Outage Last Month," May 11, 2011.

Patriot Missile

On February 25, 1991 and American *Patriot* antimissile battery failed to intercept an Iraqi *Scud* missile. The missile strike killed 28 American soldiers in a barracks.

Architecture, CPU, Memory, I/O

Classified.

Software

Classified.

Sensors, Actuators

Tracking and distance radar; tracking intercept steering commands to the missile.

Root Cause

Timing inaccuracy due to excessive clock drift lead to incorrect intercept information.

References

"Two disasters caused by computer arithmetic errors"

http://www.math.psu.edu/cao/disasters.html

Patriot Missile Defense, Software Problem Led to System Failure at Dharan, Saudi Arabia, Feb 1992, US Government General Accounting Office, GAO/IMTEC-92-25.

Therac-25

The classical embedded system failure was the Therac-25 Medical Imager issue. There were six known accidents involving radiation overdoses leading to death and serious injury.

Architecture, CPU, Memory, I/O

PDP-11 minicomputer, 16-bit.

Software

Custom. There were 8 main subroutines. "Treat" was the main monitor task. It rescheduled itself after every subroutine. The housekeeper task took care of status interlocks and limit checks.

Sensors, Actuators

Servo-controlled radiation gun positioning and intensity control.

Root Cause

Overly complex programs written in unreliable styles. Confusing user interface.

USS Yorktown

The US Navy Aegis Missile Cruiser Yorktown (CG-48) was dead in the water during an exercise in September of 1997. All ships systems were shut down, and the ship had to be towed to port

Architecture, CPU, Memory, I/O

Twenty-seven dual 200 MHz Pentium Pro based desktop computers and a PentiumPro server on a fibre optic lan.

Software

Windows-NT 4.0 with custom application software.

Sensors, Actuators

All ships systems, bridge, damage control, steering, engine control, weapons, navigation, radar, missiles, guns, 80,000 horsepower turbine engine.

Root Cause

Software. A database error caused a critical error in engine room control, resulting in shutdown. It was an attempted division by zero, entered by mistake. (Was this human error? Why no bounds checking?) There was a lack of redundancy, no error segmentation, and insufficient or non-existent backup systems.

NEAR spacecraft

The Near Earth Asteroid Rendezvous – Shoemaker was launched in 1996 to study the asteroid Eros. It was a JHU/APL spacecraft, and a NASA mission. On Monday, 12 February 2001, the NEAR spacecraft touched down on asteroid Eros, after transmitting 69 close-up images of the surface during its final descent.

However, previously, the first of four scheduled rendezvous burns had been attempted on December 20, 1998. The burn sequence was initiated but immediately aborted. The spacecraft subsequently entered safe mode and began tumbling. The spacecraft's thrusters fired thousands of times during the anomaly, which expended 29 kg of propellant reducing the spacecraft's propellant margin to zero. This anomaly almost resulted in the loss of the spacecraft due to lack of solar orientation and subsequent battery drain. Contact between the spacecraft and mission control could not be established for over 24 hours.

Architecture, CPU, Memory, I/O

Three sets of computers, AIU, FC, and tbd. Two each.

Two redundant 1553 standard data buses, two solid state recorders with 1.1 gigabits and 0.67 gigabits respectively.

Software

80,000 lines of guidance and control code.

AIU: 21,000 lines of c code; 10,000 lines of assembly.

FC: 42,000 lines of ADA, 7,000 lines of assembly.

During the Anomaly Board review, seventeen software errors were uncovered. One of these which reported the momentum wheel speed as zero when it was actually at maximum. There were two different archived versions of the software flight load.

Sensors, Actuators

Five digital solar attitude detectors, an inertial measurement unit, (IMU) and a star tracker camera. Four reaction wheels for attitude control. Thrusters to dump angular momentum from the reaction wheels, and for rapid slew and propulsive maneuvers. Gyros.

Root Cause

Startup transient of the main engine exceeded an (incorrect) lateral acceleration safety threshold; leading to engine shutdown. There was a missing command in the burn-abort contingency script.

References

http://near.jhuapl.edu/

http://klabs.org/richcontent/Reports/Failure_Reports/NEAR_Rendezvous_Burn.pdf

"The NEAR Rendezvous Burn Anomaly of December 1990, Final Report of the NEAR (Near Earth Asteroid Rendezvous) Anomaly Review Board, Nov. 1999, JHU/APL.

Clementine Spacecraft

The Clementine spacecraft suffered a catastrophic loss of propellant on May 7, 1994, leading to loss of the primary mission.

Architecture, CPU, Memory, I/O

Dual Command and Telemetry Processors (CTP), MIL-STD-1750A architecture

Sensors, Actuators

Dual star trackers, dual inertial measurement units, attitude control thrusters, reaction wheels.

Root Cause

The thrusters were erroneously held open for 11 minutes by the flight computer because the thruster protection timer (in software) contained an undetected bug. This depleted the spacecraft propellant.

References

nssdc.gsfc.nasa.gov/planetary/clementine.html

www.ganssle.com/watchdogs.pdf

Dive Computer fault

Dive computer provided incorrect information on safe dive and depth limits, leading to multiple instances of diver injury from the bends (nitrogen narcosis).

Root Cause

Software error caused underestimation of nitrogen levels. An incorrect algorithm was used.

References

Risks Digest, v 22, Issue 57, Feb. 2003.

Holding, Reynolds "Corporate cover-up exposed divers to grave risk," SF Chronicle, May 25, 2003.

This is Volume 1 of a 2-volume series on Embedded Computers. The material was derived from a class I teach for the Johns Hopkins University, Engineering for Professionals Program. This volume is supposed to be about the "what", and volume 2 about the "how." Volume 2 should be release about a year after Volume 1. Technology is changing faster and faster, and new material becomes available daily. The second volume will address updates and corrections to Volume 1 as well. I hope you enjoyed this as much as I did pulling the information together.

Appendix – Binary System and Math operations

This section provides a brief overview of computer mathematics and architecture in general. It is intended as a reference.

Definitions

A *bit* is the smallest unit of binary information. It represents a yes/no, on/off, left/right, north/south type of decision. It can be represented in mathematics as the digits zero or one. Any technology that can represent two states can represent a bit. Red light/green light, voltage or no voltage, current or no current, light or darkness, north magnetic or south magnetic, etc. We have to be careful to distinguish between the mathematical concept of a bit (one of two possible states) and its implementation.

Also, we don't necessarily need to use base-2 for computers, but it matches the implementation in microelectronics fairly well. Early computers (and calculators) used base-10, which we use because we have ten fingers.

The choice of a base number in mathematics will influence how easy or hard it is to manipulate the numbers. If we just want to know that we have 1 sheep, 2 sheep, or many sheep, we don't need very sophisticated math. The ancient Babylonians used a base-60 math, which survives in the way we tell time (seconds, minutes). They also had computers, abacus units designed to handle their representation. The Romans did not use a positional number system, which is why it is very hard to do long division in Roman numerals.

A *positional number system* allows us to choose a base number, and use the number digits to represent different orders of magnitude, even fractions. In Roman numerals, we have a specific symbol for fifty, and that is "L". In decimal, we use "50." That is to say, 5 x 10 (the base) plus 0 times 1.

We also need to consider the important concept of zero, which was used in Mesoamerica, China, India, and other places. The Romans had the concept of zero, just not a specific symbol for it. The zero symbol become important in positional notation, to keep the symbols in the right place, not just to indicate that we have no sheep.

We like to use ten as a base, because we have ten fingers. Actually, we can use any number for a base. The ones of interest to use in computing are base-2 and base-16. For microelectronics, the base-2 is used, because the physics of the devices allow for representation and recognition of two different states easily and efficiently. Base-16 is for our convenience (keep telling yourself that.)

So we like to use base 10 and computers like to use base 2, we need to discuss how to convert numbers between these bases.

Bytes, Words, and other collections

A *byte* is a collection of 8 bits. This makes for a handy size. In binary, a byte can represent 1 of 256 (2^8) possible states or values.

A computer *word* is a collection of 8, 16, 24, 13, 97, or some other number of bits. The number of bits collected into a word does not need to be a power of two. The range of numbers we can represent depends on how many bits we have in the word. This determines the complexity of the implementation.

Integers

All the numbers we talk about will be *integers* (until we get to floating point). Integers have a finite range. Eight bits gives us 256 (2^8) numbers, and 16 bits gives us nearly 65000. We need to give up one bit (or, 1/2 our range of numbers) for a sign position. There will more discussion of this in the floating point section.

One thing to keep in mind is that the hardware keeps track of the bookkeeping for integer mathematical operations. The binary point is assumed to be on the right side of the word. This means there are no fractional parts. We can, in software, choose to have the binary point anywhere in the word, in which case the bookkeeping problem is ours, in the software. For example, for addition or subtraction, the binary points of the two values must be aligned This technique is referred to as *scaled integer* representation.

Another technique is used to simplify the processing of angles. Recall that our angles are decimal, but we use 360 degrees, or 2 X Pi radians. In binary, we can use binary radians, where we divide the circle into 256 or 1024. Calculations can be done on these *binary radian* ("brad") values quickly and efficiently, and the final conversion to decimal degrees or angles done at the end of the calculation, if required.

BCD Format

Binary Coded Decimal uses 10 of the possible 16 codes in 4 bits. The other bit patterns are not used, or could be used to indicate sign, error, overflow, or such. BCD converts to decimal easily, and provides a precise representation of decimal numbers. It requires serial by digit calculations, but gives exact results. It uses more storage than binary integers, and the implementation of the logic for operations is a bit more complex. It is an alternative to the limited range or precision of binary integers, and the complexity of floating point. BCD is used extensively in instrumentation and personal calculators. Support for operations on BCD numbers were provided in IBM mainframes, and the Intel x86 series of microprocessors.

BCD 4 bit code, only 10 valid values:

0000 = 0   0001 = 1   0010 = 2   0011 = 3   0100 = 4
0101 = 5   0110 = 6   0111 = 7   1000 = 8   1001 = 9

1010, 1011, 1100, 1101, 1110, 1111 = invalid number codes

BCD numbers (4 bits) can be stored in a byte, which uses more storage, but makes calculations easier. These are sometimes referred to as BCD nibbles. Alternately, BCD digits can be packed 2 to a byte.

Arithmetic operations in BCD format numbers are usually done in binary, and then adjusted to handle the carry (or borrow). For example, in packed BCD, we may generate a carry between the 3rd and 4th bit position. Subtraction is usually implemented by adding the 10's complement of the subtrahend. The 10's complement is formed by taking the 9's complement, and then adding one. The 9's complement can be formed by subtracting the digits from 9. If a BCD arithmetic operation generates an invalid BCD result, 6 can be added to force a carry. BCD strings of numbers can have a "decimal point" inserted wherever convenient. Additional bookkeeping is then needed to keep the numbers commensurate for addition and subtraction, and to adjust in multiplication and division.

Prefixes

These are standard metric system (SI) prefixes used to represent orders of magnitude in decimal. The same prefixes are used to designate binary powers, but are not part of the SI system.

The prefixes are defined for decimal values, but are also applied to binary numbers. The percent difference is not much, but in the larger magnitudes, can be significant. When someone in the computer or communications industry quotes you a number of giga-something, stop them and ask if that is decimal or binary.

Generally, memory size is measured in the powers of two, and communication speed measured in decimal powers. Hard disk sizes are specified in decimal units. Clock frequencies are usually specified in decimal. For your convenience.

Prefix	Decimal	Binary	deviation
K = *kilo*	10^3	2^{10}	2.4%
M = *mega*	10^6	2^{20}	4.9%
G = *giga*	10^9	2^{30}	7.4%
T = *tera*	10^{12}	2^{40}	10%
P = *peta*	10^{15}	2^{50}	12.6%
E = *exa*	10^{18}	2^{60}	15.3%

To date, there has been no reported major failure related to misinterpreting or confusion over units. There have been class action lawsuits regarding confusing information on packaging.

Positional notation

In a *positional number system*, the same symbols are used in different positions to represent multiples of the powers of the base. It is a system for representing numbers by symbols. An alternative, such as Roman numerals, is not a positional system, with unique symbols for different values. Our Arabic-derived decimal number system is positional. The Babylonians used a positional number system with base 60. The Maya used base 20.

A number system of a certain base, N, needs N symbols. At the right hand side of our decimal numbers, we have a *decimal point*. This separates the positive from the negative powers of the base (i.e., fractions). Similarly, we can have an *octal point* or a *hexadecimal point* or a *binary point*. By convention, digits to the left represent high values of the base.

The decimal systems uses ten unique symbols to represent quantities (0,1,2,3,4,5,6,7,8,9). The binary systems uses two (0,1).

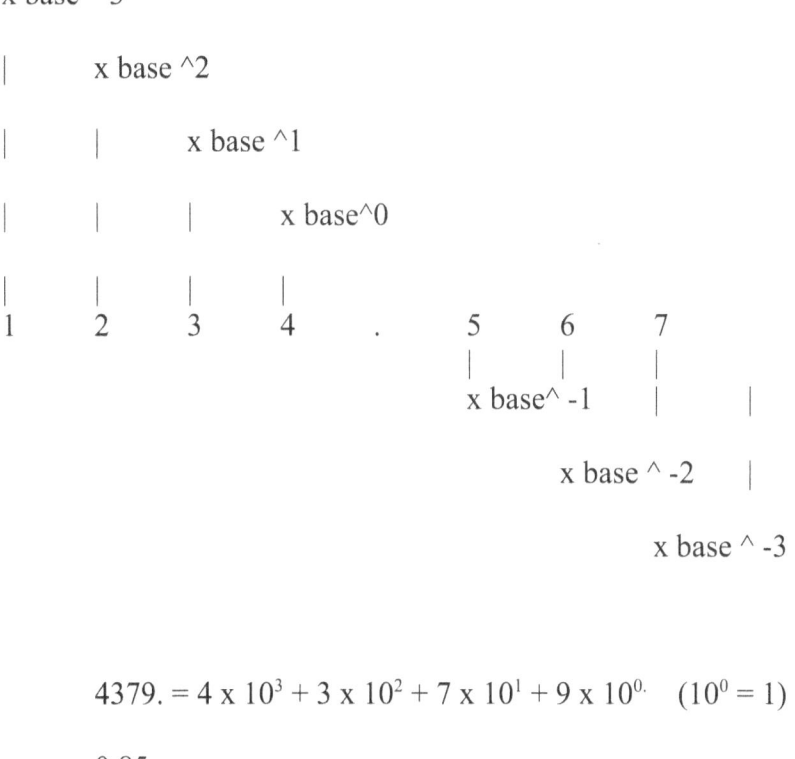

$$4379. = 4 \times 10^3 + 3 \times 10^2 + 7 \times 10^1 + 9 \times 10^0 \quad (10^0 = 1)$$

$$0.85 \; = \; 0.86$$

Infinities, overflows, and underflows

Infinity is the largest number that can be represented in the number system. Adding 1 to infinity results in infinity, by definition. In a closed number system imposed by the finite word size of the computer, adding one to infinity results in an *overflow*, a change of sign.

Negative infinity is the most negative number that can be represented in the number system, not the smallest number.

The least positive number, or the smallest amount that can be represented in the finite number systems is 1. That is because the numbers are usually considered integers, with the binary point on the right of the word. In floating point representation it is different; this will be discussed in the floating point section.

Overflow is the condition in a finite word size machine, where the result of an arithmetic operation is too large to fit in the register. For example, when adding two of the largest positive numbers in a 16-bit representation, the result would not fit in 16 bits. With the use of a two's complement representation scheme for negative numbers, the overflow would result in a sign change, from a large positive to a small negative number.

Overflows can be a problem, as the one that caused the premature termination of the Ariane 5 launch vehicle flight 501. The lost payload was worth more than $300 million.

Underflow is a condition where, as the result of an arithmetic operation, the result is smaller in value than the smallest representable number. The result will be reported as zero in integer representation, even if it is positive, greater than zero, but less than 1. The resolution of binary integers is 1.

Elementary Math operations

The elementary math operations include add, subtract, multiply, divide.

The laws of binary addition

0+0=0

1+0=1
0+1=1
1+1=0 (with a carry)

Laws of binary subtraction (Remember a-b does not equal b-a)

0-0=0
0-1=1 (with a borrow)
1-0=1
1-1=0

Laws of binary multiplication

0 x 0 = 0
0 x 1 = 0
1 x 0 = 0
1 x 1 = 1

(that's easy; anything times 0 is 0))

Laws of binary division

(Division by zero is not defined. There is no answer.)

0 / 0 = not allowed
1 / 0 = not allowed
0 / 1 = 0
1 / 1 = 1

Hexadecimal numbers

Hexadecimal (Hex) is a positional number system using base 16. It is a way of grouping four consecutive binary digits into something that looks like a decimal symbol to us humans. Earlier, the octal or base 8 system was used, but this has fell from favor. The idea behind the concept of grouping is that we humans find it difficult to work with very long numbers. On the other hand (no pun intended) some cultures count on the spaces between their fingers rather than the fingers themselves, using an octal system.

To form a hex number, we group binary digits in 4's. The base is 16. For our decimal numbers, we have 10 symbols, so we will need some more for hex – 6 more. These are the hex symbols for the first 16 numbers: 0,1,2,3,4,5,6,7,8,9,A,B,C,D,E,F. They seem a little strange to us, because there are letters mixed in with our numbers. Don't worry, they are all symbols. The computer doesn't care - it uses binary.

Hex is also a positional number system, but here, the position indicates a power of 16.

$16^0 = 1$
$16^1 = 16$
$16^2 = 256$
$16^3 = 4096$, etc.

There are also numbers to the right of the hexadecimal point, for quantities that are smaller.

$16^{-1} = 1/16$
$16^{-2} = 1/256$
$16^{-3} = 1/4096$

Conversion between bases is fairly simple, but has to be learned, just like the laws of mathematics. Most calculators can do it, but it is a useful skill. Some day you may find yourself on a deserted island without a calculator as a crutch.

To go from hex to decimal is a simple algorithm. In mathematics, algorithm is a method, expressed as a list of well-defined instructions for calculating a function. We can have an algorithm for baking a cake, or calculating conversion between bases.

The key to our conversion algorithm is that both systems are positional, on for base 16 and one for base 10. To see the correspondences between the symbols, A=10, B=11, C=12, D=13, E=14, F=15.

As an example, $13B7_{16}$ equals:

1 x 4096 = 4096
3 x 256 = 768
B x 16 = 176   (11x16)
7 x 1 = 7
5047_{10}

The conversion from decimal to hex is a little more complicated. We have to apply successive divisions of powers of the base, saving the remainder for the next step.

What is 943_{10} in hex?

First, 4096 < 943 < 256, so, 943 will have 3 hex digits. More than 2, less than 4.

Then the successive divisions:

943 / 256 = 3 remainder 175
175 / 16 = 10 remainder 15
15 / 1 = 15 remainder 0

$3/10/15_{10} = 3AF_{16}$

So, what if we see a number like 8A7? We could guess it is hex, because it has one of those hex characters included. But if we saw

894, we really wouldn't know. It is a valid hex and a valid decimal value. When in doubt, indicate the base by a subscript.

First, 4096 < 943 < 256, so, 943 will have 3 hex digits. More than 2, less than 4.

Then the successive divisions:

943 / 256 = 3 remainder 175
175/ 16 = 10 remainder 15
15 / 1 = 15 remainder 0

$3/10/15_{10} = 3AF_{16}$

So, what if we see a number like 8A7? We could guess it is hex, because it has one of those hex characters included. But if we saw 894, we really wouldn't know. It is a valid hex and a valid decimal value. When in doubt, indicate the base by a subscript.

Logical operations on data

Logical operations are done on a bit-by-bit basis. There is no interaction between adjacent bit positions.

The *Unary function*, (function of 1 variable) is "negate". This changes a 0 to a 1, or a 1 to a 0. there is one input, and one output.

There are 16 possible *binary functions* (function of 2 input variables). These include AND, OR, and XOR, and their negations, NAND, NOR, and NXOR. The other 10 don't have specific names.

Math in terms of logic functions

Here, we see that mathematical functions can be implemented by logical operations. That's good, because microelectronics implements logical functions easily. George Boole worked out the theoretical basis of this in the middle 1800's.

Addition

+		half-add	carry	
0	0	0	0	0 + 0 = 0
0	1	1	0	0 + 1 = 1
1	0	1	0	1 + 0 = 1
1	1	0	1	1 + 1 = 0, with a carry (this is like saying, 5 + 5 = 0, with a carry, in the decimal system)

ADD = half-add (XOR) plus carry (AND)

Similarly, for subtraction

-		half-add	borrow	
0	0	0	0	0 - 0 = 0
0	1	1	1	0 - 1 = 0, with a borrow
1	0	1	0	1 - 0 = 0
1	1	0	0	1 – 1 = 0

SUB = half-add (XOR) plus borrow (one of the unnamed functions)

We can see that mathematics in the binary system can be implemented with logical functions.

X (times)			multiply
0	0	0	0 x 0 = 0

0	1	0	0 x 1 = 0
1	0	0	1 x 0 = 0
1	1	1	1 x 1 = 1

Multiplication is the AND function.

Division
/

0	0	not allowed operation		0/0 = not an allowed operation
0	1	0		0/1 = 0
1	0	not allowed operation		1/0 = not an allowed operation
1	1	1		1/1 = 1

Binary division is another of the unnamed operations.

<u>Negative numbers</u>

There are many ways to do represent *negative numbers*. The case we are familiar with from our use of decimal is the use of a special symbol "-". This gives us the sign-magnitude format.

We could do this in binary as well, and in addition, there are the *1's complement* and *2's complement* schemes of representing negative numbers. To form the 1's complement of a binary number, change all bits to their complement. Problem is, in a finite (closed) number system, the 1's complement system gives two different representations of zero (i.e., +0 and -0), both valid. To form the 2's complement, do the 1's complement and add 1. This is a more complex operation, but the advantage is, there is only one representation of zero. Because zero is considered a positive number, there is one more negative number than positive number in this representation. Two's complement has become the dominant choice for negative number representation in computers.

One's complement was used on the Univac 1108 series mainframes. A problem was that 0 and -o did not test equal.

The analog to the complements in the decimal system is 9's complement and 10's complement, but these are not taught, and don't get used much anymore.

Subtraction

Subtraction can be accomplished by addition of the complement. We don't need a separate subtract-er circuit. We can use the adder, and we need a complement (inverter) circuit, which is easy. Logical operations such as complement operate on a bit-by-bit basis with no "carry" or "borrow" from adjacent bits, like we would find in mathematical operations.

Subtraction example

```
-      0   1              b    0    1
       b=borrow
0      0   1              0    0    0
1      1   0              1    1    0
```

remember a-b does not equal =b-a

```
    D            11 11
    E 8 h  ->    1110 1000
    -5 A h ->    0101 1010
    8 E h  ->    1000 1110
```

Add 2's complement

```
         5 A h = 0101 1010
1's comp = 1010 0101 (A5h)
2's comp = 1010 0110 (A6h)
```

```
    E 8 h -> 1110 1000
+ A 6 h -> 1010 0110
 1 8 E h1 10001110 ignore overflow
```

Overflow

Overflow is the case where a calculation has produced a result that I larger in magnitude than can be held in a finite register or storage location. It is a result of using a finite number system, such as 16-bits. Adding two of the largest numbers in 16-bits will result in a 17-bit number, for example. A carry is a type of overflow indicator.

Overflows can be a problem, as one caused the premature termination of Ariane 5 launch vehicle flight 501. The lost payload was worth more than $300 million.

Underflow is a condition where the result is smaller in value than the smallest representable number. This can't happen in binary, but can occur in floating point representation.

If division is equivalent to repeated subtraction, and subtraction is the same as addition of the complement, and multiplication is repeated addition, then all we really need is an additional circuit, and a complementer. Since addition can be accomplished by the logic circuits AND and XOR, we can in theory implement all binary mathematical operations in terms of logic functions. That's the theory. There's better ways to do it.

Multiplication

Multiplication by digit is possible, but can take excessive time, with long digits. The multiplication table in binary is rather simple, though. Only one of four cases results in a non-zero result. The multiplication of two n-bit numbers requires n^2 operations. The results for a multiplication of two n-bit numbers can be 2n bits wide.

Shift-and-add is a common multiplication technique in binary. Shifting gives us successive powers of two.

There do exist special algorithms for multiplication and division, so we don't need to do repeated adds or subtracts. Examples are the Karatsuba method, and the Toom-Cook algorithm. We can also design a digital multiplier for hexadecimal numbers, so we do 4 binary digits per clock. This can make use of a look-up table.

Multiplication of fractions takes the form of normal multiplication, with due diligence of the resulting binary point.

In optimizing integer multiplications, we can speed up the process where we have a variable times a constant. First, if the constant is a power of two, the multiplication can be accomplished with shifts. Similarly, multiplication by sums of powers of two is also easily handled (i.e., 6 = 4+2, 10 = 8+2). With a bit more work, we can factor the fixed multiplicand into powers of two (i.e., 13 = 8 + 4 + 1; 15 = 16 - 1) and accomplish the multiplication with shifts and adds. This works for fairly complex numbers, because the cost of a multiply instruction is high, whereas the shifts, adds, and subtracts are usually optimized to be single clock operations. This technique requires knowledge of the individual instruction times.

Division

Division is a big, ugly, and time-consuming operation, to be avoided whenever possible. The division operation is usually the longest one in the instruction set. This sets a lower limit to interrupt latency in real-time systems, and can certainly effect throughput.

A special case, of division is the *reciprocal*, 1/X. Here, the numerator of the fraction is known, and the division easier. After forming the reciprocal, which takes less time than an arbitrary division, a multiplication is required.

A/B = 1/A x B

In integer multiplication, division of a value by a power of two can be accomplished by shifts.

Appendix - Floating Point

This section describes the *floating point* number representation, and explains when it is used, and why. Floating point is an old computer technique for gaining dynamic range in scientific and engineering calculations, at the cost of accuracy. First, we look at fixed point, or integer, calculations to see where the limitations are. Then, we'll examine how floating point helps expand the limits.

In a finite word length machine, there is a tradeoff between dynamic range and accuracy in representation. The value of the most significant bit sets the dynamic range because the effective value of the most positive number is infinity. The value of the least significant bit sets the accuracy, because a value less than the LSB is zero. And, the MSB and the LSB are related by the word length.

In any fixed point machine, the number system is of a finite size. For example, in 18 bit word, we can represent the positive integers from 0 to $2^{18}-1$, or 262,143. A word of all zeros = 0, and a word of all ones = 262,143. I'm using 18 bits as an example because it's not too common. There's nothing magic about 8, 16, or 32 bit word sizes.

If we want to use signed numbers, we must give up one bit to represent the sign. Of course, giving up one bit halves the number of values available in the representation. For a signed integer in an 18 bit word, we can represent integers from + to - 131,072. Of course, zero is a valid number. Either the positive range or the negative range must give up a digit so we can represent zero. For now, let's say that in 18 bits, we can represent the integers from -131,072 to 131,071.

There are several ways of using the sign bit for representation. We can have a sign-magnitude format, a 1's complement, or a two's complement representation. Most computers use the 2's complement representation. This is easy to implement in hardware. In this format, to form the negative of a number, complement all of the bits (1->0, 0->1), and add 1 to the least significant bit position.

This is equivalent to forming the 1's complement, and then adding one. One's complement format has the problem that there are two representations of zero, all bits 0 and all bits 1. The hardware has to know that these are equivalent. This added complexity has led to 1's complement schemes falling out of use in favor of 2's complement. In two's complement, there is one representation of zero (all bits zero), and one less positive number, than the negatives. (Actually, since zero is considered positive, there are the same number. But, the negative numbers have more range.) This is easily illustrated for 3 bit numbers, and can be extrapolated to any other fixed length representation.

Remember that the difference between a signed and an unsigned number lies in our interpretation of the bit pattern.

Interpretation of 4-bit patterns

Up to this point we have considered the bit patterns to represent integer values, but we can also insert an arbitrary binary point (analogous to the decimal point) in the word. For integer representations, we have assumed the binary point to lie at the right side of the word, below the LSB. This gives the LSB a weight of 2^0, or 1, and the msb has a weight of 2^{16}. (The sign bit is in the 2^{17} position). Similarly, we can use a fractional representation where the binary point is assumed to lie between the sign bit and the MSB, the MSB has a weight of 2^{-1}, and the LSB has a weight of 2^{-17}. For these two cases we have:

The MSB sets the range, the LSB sets the accuracy, and the LSB and MSB are related by the word length. For cases between these extremes, the binary point can lie anywhere in the word, or for that matter, outside the word. For example, if the binary point is assumed to be 2 bits to the right of the LSB, the LSB weight, and thus the precision, is 2^2. The MSB is then 2^{19}. We have gained dynamic range at the cost of precision. If we assume the binary point is to the left of the MSB, we must be careful to ignore the sign, which does not have an associated digit weight. For an assumed binary point 2 bit positions to the right of the MSB, we have a MSB weight of 2^{-3}, and an LSB weight of 2^{-20}. We have gained precision at the cost of dynamic range.

It is important to remember that the computer does not care where we assume the binary point to be. It simply treats the numbers as integers during calculations. We overlay the bit weights and the meanings.

A 16-bit integer can represent the values between -16384 to 16383

A 32-bit integer can represent the values between $-2*10^9$ to $2*10^9$

A short real number has the range 10^{-37} to 10^{38} in 32 bits.

A long real number has the range 10^{-307} to 10^{308} in 64 bits

We can get 18 decimal (BCD) digits packed into 80 bits.

To add or subtract scaled values, they must have the same scaling factor; they must be commensurate. If the larger number is normalized, the smaller number must be shifted to align it for the operation. This may have the net result of adding or subtracting zero, as bits fall out the right side of the small word. This is like saying that 10 billion + .00001 is approximately 10 billion, to 13 decimal places of accuracy.

In multiplication, the scaling factor of the result is the sum of the scaling factors of the products. This is analogous to engineering notation, where we learn to add the powers of 10.

In division, the scaling factor of the result is the difference between the scaling factor of the dividend and the scaling factor of the divisor. The scaling factor of the remainder is that of the dividend. In engineering notation, we subtract the powers of 10 for a division.

In a normal form for a signed integer, the most significant bit is one. This says, in essence, that all leading zeros have been squeezed out of the number. The sign bit does not take part in this procedure. However, note that if we know that the most significant bit is always a one, there is no reason to store it. This gives us a free bit in a sense; the most significant bit is a 1 by definition, and the msb-1 th bit is adjacent to the sign bit. This simple trick has doubled the effective accuracy of the word, because each bit position is a factor of two.

The primary operation that will cause a loss of precision or accuracy is the subtraction of two numbers that have nearly but not quite identical values. This is commonly encountered in digital filters, for example, where successive readings are differenced. For an 18 bit word, if the readings differ in, say, the 19th bit position, then the difference will be seen to be zero. On the other hand, the scaling factor of the parameters must allow sufficient range to hold the largest number expected. Care must be taken in subtracting values known to be nearly identical. Precision can be retained by pre-normalization of the arguments.

During an arithmetic operation, if the result is a value larger than the greatest positive value for a particular format, or less than the most negative, then the operation has overflowed the format. Normally, the absolute value function cannot overflow, with the exception of the absolute value of the least negative number, which has no corresponding positive representation, because we made room for the representation of zero.

In addition, the scaling factor can increase by one, if we consider the possibility of adding two of the largest possible numbers. We can also consider subtracting the largest (absolute value) negative number from the largest (in an absolute sense) negative number.

A one bit position left shift is equivalent to multiplying by two. Thus, after a one position shift, the scaling factor must be adjusted to reflect the new position of the binary point. Similarly, a one bit position right shift is equivalent to division by two, and the scaling factor must be similarly adjusted after the operation.

Numeric overflow occurs when a nonzero result of an arithmetic operation is too small in absolute value to be represented. The result is usually reported as zero. The subtraction case discussed above is one example. Taking the reciprocal of the largest positive number is another.

As in the decimal representation, some numbers cannot be represented exactly in binary, regardless of the precision. Non-terminating fractions such as 1/3 are one case, and the irrational numbers such as e and pi are another. Operations involving these will result in inexact results, regardless of the format. However, this is not necessarily an error. The irrationals, by definition, cannot exactly be represented by a ratio of integers. Even in base 10 notation, e and pi extend indefinitely.

When the results of a calculation do not fix within the format, we must throw something away. We normally delete bits from the right (or low side) side of the word (the precision end). There are several ways to do this. If we simply ignore the bits that won't fit within the format, we are *truncating*, or rounding toward zero. We choose the closest word within the format to represent the results. We can also round up by adding 1 to the LSB of the resultant word if the first bit we're going to throw away is a 1. We can also choose to round to even, round to odd, round to nearest, round towards zero, round towards + infinity, or round towards - infinity. Consistency is the desired feature.

If we look at typical physical constants, we can get some idea of the dynamic range that we'll require for typical applications. The mass of an electron, you recall, is 9.1085×10^{-31} grams. Avogadro's number is 6.023×10^{23}. If we want to multiply these quantities, we need a dynamic range of $10^{(23+31)} = 10^{54}$, which would require a 180 bit word (10^{54} approx.= 2^{180}). Most of the bits in this 180 bit word would be zeros as place holders. Well, since zeros don't mean anything, can't we get rid of them? Of course.

We need dynamic range, and we need precision, but we usually don't need them simultaneously. The floating point data structure will give us dynamic range, at the cost of being unable to exactly represent data.

So, finally, we talk about floating point. In essence, we need a format for the computer to work with that is analogous to engineering notation, a mantissa and a power of ten. The two parts of the word, with their associated signs, will take part in calculation exactly like the scaled integers discussed previously. The exponent is the scaling factor that we used. Whereas in scaled integers, we had a fixed scaling factor, in floating point, we allow the scaling factor to be carried along with the word, and to change as the calculations proceed.

The representation of a number in floating point, like the representation in scientific notation, is not unique. For example,

$$6.54 \times 10^2 = .654 \times 10^3 = 654. \times 10^0$$

We have to choose a scheme and be consistent. What is normally done is that the exponent is defined to be a number such that the leftmost digit is non-zero. This is defined as the normal form.

In the floating point representation, the number of bits assigned to the exponent determines *dynamic range*, and the number of bits assigned to the mantissa determine the *precision*, or resolution. For a fixed word size, we must allocate the available bits between the precision (mantissa), and the range (exponent).

Granularity is defined as the difference between representable numbers. This term is normally equal to the absolute precision, and relates to the least significant bit.

Denormalized numbers

This topic is getting well into the number of theory, and I will only touch on these special topics here. There is a use for numbers that are not in normal form, so-called de-normals. This has to do with decreasing granularity, and the fact that numbers in the range between zero and the smallest normal number. A *denorm* has an exponent which is the smallest representable exponent, with a leading digit of the mantissa not equal to zero. An un-normalized number, on the other hand, has the same mantissa case, but an exponent which is not the smallest representable. Let's get back to engineering...

Overflow and Underflow

If the result of an operation results in a number too large (in an absolute magnitude case) to be represented, we have generated an overflow. If the result is too small to be represented, we have an underflow. Results of an overflow can be reported as infinity (+ or - as required), or as an error bit pattern. The underflow case is where we have generated a denormalized number. The IEEE standard, discussed below, handles denorms as valid operands. Another approach is to specify resultant denorms as zero.

Standards

There are many standards for the floating point representation, with the IEEE standard being the defacto industry choice. In this section, we'll discuss the IEEE standard in detail, and see how some other industry standards differ, and how conversions can be made.

IEEE floating point

The IEEE standard specifies the representation of a number as +/- mantissa x $2^{(+/- exponent)}$. Note that there are two sign bits, one for the mantissa, and one for the exponent. Note also that the exponent is an exponent of two, not ten. This is referred to as radix-2 representation. Other radices are possible. The most significant bit of the mantissa is assumed to be a 1, and is not stored. Take a look at what this representation buys us. A 16 bit integer can cover a range of +/- 10^4. A 32 bit integer can span a range of +/- 10^9. The IEEE short real format, in 32 bits, can cover a range of +/- $10^{+/-38}$. A 64 bit integer covers the range +/- 10^{19}. A long real IEEE floating point number covers the range +/- $10^{+/- 308}$. The dynamic range of calculations has been vastly increased for the same data size. What we have lost is the ability to exactly represent numbers, but we are close enough for engineering.

In the short, real format, the 32 bit word is broken up into fields. The mantissa, defined as a number less than 1, occupies 23 bits. The most significant bit of the data item is the sign of the mantissa. The exponent occupies 8 bits. The represented word is as follows:

$(-1)^S (2^{E+bias}) (F1...F23)$

where F0...F23 < 1. Note that F0=1 by definition, and is not stored.

The term $(-1)^S$ gives us + when the S bit is 0 and - when the S bit is 1. The bias term is defined as 127. This is used instead of a sign bit for the exponent, and achieves the same results. This format simplifies the hardware, because only positive numbers are then involved in exponent calculations. As a side benefit, this approach ensures that reciprocals of all representable numbers can be represented.

In the long real format, the structure is as follows:

$(-1)^S (2^{E+bias}) (F1...F52)$

where F0...F52 < 1. Note that F0=1 by definition, and is not stored.

Here, the bias term is defined as 1023.

For intermediate steps in a calculation, there is a temporary real data format in 80 bits. This expands the exponent to 15 bits, and the mantissa to 64 bits. This allows a range of +/- 10^{4932}, which is a large number in anyone's view.

In the IEEE format, provision is made for entities known as *Not-A-Number* (NaN's). For sample, the result of trying to multiply zero times infinity is NaN. These entities are status signals that particular violation cases took place. IEEE representation also supports four user selectable rounding modes. What do we do with results that won't fit in the bits allocated? Do we round or truncate? If we round, is it towards +/- infinity, or zero? Not all implementations of the IEEE standard implement all of the modes and options.

Floating point hardware is specialized, optimized computer architecture for the floating point data structure. It usually features concurrent operation with host, or the integer unit. Initially, floating point units were separate chips, but now the state of the art allows these functional units to be included on the same silicon real estate as the integer processor. The hardware of the floating point unit is specialized to handle the floating point data format. For example, in a floating multiply, we simultaneously integer multiply the mantissas and add the exponents. A barrel shifter is handy for normalization/renormalization by providing a shift of any number of bits in one clock period. Floating point units usually implement the format conversions in hardware (integer to floating, Float, floating to integer, Fix), and can handle extended precision (64 bit) integers. Both external and internal floating point units usually rely on the main processor's instruction fetch unit. The coprocessor may have to do a memory access for load/store. In this case, it may use a dma-like protocol to get use of the memory bus resource from the integer processor.

Floating point hardware gives us the ability to add, subtract, multiply, and sometimes divide. Some units provide only the reciprocal function, which is a simple divide into a known fixed quantity (1), and thus easy to implement. A divide requires two operations, then, a reciprocal followed by a multiply. Some units also include square root, and some transcendental primitives. In general, these functions are implemented in a microstep fashion, with Taylor or other series expansions of the functions of interest.

signed integer range $2 \wedge$ (bits - 1)

10 bits 1×10^3 a good approximation is 2^{10} is approx. 10^3)

16 bits 3×10^4

32 bits 2×10^9

64 bits 9.2×10^{18}

128 bits 1.7×10^{38}

256 bits 1.1×10^{77}

Floating Point operations

This subsection discuses operations on floating point numbers. This forms the basis for the specification of a floating point emulation software package, or for the development of custom hardware.

Before the addition can be performed, the floating point numbers must be *commensurate* with addition; in essence, they must have the same exponent. The mantissa of the number with the smaller exponent will be right shifted, and the exponent adjusted accordingly. However, if the right shift is equal to or more than the number of bits in the mantissa representation, we will lose something. This is analogous to the case where we add 0.000001 to 1 million and get approximately 1 million.

After the addition of mantissas, we may need to right shift the resultant by 1, and adjust the exponent accordingly, to account for mantissa overflow. This is analogous to the case of adding $4.1 \times 10^{16} + 6.3 \times 10^{16}$, with the result of 10.4×10^{16}, or $1.04 * 10^{17}$, in normal form.

If we add two numbers of almost equal magnitude but opposite sign, we get a case of massive cancellation. Here, the leading digits of the mantissa may be zero, with a loss of precision. Renormalization is always called for after addition.

example: $1.23456 * 10^{16}$ plus $-1.23455 * 10^{16} = 0.00001 \times 10^{16}$, or $1.0 * 10^{11}$, in normal form.

In multiply, we may simultaneously multiply the mantissas, and add the exponents. After the operation, we need to renormalize the results. In division, we divide the mantissas and subtract the exponents, then renormalize.

The easiest division to do is a *reciprocal*, where the dividend is a known quantity. Some systems implement only the reciprocal operation, requiring a following multiplication to complete the division operation. Even so, this may be faster than a division, because the reciprocal is much easier to implement in algorithmic form than the general purpose division.

Transcendentals

The floating point unit can also implement *transcendental functions*. These are usually represented as Taylor series expansions of common trigonometric and log functions. Enough transcendentals are included to provide basis functions for all we might need to calculate.

- F2XM1 - 2X-1
- FYL2X - Y * log2 (X)
- FYL2XP1 - Y * log2(X+1)
- FPTAN - tangent
- FPATAN - arctangent

From the basis functions, if x=tan(a), then a = atan (x), then

- Sin (a) = x / sqrt (1 + x2)
- cos (a) = 1 / sqrt (1 + x2)
- asin (x) = atan [x/sqrt (1-x2)]

There are known functions to calculate 2^x, e^x, 10^x, and y^x in terms of the F2MX1 (2^x-1) function. Similarly, the log base e and base 10 can be calculated in terms of the FYL2X (log base 2) function. All of the trigonometric, inverse trigonometric, hyperbolic, and inverse hyperbolic functions can be calculated in terms of the supplied basis functions.

Glossary of Embedded System Terms and Acronyms

1's complement – a binary number representation scheme for negative values.

2's complement – another binary number representation scheme for negative values.

2-wire – twisted pair wire channel for full duplex communications. Still needs a common ground.

802.11 – a radio frequency wireless data communications standard.

Accumulator – a register to hold numeric values during and after an operation.

ACM – Association for Computing Machinery; professional organization.

Actuator – device which converts a control signal to a mechanical action.

Ada – a programming language named after Ada Augusta, Countess of Lovelace, and daughter of Lord Byron; arguably, the first programmer. Collaborator with Charles Babbage.

A/D, ADC – analog to digital converter.

ALU – arithmetic logic unit.

Android – an operating system based on Gnu-Linux, popular for smart phones and tablet computers.

Analog – concerned with continuous values.

ANSI – American National Standards Institute

API – application program interface; specification for software modules to communicate.

Arduino – open source, single board microcontroller using an Atmel AVR (8-bit risc) cpu.

Arinc – Aeronautical Radio, Inc. commercial company supporting transportation, and providing standards for avionics.

ARM – Acorn RISC machine; a 32-bit architecture with wide application in embedded systems.

ArpaNet – Advanced Research Projects Agency (U.S.), first packet switched network, 1968.

ASCII - American Standard Code for Information Interchange, a 7-bit code; developed for teleprinters.

ASIC – application specific integrated circuit, custom or semicustom,.

Assembly language – low level programming language specific to a particular ISA.

Async – asynchronous; using different clocks.

ATCA- Advanced Telecomm Computing Architecture (spec).

Babbage, Charles –early 19th century inventor of mechanical computing machinery to solve difference equations, and output typeset results; later machines would be fully programmable.

Baud – symbol rate; may or may not be the same as bit rate.

Baudot – a five-bit code used with teleprinters.

BCD – binary coded decimal. 4-bit entity used to represent 10 different decimal digits; with 6 spare states.

Beowulf – clustering technology for Gnu-Linux-based computers.

Big-endian – data format with the most significant bit or byte at the lowest address, or transmitted first.

BIOS – basic input output system; first software run after boot.

BIST – built-in self test.

Bit – smallest unit of digital information; two states.

Blackbox – functional device with inputs and outputs, but no detail on the internal workings.

Bluetooth – short range open wireless communications standard.

Boolean – a data type with two values; an operation on these data types; named after George Boole, mid-19th century inventor of Boolean algebra.

Bootstrap – a startup or reset process that proceeds without external intervention.

BSD – Berkeley Software Distribution version of the Bell Labs Unix operating system.

BSP – board support package; information and drivers for a specific circuit board.

Buffer – a temporary holding location for data.

Bug – an error in a program or device.

C – programming language from Bell Labs, circa 1972.

Cache – faster and smaller intermediate memory between the processor and main memory.

Cache coherency – process to keep the contents of multiple caches consistent,

CAN – controller area network.

CAS – column address strobe (in DRAM refreshing)

Chip – integrated circuit component.

Clock – periodic timing signal to control and synchronize operations.

CMOS – complementary metal oxide semiconductor; a technology using both positive and negative semiconductors to achieve low power operation.

Complement – in binary logic, the opposite state.

Compilation – software process to translate source code to assembly or machine code (or error codes).

Configuware – equivalent of software for FPGA architectures; configuration information.

Control Flow – computer architecture involving directed flow through the program; data dependent paths are allowed.

COP – computer operating properly.

Coprocessor – another processor to supplement the operations of the main processor. Used for floating point, video, etc. Usually relies on the main processor for instruction fetch; and control.

Core – early non-volatile memory technology based on ferromagnetic toroid's.

CRC – cyclic redundancy code, an error-control mechanism.

D/A – digital to analog conversion.

DAC – digital to analog converter.

Daemon – in multitasking, a program that runs in the background.

Dalvik – the virtual machine in the Android operating system.

Dataflow – computer architecture where a changing value forces recalculation of dependent values.

Datagram – message on a packet switched network; the delivery, arrival time, and order of arrival are not guaranteed.

D-cache – data cache

DDR – dual data rate (memory).

Deadlock – a situation in which two or more competing actions are each waiting for the other to finish, and thus neither ever does.

DCE – data communications equipment; interface to the network.

Denorm – in floating point representation, a non-zero number with a magnitude less than the smallest normal number.

Digital – using discrete values for representation of states or numbers.

Dirty bit – used to signal that the contents of a cache have changed.

DMA - direct memory access (to/from memory, for I/O devices).

Double word – two words; if word = 8 bits, double word = 16 bits.

Dram – dynamic random access memory.

Drum memory – obsolete storage media using large cylindrical magnetic media.

DSP – digital signal processing.

DTE – data terminal equipment; communicates with the DCE to get to the network.

DVI – digital visual interface (for video).

ECL – emitter coupled logic, a bipolar transistor logic that is fast and power hungry.

EIA – Electronics Industry Association.

Embedded system – a computer systems with limited human interfaces and performing specific tasks. Usually part of a larger system.

Epitaxial – in semiconductors, have a crystalline overlayer with a well-defined orientation.

Eprom – erasable programmable read-only memory.

EEprom – electrically erasable read-only memory.

Ethernet – 1980's networking technology. IEEE 802.3.

Exception – interrupt due to internal events, such as overflow.

Fail-safe – a system designed to do no harm in the event of failure.

FET – field effect transistor.

Fetch/execute cycle – basic operating cycle of a computer; fetch the instruction, execute the instruction.

File – a container of information, usually stored as a one dimensional array of bytes.

Firewire – serial communications protocol (IEEE-1394).

Firmware – code contained in a non-volatile memory.

Fixed point – computer numeric format with a fixed number of digits or bits, and a fixed radix point. Integers.

Flag – a binary indicator.

Flash memory – a type of non-volatile memory, similar to EEprom.

Flip-flop – a circuit with two stable states; ideal for binary.

Floating point – computer numeric format for real numbers; has significant digits and an exponent.

Forth – stack-oriented programming language

FPGA – field programmable gate array.

FPU – floating point unit, an ALU for floating point numbers.

Full duplex – communication in both directions simultaneously.

Gate – a circuit to implement a logic function; can have multiple inputs, but a single output.

Giga - 10^9 or 2^{30}

Gnu – recursive acronym; gnu (is) not unix. Operating system that is free software.

GPIO – general purpose input output

GPL – gnu public license used for free software; referred to as the "copyleft."

GPS – global positioning system (U.S.) system of navigation satellites.

GPU – graphics processing unit. ALU for graphics data.

GUI – graphics user interface.

Half-duplex – communications in two directions, but not simultaneously.

Hall effect - production of a voltage across an electrical conductor, transverse to an electric current in the conductor and a magnetic field perpendicular to the current. Used in sensors.

Handshake – co-ordination mechanism.

Harvard architecture – memory storage scheme with separate instructions and data.

Hexadecimal – base 16 number representation.

Hexadecimal point – radix point that separates integer from fractional values of hexadecimal numbers.

Hotplug – to connect equipment without turning the power off first.

HP – Hewlett-Packard Company. Instrumentation and computers.

Hypervisor – virtual machine manager. Can manage multiple operating systems.

Hysteresis – system dependency on current state and path (or history).

I-cache – instruction cache.

I^2C – inter-integrated circuit; a multi-master serial single-ended computer bus invented by Philips.

Icon – a graphical representation or pictogram.

IDE – Integrated development environment for software or configware.

IEEE – Institute of Electrical and Electronic Engineers. Professional organization and standards body.

IEEE-754 – standard for floating point representation and operations.

Infinity - the largest number that can be represented in the number system.

Integer – the natural numbers, zero, and the negatives of the natural numbers.

Interrupt – an asynchronous event to signal a need for attention (example: the phone rings).

Interrupt vector – entry in a table pointing to an interrupt service routine; indexed by interrupt number.

I/O – Input-output from the computer to external devices, or a user interface.

IP – intellectual property; also internet protocol.

IP core – IP describing a chip design that can be licensed to be used in an FPGA or ASIC.

IR – infrared, 1-400 terahertz. Perceived as heat.

ISA – instruction set architecture, the software description of the computer.

ISO – International Standards Organization.

ISR – interrupt service routine, a subroutine that handles a particular interrupt event.

Java – programming language that targets the Java Virtual Machine.

Jazelle – direct execution of Java bytecodes, as opposed to execution in the Java Virtual Machine.

Joystick – human interface device for rotation and direction control. Used in aircraft and video games.

JTAG – Joint Test Action Group; industry group that lead to IEEE 1149.1, Standard Test Access Port and Boundary-Scan Architecture.

Junction – in semiconductors, the boundary interface of the n-type and p-type material.

JVM – Java Virtual Machine – software that allows any architecture to execute Java bytecodes by emulation.

Kernel – main portion of the operating system. Interface between the applications and the hardware.

Kilo – a prefix for 10^3 or 2^{10}

Ladder logic – description of relay-based logic circuits. Obsolete.

LAN – local area network.

Latency – time delay.

LCD – liquid crystal display.

LED – light emitting diode.

LET – linear energy transfer. Used to characterize ionizing radiation.

Linux – unix-like operating system developed by Linus Torvalds; open source.

LISP – programming language for list processing (1958).

List – a data structure.

Little-endian – data format with the least significant bit or byte at the highest address, or transmitted last.

Logic operation – generally, negate, AND, OR, XOR, and their inverses.

Logo – programming language for education and robotics, based on LISP (1967).

Loop-unrolling – optimization of a loop for speed at the cost of space.

LRU – least recently used; an algorithm for item replacement in a cache.

LSB – least significant bit or byte.

LUT – look up table.

Mac – media access control; a mac address is unique on a network.

Machine language – native code for a particular computer hardware.

Mainframe – a computer you can't lift.

Malware – malicious software; virus, worm, Trojan, spyware, adware, and such.

Mantissa – significant digits (as opposed to the exponent) of a floating point value.

Master-slave – control process with one element in charge. Master status may be exchanged among elements.

Mega - 10^6 or 2^{20}

Memory leak – when a program uses memory resources but does not return them, leading to a lack of available memory.

Memory scrubbing – detecting and correcting bit errors.

MEMS – Micro Electronic Mechanical System

Mesh – a highly connected network.

MESI – modified, exclusive, shared, invalid state of a cache coherency protocol.

Metaprogramming – programs that produce or modify other programs.

Microcode – hardware level data structures to translate machine instructions into sequences of circuit level operations.

Microcontroller – microprocessor with included memory and/or I/O.

Microkernel – operating system which is not monolithic. So functions execute in user space.

Microprocessor – a monolithic cpu on a chip.

Microprogramming – modifying the microcode.

Middleware – software layer between the application and the operating system, providing services.

MIL-STD-1553 – military standard (US) for a serial communications bus for avionics.

MIMD – multiple instruction, multiple data

Minicomputer – smaller than a mainframe, larger than a pc.

Minix – Unix-like operating system; free and open source.

MIPS – millions of instructions per second; sometimes used as a measure of throughput. also a RISC architecture from Stanford University.

MMU – memory management unit; translates virtual to physical addresses.

Modem – modulator/demodulator; digital communications interface for analog channels.

MPU – memory protection unit – like an MMU, but without address translation.

MRAM – Magnetorestrictive random access memory. Non-volatile memory approach using magnetic storage elements and integrated circuit fabrication techniques.

MSB – most significant bit or byte.

Multiplex – combining signals on a communication channel by sampling.

Mutex – a data structure and methodology for mutual exclusion.

Multicore – multiple processing cores on one substrate or chip; need not be identical.

NAN – not-a-number; invalid bit pattern.

NAND – negated (or inverse) AND function.

NASA – National Aeronautics and Space Administration.

NDA – non-disclosure agreement; legal agreement protecting IP.

Nibble – 4 bits, ½ byte.

NIST – National Institute of Standards and Technology (US), previously, National Bureau of Standards.

NMI – non-maskable interrupt; cannot be ignored by the software.

NOP – no operation.

NOR – negated (or inverse) OR function

Normalized number – in the proper format for floating point representation.

Northbridge – a custom chip on a cpu motherboard that handles all of the cpu interfacing to memory and I/O.

NRE – non-recurring engineering; one-time costs for a project.

Null modem – acting as two modems, wired back to back. Artifact of the RS-232 standard.

NUMA – non-uniform memory access for multiprocessors; local and global memory access protocol.

NVM – non-volatile memory.

Nyquist rate – in communications, the minimum sampling rate, equal to twice the highest frequency in the signal.

OBD – On-Board diagnostics; for automobiles, a state-of-health systems for emissions control.

Octal – base 8 number.

Off-the-shelf – commercially available; not custom.

Opcode – part of a machine language instruction that specifies the operation to be performed.

Open source – methodology for hardware or software development with free distribution and access.

Operating system – software that controls the allocation of resources in a computer.

OSI – Open systems interconnect model for networking, from ISO.

Overflow - the result of an arithmetic operation exceeds the capacity of the destination.

Packet – a small container; a block of data on a network.

Paging – memory management technique using fixed size memory blocks.

Paradigm – a pattern or model

Paradigm shift – a change from one paradigm to another. Disruptive or evolutionary.

Parallel – multiple operations or communication proceeding simultaneously.

Parity – an error detecting mechanism involving an extra check bit in the word.

Pascal – a programming language (circa 1970).

PC – personal computer, politically correct, program counter.

PCB – printed circuit board.

PCI – peripheral interconnect interface (bus).

PCM – pulse code modulation.

PDA – personal digital assistant; pocket-sized device; palmtop; 1984; superseded by functions in mobile phones.

Peta - 10^{15} or 2^{50}

PIC – a microcontroller from Microchip Technology.

Piezo – production of electricity by mechanical stress.

Pinout – mapping of signals to I/O pins of a device.

Pipeline – operations in serial, assembly-line fashion.

Pixel – picture element; smallest addressable element on a display or a sensor.

PLC – Programmable logic controller, embedded device for automation.

PLD – programmable logic device; generic gate-level part that can be programmed for a function.

PMOS – positive metal oxide semiconductor, in which the carriers are positively charged.

Posix – portable operating system interface, IEEE standard.

POWER – a risc architecture from IBM.

PROM – programmable read-only memory.

Pullup – a resistor to tie a signal point to + voltage to establish a logic state. Used with an open-collector transistor architecture. Without the pullup, the output of the transistors floats to a random voltage level, and the transistor has no drive capability.

PWM – pulse width modulation.

Python – programming language.

Quad word – four words. If word = 16 bits, quad word is 64 bits.

Quadrature encoder – an incremental rotary encoder providing rotational position information.

Queue – first in, first out data buffer structure; hardware of software.

Rad – unit of absorbed radiation dose; 100 ergs per gram; also, radian, angular measurement.

RAID – random array of inexpensive disks; using commodity disk drives to build large storage arrays.

Radix point – separates integer and fractional parts of a real number.

RAM – random access memory; any item can be access in the same time as any other.

RAS – Row address strobe, in dram refresh.

Register – temporary storage location for a data item.

Reset – signal and process that returns the hardware to a known, defined state.

RISC – reduced instruction set computer.

Router – networking component for packets.

Real-time – system that responds to events in a predictable, bounded time.

RS-232 – EIA telecommunications standard (1962), serial with handshake.

SAM – sequential access memory, like a magnetic tape.

SATA – serial ATA, a storage media interconnect.

Sandbox – an isolated and controlled environment to run untested or potentially malicious code.

SCADA – Supervisory Control and Data Acquisition – for industrial control systems.

Script – a program for an interpreter. Used to automate tasks.

SDRAM – synchronous dynamic random access memory.

Segmentation – dividing a network or memory into sections.

Self-modifying code – computer code that modifies itself as it run; hard to debug

Semiconductor – material with electrical characteristics between conductors and insulators; basis of current technology processor and memory devices.

Semaphore –signaling element among processes.

Sensor – a device that converts a physical observable quantity or event to a signal.

Serial – bit by bit.

Server – a computer running services on a network.

Servo – a control device with feedback.

Set-top box – embedded system to provide interface to a television from cable and internet.

Seu – single event upset; radiation induced upset in a device.

Shannon limit – in communications theory, the theorem that it is possible to communicate digital data nearly error-free up to a maximum rate through the channel, based on the noise. This result was presented by Claude Shannon in 1948.

Shift – move one bit position to the left or right in a word.

Sign-magnitude – number representation with a specific sign bit.

Signed number – representation with a value and a numeric sign.

SIMD – single instruction, multiple data.

Simm – single in-line memory module.

SOC – system on chip

Software – set of instructions and data to tell a computer what to do.

Southbridge – a custom chip on a cpu motherboard that implements the all of the I/O functionality.

SMP – symmetric multiprocessing.

Snoop – monitor packets in a network, or data in a cache

SRAM – static random access memory.

Stack – first in, last out data structure. Can be hardware or software.

Stack pointer – a reference pointer to the top of the stack.

State machine – model of sequential processes.

Superscalar – computer with instruction-level parallelism, by replication of resources.

SWD – serial wire debug.

Synchronous – using the same clock to coordinate operations.

System – a collection of interacting elements and relationships with a specific behavior.

System of Systems – a complex collection of systems with pooled resources.

Table – data structure. Can be multi-dimensional.

Tera - 10^{12} or 2^{40}

Test-and-set – coordination mechanism for multiple processes that allows reading to a location and writing it in a non-interruptible manner.

TCP/IP – transmission control protocol/internet protocol; layered set of protocols for networks.

Thread – smallest independent set of instructions managed by a multiprocessing operating system.

Thumb – a 16-bit instruction subset and operating mode for the ARM processor.

TLB – translation lookaside buffer – a cache of addresses.

TMR – Triple Modular Redundancy; an error control mechanism using redundant components.

Transceiver – receiver and transmitter in one box.

Transducer – a device that converts one form of energy to another (example: the Grand Coulee Dam).

Transputer – a microcomputer on a chip by Inmos Corp., circa 1980. Innovative communication mechanism using serial links.

TRAP – exception or fault handling mechanism in a computer; an operating system component.

Triplicate – using three copies (of hardware, software, messaging, power supplies, etc.). for redundancy and error control.

Tri-state – logic with 0, 1, and a high impedance for output port to allow line sharing.

Truncate – discard. Cutoff, make shorter.

TTL – transistor-transistor logic in digital integrated circuits. (1963)

UART – universal asynchronous receiver-transmitter. Parallel-to-serial; serial-to parallel device with handshaking.

Ubuntu – Gnu-Linux variant.

UDP – User datagram protocol; part of the Internet Protocol.

USART – universal synchronous (or) asynchronous receiver/transmitter.

Underflow – the result of an arithmetic operation is smaller than the smallest representable number.

UPS – uninterruptable power supply. Backup power source.

USAF – United States Air Force.

USB – universal serial bus.

Unsigned number – a number without a numeric sign.

Vector – single dimensional array of values.

VHDL- very high level description language; a language to describe integrated circuits and asic/ fpga's.

VIA – vertical conducting pathway through an insulating layer in a semiconductor.

Virtual memory – memory management technique using address translation.

Virtualization – creating a virtual resource from available physical resources.

Virus – malignant computer program.

Viterbi Decoder – a maximum likelihood decoder for data encoded with a Convolutional code for error control. Can be implemented in software or hardware

VLIW – very long instruction word – mechanism for parallelism.

VxWorks – real time operating system from WindRiver Corp.

von Neumann – John, a computer pioneer and mathematician; realized that computer instructions are data.

Watchcat – watches the watchdog

Watchdog – hardware/software function to sanity check the hardware, software, and process; applies corrective action if a fault is detected; fail-safe mechanism.

Wiki – the Hawaiian word for "quick." Refers to a collaborative content website.

Word – a collection of bits of any size; does not have to be a power of two.

Write-back – cache organization where the data is not written to main memory until the cache location is needed for re-use.

Write-only – of no interest.

Write-through – all cache writes also go to memory.

X86 – Intel -16, -32, 64-bit ISA.

Xen – Hypervisor, U. Cambridge.

XOR – exclusive OR; either but not both.

Zener – voltage reference diode.

Zero address – architecture using implicit addressing, like a stack.

Selected Bibliography on Embedded

www.embedded.com

Abut, Huseyin (ed.) et all *Advances for In-Vehicle and Mobile Systems: Challenges for International Standards* Springer; 1 edition, 2007, ISBN-1 038733503X.

Analog Devices, *Analog-Digital Conversion Handbook*, Prentice-Hall, 3rd ed, 1986, ISBN 0-13-032848-0.

Arnold, Ken *Embedded Controller Hardware Design*, Newnes; 1 edition, 2001, ISBN-1878707523.

Bailey, Oliver H. *Embedded Systems: Desktop Integration*, Wordware Publishing, 2005, ISBN-1556229941.

Ball, Stuart, *Embedded Microprocessor Systems: Real World Design*, 3rd ed, Newnes, 2002, ISBN 0-0-7506-7534-9.

Ball, Stuart, *Analog Interfacing to Embedded Microprocessors*, Real World Design, 2nd ed, Newnes, 2004, ISBN 1-878-70798-1.

Ball, Stuart, *Debugging Embedded Microprocessor Systems*, Newnes; 1st edition, 1998, ISBN 0750699906

Berger, Arnold S. *Embedded Systems Design: An Introduction to Processes, Tools and Techniques*, CMP Books, 2001, ISBN- 978-1578200733.

Berger, Arnold S. *Hardware and Computer Organization*, Newnes; 1st edition, 2005, ISBN- 0750678860

Bräunl, Thomas *Embedded Robotics: Mobile Robot Design and Applications with Embedded Systems* Springer; 2nd ed., 2006, ISBN- 3540343180.

Clarke, Peter, "Why the ARM architecture is shaped the way it is," EETimes, 11/26/2012.

DeMuth, Brian and Eisenreich, Dan *Designing Embedded Internet Devices*, Newnes, 2002, ISBN 1878707981.

Doboli, Alex and Currie, Edward H. *Introduction to Mixed-Signal, Embedded Design,* Springer, 2010 ISBN- 1441974458.

Donaldson, Alastair F. et all "Analysing DMA Races in Multicore Software" Oxford University Computing Laboratory.

Eady, Fred *Implementing 802.11 with Microcontrollers: Wireless Networking for Embedded Systems Designers*, Newnes, 2005, ISBN 0750678658.

Edwards, Lewin *Embedded System Design on a Shoestring Achieving High Performance with a Limited Budget*, Newnes, 2003, ISBN 0750676094.

Edwards, Lewin *So You Wanna Be an Embedded Engineer The Guide to Embedded Engineering, From Consultancy to the Corporate Ladder*, Newnes; 1st edition, 2006, ISBN 0750679530.

Edwards, Lewin *Open-Source Robotics and Process Control Cookbook: Designing and Building Robust, Dependable Real-time Systems,* Newnes, 2004, ISBN- 0750677783.

Eskandarian, Azim (Ed) *Handbook of Intelligent Vehicles* Springer; 2012 edition, ISBN- 085729086X.

Fisher, Joseph A. et al *Embedded Computing, A VLIW Approach to Architecture, Compilers and Tools*, Morgan Kaufmann; 1st edition, 2004, ISBN 1558607668.

Fowler, Kim R. *What Every Engineer Should Know About Developing Real-Time Embedded Products*, CRC Press, 2007, ISBN- 0849379598.

Ganssle, Jack; Noergaard, Tammy; Eady, Fred; and Edwards, Lewin; *Embedded Hardware*, Newnes, 2007, ISBN-978-0750685849.

Ganssle, Jack, *The Art of Designing Embedded Systems* (EDN Series for Design Engineers) Newnes, 1999, ISBN-978-0750698696.

Ganssle, Jack and Barr Mike *Embedded Systems Dictionary*, CMP; 1st edition, 2003, ISBN- 1578201209.

Ganssle, Jack *The Firmware Handbook*, Newnes; 1st edition, 2004, ISBN- 075067606X.

Hartman, Kim "Embedded Virtualization Enables Scalability of Real-time Applications on Multicore," 2011, www.embedded-computing.com/

Heath, Steve, *Embedded Systems Design, Second Ed,* Newnes; 2 edition, 2002, ISBN-0750655461.

Ibrahim, Ahmad *Fuzzy Logic for Embedded Systems Applications,* Newnes, 2003, ISBN- 0750676051.

Ienne, Paolo and Leupers, Rainer *Customizable Embedded Processors Design Technologies and Applications*, Morgan Kaufmann; 1st edition, 2006, ISBN-0123695260.

Insam, Edward *TCP/IP Embedded Internet Applications*, Newnes; 1st edition, 2003, ISBN 0750657359.

Intel, Embedded Controller Handbook, (80186, 80188), 1987, 210918, ISBN 1555121217.

Intel Microprocessor and Peripheral Handbook, 2 Vol., 1987, 230843.

Jantsch, Axel *Modeling Embedded Systems and SoC's Concurrency and Time in Models of Computation*, Morgan Kaufmann; 1st edition, 2003, ISBN- 1558609253.

Kalinsky, David, *Architecture of Safety-Critical Systems*, http://www.embedded.com/columns/technicalinsights/169600396.

Katz, David and Gentile, Rick, *Embedded Media Processing*, Newnes, 2005, ISBN-0750679123.

Kleman, Alan *Interfacing Microprocessors in Hydraulic Systems*, CRC Press 1st. ed, 1989, ISBN 0824780639.

Koopman, Philip "Embedded System Security," IEEE Computer, July 2004.

Lee, Insup (ed), *Handbook of Real-Time and Embedded Systems*, Chapman and Hall/CRC, 2007, ISBN- 1584886781.

Leveson, Nancy G. *System Safety and Computers*, Addison-Wesley, 1995, ISBN: 0-201-11972-2.

Li, Qing and Yao, Caroline *Real-Time Concepts for Embedded Systems*, CMP; 1st edition, 2003, ISBN- 1578201241.

Martinez, David R. (ed) et al *High Performance Embedded Computing Handbook: A Systems Perspective* CRC Press; 1st edition, 2008, ISBN- 084937197X.

Matalon, Shabtay, et al "Embedded System Power Consumption: A Software or Hardware issue?" Mentor Graphics.

Mattos, Philip and Packer, Jamie, *Using Transputers as Embedded Controllers,* Inmos Technical Note 57, April 1989.

Maxfield, Clive *The Design Warrior's Guide to FPGA's*, 2004, Newnes Elsevier, ISBN 0-7506-7604-3.

Neumann, Peter G. *Computer Related Risks*, ACM Press Books, 1995. ISBN: 0-201-55805-X.

Nicolescu, Gabriela; Mosterman, Pieter J. *Model-Based Design for Embedded Systems* (Computational Analysis, Synthesis, and Design of Dynamic Systems), CRC Press; 1st edition, 2009, ISBN-1420067842.

Nicolescu, Gabriela; Jerraya, Ahmed A. *Global Specification and Validation of Embedded Systems: Integrating Heterogeneous Components,* Springer; Softcover reprint of hardcover 1st ed. 2007 edition, 2010, ISBN- 904817550X.

Noergaard, Tammy, *Embedded Systems Architecture: A Comprehensive Guide for Engineers and Programmers*, Newnes, 2005, ISBN-978-0750677929.

O'Brien, Frank *The Apollo Guidance Computer: Architecture and Operation,* Praxis; 1st edition, 2010, ISBN 1441908765

Olson, Alan R. and Langlois, Denis J. "Solid State Drives Data Reliability and Lifetime," April 2008, whitepaper, Imation, www.Imation.com

Ortiz, David A. and Santiago, Nayda G. *High-Level Optimization for Low Power Consumption on Microprocessor-Based Systems,* 2007, IEEE 1-4244-1176-9/07.

Parab, Jivan et al, *Practical Aspects of Embedded System Design using Microcontrollers,* Springer; Softcover reprint of hardcover 1st ed. 2008 edition, 2010, ISBN: 9048178657.

Parker. Kenneth O. (ed) *The Boundary-Scan Handbook*, Springer; 3rd edition, 2003, ISBN- 1402074964

Parnell, Karen and Mehta, Nick *Introduction to Programmable Logic*, Xilinx, April 2004, 0402230.

Redmond, Kent C.; Thomas M. Smith (1980). *Project Whirlwind: The History of a Pioneer Computer*. Bedford, MA: Digital Press. ISBN 0-932376-09-6.

Rettberg, Achim; Zanella, Mauro C.; Rammig, Franz J. *From Specification to Embedded Systems Application* Springer; Softcover reprint of hardcover 1st ed. 2005 edition, November 23, 2010, ISBN 1441938990.

Siegwart, Roland and Nourbakhsh, Illah R. *Introduction to Autonomous Mobile Robots,* The MIT Press, 2004, ISBN-026219502X.

Simone, Lisa *If I Only Changed the Software, Why is the Phone on Fire?: Embedded Debugging Methods Revealed Technical Mysteries for Engineers,* Newnes (March 23, 2007, ISBN 0750682183.

Smith, Warwick A. *Arm Microcontroller Interfacing*, Elektor International, September 1, 2010, ISBN- 0905705912.

Spaanenburg, Lambert and Spaanenburg, Hendrik, *Cloud Connectivity and Embedded Sensory Systems,* Springer; 1st Edition, 2010, ISBN-1441975446.

Spitzer, Cary R. *Avionics: Elements, Software and Functions (The Avionics Handbook, Second Edition)*, CRC Press, December 13, 2006, ISBN- 0849384389.

Stakem, Patrick H. "Hardware/Software Trade-offs in Microprocessor Design," Electronic Design, Vol. 26, no.19, Sept 1978.

Stakem, Patrick H. "A Practitioner's Guide to RISC Microprocessor Architecture," 1996, Wiley-Interscience, J. Wiley & Sons, New York, ISBN 0-471-13018-4.

Stapko, Timothy *Practical Embedded Security: Building Secure Resource-Constrained Systems,* Newnes; 1st edition, 2007, ISBN-: 0750682159.

Storey, Neil *Safety-Critical Computer Systems,* Addison-Wesley, 1996. ISBN: 0-201-42787-7.

Sutter, Ed *Embedded Systems Firmware Demystified*, Publisher: CMP, 2002, ISBN 1578200997.

Truszkowski, Walt *Autonomous and Autonomic Systems: With Applications to NASA Intelligent Spacecraft Operations and Exploration Systems,* Springer; 1st Edition. edition, 2009, ISBN- 1846282322

Vahid, Frank and Givargis, Tony D., *Embedded System Design: A Unified Hardware/Software Introduction*, Wiley, 2001, ISBN-978-0471386780.

Valvano, Jonathan W. *Embedded Microcomputer Systems: Real Time Interfacing*, Cengage-Engineering, 2006, ISBN- 978-0534551629.

Valvano, Jonathan W. *Embedded systems: Real time Interfacing to the ARM Cortex-M3,* CreateSpace Independent Publishing Platform, November 10, 2011, ISBN- 1463590156.

Valvano, Jonathan W. *Embedded systems: Real-Time Operating systems for the ARM Cortex-M3,* CreateSpace Independent Publishing Platform, January 3, 2012, ISBN- 1466468866.

Walder, Herbert; Platznet, Marco "Reconfigurable Hardware Operating systems: From Design Concept to Realizations," Swiss Federal Institute of Technology.

Williams, Al *Embedded Internet Design* McGraw-Hill/TAB Electronics; 1st edition (March 12, 2003) ISBN-10071374361.

Wilson, Graham R. *Embedded Systems & Computer Architecture,* Newnes, 2002, ASIN: B008AUG2U4.

Wolf, Wayne, *High-Performance Embedded Computing: Architectures, Applications, and Methodologies,* Morgan Kaufmann, 2006, ISBN- 978-0123694850.

Wolf, Wayne *Computers As Components, Principles of Embedded Computing System Design,* Publisher: Morgan Kaufmann; 2nd edition, 2008, ISBN 0123743974.

Zander, Justyna (Ed), Schieferdecker, Ina (Ed), Mosterman, Pieter J. (Ed), *Model-Based Testing for Embedded Systems* (Computational Analysis, Synthesis, and Design of Dynamic Systems), CRC Press; 1st edition (September 15, 2011, ISBN- 1439818452.

The Concise Handbook of Real-Time Systems, TimeSys Corp., www.timesys.com

"Implementing DMA on ARM SMP Systems," Application Note 228, August 2009, Document ARM-DAI-0228-A.

"ARINC 653 - An Avionics Standard for Safe, Partitioned Systems". WindRiver Systems - IEEE Seminar. August 2008.

www.opencores.org

wikipedia, various. Material from Wikipedia (www.wikipedia.org) is used under the conditions of the Creative commons Attribution-ShareAlike #.0 Unported License.
http://creativecommons.org/licenses/by-sa/3,0

Operating systems
Android

Gargenta, Marko *Learning Android* O'Reilly Media; 1st edition, 2011, ISBN- 1449390501.

Milette, Greg and Stroud, Adam *Professional Android Sensor Programming*, Wrox, 1st edition, 2012, ISBN- 1118183487.

Steele, James and To, Nelson *The Android Developer's Cookbook: Building Applications with the Android SDK: Building Applications with the Android SDK* (Developer's Library), Addison-Wesley Professional; 1st edition, 2010, ISBN- 0321741234.

Yaghmour, Karim *Embedded Android: Porting, Extending, and Customizing* O'Reilly Media, 2012, ISBN- 144930829.

Gnu/Linux and BSD

Abbott, Doug, *Linux for Embedded and Real-time Applications* (2nd Edition), Newnes; 2nd edition, 2006, ISBN 0750679328.

Cevoli, Paul *Embedded FreeBSD Cookbook*, Newnes, 2002, ISBN 1589950046.

Hallinan, Christopher *Embedded Linux Primer: A Practical Real-World Approach,* Prentice Hall PTR; 1 edition, 2006, ISBN- 0131679848.

Hollabaugh, Craig; *Embedded Linux: Hardware, Software, and Interfacing*, Addison-Wesley Professional; 1st edition, 2002, ISBN- 0672322269.

Lombardo, John *Embedded Linux*, New Riders Publishing, 2001, ISBN 0-7357-0998-X.

Nicholson, J. *Starting Embedded Linux Development on an ARM Architecture*, Newnes, July 2013, ISBN 9780080982366.

Raghavan, P. *Embedded Linux System Design and Development*, Auerbach, 2005, ISBN- 978-0849340581.

Raymond, Eric S. *The Cathedral and the Bazaar : Musings on Linux and Open Source by an Accidental Revolutionary,* O'Reilly Media; Revised edition, 2001, ISBN 0596001088.

Salus, Peter H. *The Daemon, the GNU, and the Penguin,"* 2008, Reed Media Services, ISBN 978-0-9790342-3-7.

Smith, Bob; Hardin, John; Phillips, Graham; Pierce, Bill; *Linux Appliance Design: A Hands-On Guide to Building Linux Appliances*, No Starch Press; (March 31, 2007) ISBN1593271409.

Villani, Pat *FreeDOS Kernel An MS-DOS Emulator for Platform Independence & Embedded System Development*, CMP Books; 1 edition, 1996, ISBN- 0879304367

Yaghmour, Karim *Building Embedded Linux Systems,* O'Reilly Media, Inc.; 1st edition, 2003, ISBN- 059600222X.

www.Linuxdevices.com

www.elks.sourceforge.net

Freebsd architecture handbook
 http://www.freebsd.org/doc/en/books/arch-handbook/

POSIX
 http://standards.ieee.org/develop/wg/POSIX.html

RTEMS
www.rtems.com

freeRTOS
www.freertos.org

QNX

Hildebrand, Dan "An Architectural Overview of QNX". Proceedings of the Workshop on Micro-kernels and Other Kernel Architectures," 1992, pp 113–126. ISBN 1-880446-42-1.

VxWorks

www.windriver.com

Windows Embedded

Liming, Sean D. *Windows XP Embedded Advanced*, Annabooks, 2003, ISBN-978-0929392776.

Engineers Guide to Windows Embedded

http://eproductalert.com/digitaledition/windows/2012/Engineers%20Guide%20to%20Windows%20Embedded.pdf

http://www.microsoft.com/windowsembedded/en-us/windows-embedded.aspx

Embedded Software and Programming, General

Barr, Michael; Massa, Anthony; *Programming Embedded Systems: With C and GNU Development Tools*, 2nd Edition O'Reilly Media, Inc.; 2nd edition, 2006, ISBN-0596009836.

Bentley, Jon Louis, *Writing Efficient Programs*, 1982 Prentice Hall, ISBN 0139702512.

Chisnall, David "Optimizing Code for Power Consumption," Nov. 18, 2010, Addison-Wesley Professional, www.informit.com/articles/

Cofer, R. C. and Harding Benjamin F. *Rapid System Programming with FPGA's*, 2006, Newnes Elsevier, ISBN 0-7506-7866-6.

Curtis, Keith E. *Embedded Multitasking*, Newnes, 2006, ISBN 0750679182.

Ganssle, Jack *The Art of Programming Embedded Systems* Publisher: Academic Press; 1st edition, 1991, ISBN 0122748808.

Ganssle, Jack *Embedded Systems, World Class Designs*, Newnes; 1st edition, 2007, ISBN- 0750686251.

IBM RISC System/6000 PowerPC System Architecture Morgan Kaufmann; 1st ed. (September 15, 1994) ISBN 1558603441.

"IBM RISC System/6000 Technology", IBM Corp., 1990, SA23-2619.

Jerraya, Ahmed Amine et al *Embedded Software for SoC,* Springer; 1st edition, 2003, ISBN- 1402075286.

Kamal, Raj *Embedded Systems: Architecture, Programming and Design*, 2nd Edition
McGraw-Hill Education (India); 2nd Edition, 2009, ISBN 0070151253.

Labrosse, Jean J.; Ganssle, Jack; Oshana, Robert; Walls, Colin; *Embedded Software*, Newnes, 200,7 ISBN-978-0750685832.

Lamie, Edward *Real-Time Embedded Multithreading Using ThreadX and ARM*, Newnes; 2nd edition, 2009, ISBN 1856176010.

Leveson, Nancy G. "Software Safety in Embedded Computer Systems," Communications of the ACM. Vol. 34, No. 2, February 1991, pp. 34-46.

Lewis, David W. *Fundamentals of Embedded Software: Where C and Assembly Meet*, Prentice Hall; 1st edition, 2001, ISBN 0130615897.

Lewis, David W. *Fundamentals of Embedded Software with the ARM Cortex-M3,* Prentice Hall; 1st edition, February 12, 2012, ISBN- 0132916541.

Murphy, Niall *Front Panel: Designing Software for Embedded User Interfaces,* CMP; 1st edition, 1998, ISBN 0879305282.

Oshana, Robert *DSP Software Development Techniques for Embedded and Real-Time Systems*, ISBN 978-0-7506-7759-2.

Pressman, Roger, *Software Engineering: A Practitioner's Approach,* McGraw-Hill Science/Engineering/Math; 6 edition, 2004, ISBN 007301933X.

Roychoudhury, Abhik *Embedded Systems and Software Validation* (Morgan Kaufmann Series in Systems on Silicon), 1st edition, 2009, ISBN 0123742307.

Silberschatz, Avi; Galvin, Peter; Gagne, Greg (2008). *Operating Systems Concepts*. John Wiley & Sons. ISBN 0-470-12872-0.

Simon, David E. *An Embedded Software Primer*, Addison-Wesley Professional, 1990, ISBN 020161569X.

Software Engineering – Software Life Cycle Processes – Maintenance, 2006, ISO/IEC 14764, IEEE Standard 14764. 2nd edition.

Stallings, William *Operating Systems, Internals and Design Principles*. 7th edition, 2011 Pearson: Prentice Hall, ISBN 013230998X.

Sterling, Thomas Lawrence Beowulf Cluster Computing With Linux, 2001, MIT Press, ISBN- 0262692740.

Sridhar, T. *Designing Embedded Communications Software*, Publisher: CMP; 1st edition, 2003, ISBN: 157820125X.

Wichmann, Brian A. *Software in Safety Related Systems*, Wiley, 1992. ISBN 0471-93474-7.

Assembly

Mahout, Vincent *Assembly Language Programming: ARM Cortex-M3*, Wiley-ISTE; 1st edition, March 6, 2012, ISBN- 1848213298.

c/c++

Barr, Michael *Programming Embedded Systems in C and C ++*, O'Reilly Media; 1 edition, 1999, ISBN 1565923545.

Barr, Michael *Embedded C Coding Standard*, CreateSpace; 1st edition, 2008, ISBN 1442164824.

Barr, Michael *Programming Embedded Systems: With C and GNU Development Tools*, 2nd Edition, O'Reilly Media; 2nd edition, 2006, ISBN- 0596009836

Campbell, Joe *C Programmer's Guide to Serial Communications*, Sams, ISBN 0-672-22584-0.

Douglass, Bruce Powell *Design Patterns for Embedded Systems in C: An Embedded Software Engineering Toolkit*, Newnes; 2010, ISBN 1856177076.

Gehani, Narain *C: An Advanced Introduction*: ANSI C Edition, Silicon Press; 2nd edition, 1994, ISBN 0929306171.

Grenning, James W. *Test Driven Development for Embedded C*, Pragmatic Bookshelf; 1st edition, 2011, ISBN 193435662X.

Hanson, David R. *C Interfaces and Implementations: Techniques for Creating Reusable Software*, Addison-Wesley Professional; 1st edition, 1996, ISBN- 0201498413.

Harbison, Samuel P.; Steele, Guy L. *C: A Reference Manual* (5th Edition), Prentice Hall, 2002, ISBN- 013089592X.

Hatton, Les *Safer C* (McGraw-Hill International Series in Software Engineering), McGraw-Hill Companies (1995), ISBN 0077076400.

Kerrighan, Brian W. ; Ritchie, Dennis M. *C Programming Language: ANSI C,* Prentice-Hall (June 1, 1990, ISBN 0131158171.

Kerrighan, Brian W.; Pike, Rob *The Practice of Programming*, Addison-Wesley Professional; 1 edition (February 14, 1999), ISBN 020161586X.

Kochan, Stephen G. *Programming in C* (3rd Edition), Sams; 3 edition, 2004, ISBN- 0672326663.

Labrosse, Jean *Embedded Systems Building Blocks*, (2nd Edition), Complete and Ready-to-Use Modules in C, CMP; 2nd edition, 1999, ISBN 0879306041.

Ledin, Jim *Embedded Control Systems in C/C++*, CMP, 2003, ISBN 978-1-57820-127-3.

Massa, Anthony; Barr, Michael *Programming Embedded Systems: With C and GNU Development Tools*, 2nd Edition, O'Reilly Media; 2nd edition, 2006, ISBN 0596009836.

Perry, John W. *Advanced C Programming by Example,* 1998, PWS Publishing, ISBN 0534951406.

Pont, Michael J. *Embedded C*, Addison-Wesley Professional, 2002, ISBN-020179523X.

Ritchie, Dennis M. *The C Programming Language*, Brian W. Kernighan, Prentice Hall, 1978, ISBN- 0131101633.

Schildt, Herbert *C: The Complete Reference*, 4th Ed. McGraw-Hill Osborne Media; 4 edition, 2000, ISBN- 0072121246.

Smith, Warwick A. *C Programming for Embedded Microcontrollers,* Elektor, ISBN 978-0-905705-80-4.

Summit, Steve *C Programming FAQs: Frequently Asked Questions*, Addison-Wesley Professional; 2nd edition, 1995, ISBN- 0201845199.

Tondo, Clovis L.; Gimpel, Scott E. *The C Answer Book: Solutions to the Exercises in 'The C Programming Language*, Second Edition, Prentice Hall; 2nd edition, 1988, ISBN- 0131096532.

Van der Linden, Peter, *Expert C Programming,* 1994, Prentice Hall, ISBN 0131774298.

Python

Arbuckle, Daniel *Python Testing: Beginner's Guide*, Packt Publishing, 2010, ISBN- 1847198848.

Brown, Martin C. *Python: The Complete Reference*, McGraw-Hill, 2001, ISBN 007212718X.

Hughes, John M. *Real World Instrumentation with Python: Automated Data Acquisition and Control Systems*, O'Reilly Media; 1 edition, 2010, ISBN- 0596809565.

Kumar, Deepak, *Learning computing with Robots (Python),* Institute for Personal Robots in Education; 1ST edition, 2007, ISBN- 1607028832

Lutz, Mark; Ascher, David *Learning Python*, Second Edition, O'Reilly Media; Second Edition, 2003, ISBN- 0596002815.

Lutz, Mark *Programming Python*, O'Reilly Media; 3rd edition, 2006, ISBN- 0596009259.

Maruch, Stef; Maruch, Aahz *Python For Dummies*, For Dummies; 1st edition, 2006, ISBN 0471778648.

Telles, Matt *Python Power! The Comprehensive Guide*, Course Technology PTR; 1st edition, 2007, ISBN 1598631586.

Turnquist, Greg L. *Python Testing Cookbook*, Packt Publishing 2011, ISBN-1849514666.

Java

Arnold, Ken *The Java Programming Language, 4th edition*, Prentice Hall; 4th edition, 2005, ISBN: 0321349806.

Bloch, Joshua *Effective Java* (2nd Edition), Prentice Hall; 2nd edition, 2008, ISBN 0321356683.

Hayes, Mattis; Johansen, Isaaih *Java Software and Embedded Systems*, Nova Science Pub Inc., 2010, ISBN 1607416611.

Higuera-Toledano, M. Teresa; Wellings, Andy *Distributed, Embedded and Real-time Java Systems*, Springer; 2012 edition, 2012, ISBN 1441981578.

Lindholm, Tim and Yellin, Frank, *Java™ Virtual Machine Specification*, The (2nd Edition), Publisher: Prentice Hall; 2 edition, 1999, ISBN 0201432943.

Lindsey, Clark S. et al *Java Tech – Introduction to Scientific and Technical computing with Java,* 2005, Cambridge University Press.

Niemeyer, Patrick; Knudsen, Jonathan *Learning Java*, O'Reilly Media; Third Edition, 2005, ISBN 0596008732.

Walsh, Aaron E. *Java For Dummies*, For Dummies; 3rd edition, 1998, ISBN 0764504177.

Java Virtual Machine Specification, http://java.sun.com/docs/books/vmspec/

www.particle.kth.se/~lindsey/JaveaCourse/book/index.html

Computer Architecture, general

Bell, C. Gordon and Newell, Allen, *Computer Structures: Readings and Examples*, McGraw-Hill Inc., 1971, ISBN-0070043574.

Blaauw, Gerrit A. and Brooks, Frederick P. Jr. *Computer Architecture, Concepts and Evolution*, 2 volumes, 1997, Addison-Wesley, IBN 0-201-10557-8.

Boole, George *An Investigation of the Laws of Thought on which are Founded the Mathematical Theories
of Logic and Probability*, 1854, Reprinted 1958, Dover, ISBN 0-486-60028-9.

Bryant, Randal E. and O'Hallaron, David R. *Computer Systems: A Programmer's Perspective*, 2nd edition, Addison Wesley, Kindle e-book edition, ASIN: B004S81RXE.

Burks, Arthur; W. Goldstein, Herman H.; Von Neumann, John *Preliminary Discussion of the Logical Design
of an Electronic Computing Instrument*, 1987, MIT Press, originally published in Papers of John Von Neumann on Computing and Computer Theory.

Carter, Nick *Schaum's Outline of Computer Architecture*, McGraw-Hill; 1st edition, 2001, ISBN- 007136207X.

Comer, Douglas E. *Essentials of Computer Architecture*, Prentice Hall, 2004, ISBN 0131491792.

Englander, Irv *The Architecture of Computer Hardware and Systems Software: An Information Technology Approach*, Wiley; 3rd edition, 2003, ISBN-0471073253.

Everett, R. R. and Swain, F. E. Project Whirlwind, Report R-127, Whirlwind I Computer, Servomechanisms Laboratory, M.I.T., Sept 4, 1947.

Flores, Ivan The Logic of Computer Arithmetic, 1963, Prentice-Hall, ISBN 0135400392.

Flynn, Michael J. *Computer Architecture: Pipelined and Parallel Processor Design,* 1995, Jones & Bartlett Learning; 1st ed, ISBN-0867202041.

Godse, A. P. *Microcontrollers & RISC Architecture*, Technical Publications; 1st. edition, 2011, ISBN- 9350380390.

Harris, David and Harris, Sarah *Digital Design and Computer Architecture,* Morgan Kaufmann,, 2007, ISBN 0123704979.

Heath, Steve *Microprocessor Architectures*, *Second Edition: RISC, CISC and DSP* Newnes; 2nd ed, 1995, ISBN 0750623039.

Hennessy, John L. and Patterson, David A. *Computer Architecture, Fifth Edition: A Quantitative Approach*, Morgan Kaufmann,, 2011, ISBN 012383872X.

Heuring, Vincent, and Jordan, Harry F. *Computer Systems Design and Architecture*, Prentice Hall; 2nd edition, 2003, ISBN 0130484407.

Johnson, William M. *Superscalar Microprocessors Design*, Prentice Hall PTR; Facsimile edition, 1990, ISBN 0138756341.

Kidder, Tracy *The Soul of a New Machine*, Back Bay Books, 2000, ISBN 0316491977.

Kuhnel, Claus, *AVR RISC Microcontroller Handbook*, Newnes; 1st edition, 1998, ISBN- 0750699639.

Mano, M. Morris *Computer System Architecture (3rd Edition)*, Prentice Hall; 3rd edition, 1992, ISBN 0131755633.

Murdocca, Miles J. and Heuring, Vincent *Computer Architecture and Organization: An Integrated Approach*, Wiley, 2007, ISBN 0471733881.

McGeady, Steven "The i960CA SuperScalar Implementation of the 80960 Architecture", IEEE, 1990, pp. 232–240.

Nisan, Noam and Schocken, Shimon, *The Elements of Computing Systems: Building a Modern Computer from First Principles*, 2005, MIT Press, ISBN 0262640686.

Null, Linda *The Essentials of Computer Organization and Architecture,* Jones & Bartlett Pub; 2 edition, 2006, ISBN 0763737690.

Page, Daniel, *A Practical Introduction to Computer Architecture*, 2009, Springer, ISBN 1848822553.

Patterson, David A and Hennessy, John L. *Computer Organization and Design: The Hardware/Software Interface, Revised Fourth Edition*, Morgan Kaufmann, 2011, ISBN 0123744938.

Ramachandran, Umakishore, and Leahy William D. Jr., *Computer Systems: An Integrated Approach to Architecture and Operating Systems*, 2010, Addison Wesley, ISBN 0321486137.

Reid, T. R. T*he Chip: How Two Americans Invented the Microchip and Launched a Revolution,* Random House Trade Paperbacks; Revised edition, 2001, ISBN 0375758283.

Richards, R. K. *Arithmetic Operations in Digital Computers, 1955, Van Nostrand,* B00128Z00.

Shriver, Bruce D. *The Anatomy of a High-Performance Microprocessor: A Systems Perspective,* Wiley-IEEE Computer Society Press, 1998, ISBN 0818684003.

Silc, Jurji, Robic, Borut, Ungerer, Theo *Processor Architecture: From Dataflow to Superscalar and Beyond,* Springer; 1st edition, 1999, ISBN 3540647988.

Slater, Michael *Microprocessor-Based Design A Comprehensive Guide to Effective Hardware Design,* 1989, Prentice Hall, ISBN 0-13-582248-3.

Stakem, Patrick H. *A Practitioner's Guide to RISC Microprocessor Architecture,* Wiley-Interscience, 1996, ISBN 0471130184.

Stakem, Patrick H. *Computer Architecture & Programming of the Intel x86 Family*; 2012, PRB Publishing, ASIN: B0078Q39D4.

Stakem, Patrick H. *Architecture of Massively Parallel Microprocessor Systems*, PRB Publishing, 2011, ASIN: B004K1F172.

Stakem, Patrick H. *4- and 8-bit Microprocessors, Architecture and History,* PRRB Publishing, May, 2013, ASIN B00D5ZSKCC,

Stakem, Patrick H. *16-bit Microprocessors, History,* PRRB Publishing, May, 2013, ASIN B00D5ETQ3U.

Stakem, Patrick H. *The Architecture and Applications of the ARM Microprocessors,* PRRB Publishing, Feb 2013, B00BAFF4OQ.

Stakem, Patrick H. *RISC Microprocessors, History and Overview,* PRRB Publishing, 2013, B))D5SCHQ0.

Stakem, Patrick H. *The Hardware and Software Architecture of the Transputer,* 2011, PRB Publishing, ASIN: B004OYTS1K.

Stakem, Patrick H. *Virtualization and the Cloud*, 2013, PRRB Publishing, ASIN B00BAFF0JA.

Stallings, William *Computer Organization and Architecture: Designing for Performance* (7th Edition), Prentice Hall; 7 edition (July 21, 2005) ISBN 0131856448.

Standage, Tom *The Victorian Internet,* Walker & Co. 2007, ISBN 0802715040.

Stokes, Jon, *Inside the Machine An Illustrated Introduction to Microprocessors and Computer Architecture*, 2006, No Starch Press, ISBN 1593271042.

Arduino
http://arduino.cc

ARM

Atheshian, Peter and Zulaica, Daniel *ARM Synthesizable Design with Actel FPGAs: With Mixed-Signal SOC Applications*, 2010, McGraw-Hill Professional, ISBN-0071622810.

Badawy, Wael and Jullien, Graham *System-on-chip for Real-time Applications*. 2003, Kluwer, ISBN 1-4020-7254-6.

Furber, Stephen B. *ARM System-on-Chip Architecture* (2nd Edition), 2000, Addison Wesley Professional, ISBN 9780201675191.

Furber, Stephen B. *ARM System Architecture*, 1996 Addison-Wesley, ISBN 0201403528.

Gibson, J. R. *ARM Assembly Language - an Introduction*, 2007, Lulu enterprises UK Ltd. ISBN 1847536964.

Hohl, William *ARM Assembly Language: Fundamentals and Techniques,* 2009, CRC Press, ISBN 1439806101.

Jagger, Dave *ARM Architecture Reference Manual*, 1997, Prentice Hall, ISBN 0137362994.

Lindberg, Van, *Intellectual Property and Open Source, A Practical Guide to Protecting Code*, 2008, O'Reilly Media, ISBN 0596517963.

Predko, Michael *Programming and Customizing the ARM7 Microcontroller*, 2011, McGraw-Hill/Tab, ISBN 0071597573.

Seal, David ARM *Architecture Reference Manual,* 2nd Edition, 2001 Addison Wesley, ISBN 0201737191.

Sloss, Andrew; Symes, Dominic; and Wright, Chris *ARM System Developer's Guide: Designing and Optimizing System Software*, Morgan Kaufmann Series in Computer Architecture and Design, 2004, ISBN 9781558608740.

Stakem, Patrick H. T*he Architecture and Applications of the ARM Microprocessors,* 2013, PRB Publishing, ASIN .

St. Laurent, Andrew M. *Understanding Open Source and Free Software Licensing*, 2004, O'Reilly, ISBN- 0596005814.

Toulson, Rob and Wilmshurst, Tim, *Fast and Effective Embedded Systems Design: Applying the ARM embed*, Newnes; 1st edition, August 20, 2012, ISBN- 0080977685.

Valvano, Jonathan W. *Embedded Systems: Introduction to the ARM Cortex-M3*, CreateSpace Independent Publishing Platform, May 26, 2012, ISBN 1477508996.

Van Someren, Alex and Atack, Carol, *ARM RISC Chip: A Programmer's Guide*, 1994 Addison Wesley, ISBN 0201624109.

Yiu, Joseph *The Definitive Guide to the ARM Cortex-M0*; 2nd Edition; 2011, Newnes; ISBN 978-0123854773.

Yiu, Joseph *The Definitive Guide to the ARM Cortex-M3*, 2nd Edition, 2009, Newnes, ISBN 185617963X.

VL86C010 32 bit RISC CPU and Peripherals User's Manual, VLSI Technologies, Inc., 1989, Prentice-Hall, ISBN 0-13-944968-X.

ARM Product family, ARM60 Microprocessor, GEC Plessey, March, 1993, Pub. DS3553.

ARM Product family, ARM610 Microprocessor, GEC Plessey, March, 1993, Pub. DS3554.

3rd Generation Intel XScale(R) Microarchitecture Developer's Manual,
http://www.intel.com/design/intelxscale/316283.htm

www.arm.com

General References – Safety and Failure

Berk, Joseph Systems *Failure Analysis*, ASM International (November 17, 2009), ISBN- 1615030123.

Bozzano, Marco and Villafiorita, Adolfo *Design and Safety Assessment of Critical Systems,* Auerbach Publications; 1st edition, November 12, 2010, ISBN- 1439803315.

Charette, Robert N. "Air France Flight 447 Crash Causes in Part Point to Automation Paradox," July 10, 2012, http://spectrum.ieee.org.

Cressler, John D. and Mantooth, H. Alan, *Extreme Environment Electronics*, 2013, CRC Press, ISBN 978-1-4398-7430-1.

Dunn William R. *Practical Design of Safety-Critical Computer Systems*, July 2002, ISBN- 0971752702.

Fowler, Kim *Mission-Critical and Safety-Critical Systems Handbook: Design and Development for Embedded Applications,* Newnes; 1st edition, November 20, 2009, ISBN- 0750685670.

Harland, David M. and Lorentz, Ralph D. *Space Systems Failures, Disasters and Rescues of Satellites, Rockets and Space Probes*, Springer, 2005, ISBN 0-387-21519-0.

Hermann, Debra S. Software Safety and Reliability: Techniques, Approaches, and Standards of Key Industrial Sectors, Wiley-IEEE Computer Society Press, 1st ed, February 10, 2000, ISBN- 0769502997.

Jones, Capers *Patterns of Software System Failure and Success*, Intl Thomson Computer Press, December 1995, ISBN- 1850328048.

Kalinsky, David, "Architecture of Safety-Critical Systems," Aug 23. 2005, available white paper at www.embedded.com.

Klocwork, "Software on Wheels," White Paper, 2012, www.klocwork.com
Klotz, Irene "Programming Error Doomed Russian Mars Probe," Feb. 7, 2012, http://news.discovery.com/space/
Krämer, Bernd J. and Völker, Norbert (Eds.) *Safety-Critical Real-Time Systems,* December 3, 2010, ISBN-1441950192.

Leveson, Nancy G. "Software Safety in Embedded Computer Systems," Communications of the ACM. Vol. 34, No. 2, February 1991. pp. 34-46.

Leveson, Nancy G. *Engineering a Safer World: Systems Thinking Applied to Safety* The MIT Press (January 13, 2012), ISBN-0262016621.

Leveson, Nancy G. *System Safety and Computers*, Addison-Wesley, 1995, ISBN: 0-201-11972-2.

Pan, Jiantao, Software Reliability, Carnegie Mellon University, course 18-849b, Dependable Embedded Systems.

Petroski, Henry *To Forgive Design: Understanding Failure* Belknap Press of Harvard University Press (March 30, 2012), ISBN- 0674065840.

Petroski, Henry *To Engineer Is Human: The Role of Failure in Successful Design* Vintage (March 31, 1992), ISBN: 0679734163.

Petroski, Henry *Success through Failure: The Paradox of Design* Vintage, March 31, 199), ISBN- 0679734163.

Schlager, Neil (Ed) When Technology Fails: Significant Technological Disasters, Accidents, and Failures of the Twentieth Century, Gale Research (1994), ISBN- 0810389088.

Storey, Neil *Safety-Critical Computer Systems,* Addison-Wesley, 1996. ISBN: 0-201-42787-7.

Vogel, David A. *Medical Device Software Verification, Validation and Compliance* Artech House; November 30, 2010, ISBN- 1596934220.

Wichmann, Brian A. *Software in Safety Related Systems*, Wiley, 1992. ISBN: 0471-93474-7.

http://www.embedded.com/columns/technicalinsights/169600396 'Air traffic control computer failures: Hearings before a subcommittee of the Committee on Government Operations, House of Representatives, ..." second session, June 30 and August 15, 1980, University of Michigan Library 1980, ASIN: B00300GEMK.

Computer Arithmetic

Barrenechea, Mark J.; "Numeric Exception Handling", Programmer's Journal, May 1991, v 9 n 3 P 40.

Cavanagh, Joseph J. F. *Digital Computer Arithmetic Design and Implementation*, 1984, McGraw Hill, ISBN 0-07-010282-1.

Flores, Ivan T*he Logic of Computer Arithmetic*, 1963, Prentice-Hall, ISBN 0135400392.

Hwang, Kai *Computer Arithmetic, Principles, Architecture, and Design,* Wiley, 1979, ISBN 0471034967.

Muller, Jean-Michel et al, *Handbook of floating Point Arithmetic*, 2009, Birkhauser, ISBN 081764704X.

Muller, Jean-Michel *Elementary Functions: Algorithms and Implementation*, 2005, Birkhauser, ISBN 0817643729.

Overton, Michael L. *Numerical Computing with IEEE Floating Point Arithmetic*, Society for Industrial & Applied Math; 1st ed, April 2001, ISBN- 978-0898714821.

Richards, R. K. *Arithmetic Operations in Digital Computers,* 1955, Van Nostrand, B00128Z00.

Rowen, Johnson, and Ries "The MIPS R3010 Floating Point Coprocessor", IEEE Micro, June 1988.

Schmid, Hermann *Decimal Computation*, 1974, Wiley, ISBN 0-471-76180-X.

Schwartzlander, E. and Lemonds, Carl (ed) Computer Arithmetic a Complete Reference, August 2012, Springer, ISBN 0387748830.

Scott, Norman R. *Computer Number Systems & Arithmetic*, 1984, Prentice-Hall, ISBN-0-13-164211-1.

Sterbenz, Patrick H. *Floating Point Computation*, 1974, Prentice Hall, ISBN 0133224953.

MC68881/882 Floating Point Coprocessor User's Manual, 1989, 2nd ed., Motorola, Prentice-Hall, ISBN 0-13-567009-8.

80387 Programmer's Reference Manual, 1987, Intel, 231917-001

32-bit Microprogrammable Products, Am29C300/29300 Data Book, 1988, AMD.

DSP96002 IEEE Floating-Point Dual Port Processor User's Manual, Motorola, DSP96002um/ad, 1989.

ANSI/IEEE Standard 754-1985 for Binary Floating-Point Arithmetic, IEEE Computer, Jan. 1980.

Data Communications

Koppe, U. "Automatic Baud Rate Detection in CANopen Networks," ICC 2003, http://www.can-cia.de/fileadmin/cia/files/icc/9/koppe.pdf

Mackay, Steve, et al, *Practical Data Communications for Instrumentation and Control,*
Newnes; 1st edition, 2003, ISBN 0750657979.

McNamara, John E. *Technical Aspects of Data Communication*, 1977, DEC, ISBN 0-932376-01-0.

Sklar, Bernard *Digital Communications, Fundamentals and Applications*, 2nd ed, 2001, Prentice Hall, ISBN 0-13-084788-7.

Stallings, William *Data and Computer Communications* (9th Edition), Prentice Hall; August 13, 2010, ISBN 0131392050.

Thompson, Lawrence *Industrial Data Communications*, 2008, ISA: The Instrumentation, Systems, and Automation Society; 4th edition, ISBN 1934394246

Sensors & Interfacing

Bartelt, Terry L. M. *Industrial Control Electronics*, 2005, Delmar Cengage Learning; 3rd edition, ISBN 1401862926.

Bode, Sr., Peter Abiodun *Current Measurement Applications Handbook*, AN39, www.zetex.com, Issue 5, Jan. 2008.

Borowik, Bohdan, *Interfacing PIC Microcontrollers to Peripheral Devices*, 2011, Springer, 1st Ed, ISBN 9400711182.

Caruso, Michael J. *Applications of Magnetorestrictive Sensor in Navigation Systems*, Honeywell, Inc., Solid State Electronics Center, 1998.

Fraden, Jacob *Handbook of Modern Sensors,* 4th ed, Springer, Sept 2010. ISBN 144196465.

Frank, Randy *Understanding Smart Sensors*, 2000, Artech House, ISBN 08900763117.

Grimes, C. A., Dickey, E. C. and Pishko M. V., *Encyclopedia of Sensors* (10-Volume Set), American Scientific Publishers, 2006, ISBN 1-58883-056-X ISBN 1-58883-056-X.

James, Kevin *PC Interfacing and Data Acquisition: Techniques for Measurement, Instrumentation and Control,* 2000, Newnes ISBN 0750646241.

Kirianaki, Nikolay V. et al *Data Acquisition and Signal Processing for Smart Sensors,*
2002, Wiley;, ISBN 0470843179.

Tompkins, Willis J. and Webster, John G. *Interfacing Sensors to the IBM-PC*, 1987, Prentice Hall, ISBN 0134690818.

Usher, M. J. and Keating, D. A. *Sensors & Transducers: Characteristics, Application., Instrumentation & Interfacing* 1996, Scholium International; 2nd edition, ISBN 0333604873.

Webster, John G. (ed) *The Measurement, Instrumentation and Sensors Handbook* (2 volumes), 1998, CRC Press, ISBN 0849383471.

Yamasaki, H. (ed) *Intelligent Sensors*, 1996, Elsevier Science, ISBN 0444541543.

Motor and Device Control

Herman, Stephen L. *Understanding Motor Controls* Delmar Cengage Learning; 1 edition (August 4, 2005), ISBN 1401890164.

Kenjo, Takashi and Sugawara, Akira *Stepping Motors and Their Microprocessor Controls* Oxford University Press, USA; 2 edition (January 15, 1994), ISBN 0198593856.

Patrick, Dale R. and Fardo, Stephen W. *Laboratory Manual for Electrical Motor Control Systems: Electronic and Digital Controls Fundamentals and Applications* Goodheart-Willcox Co (January 1, 2000), ISBN 1566377021.

Petruzella, Frank *Electric Motors and Control Systems* Career Education; 1 edition (May 8, 2009), ISBN 0073521825.

Pfister, Cuno *Getting Started with the Internet of Things: Connecting Sensors and Microcontrollers to the Cloud*, O'Reilly Media; 1st edition, June 2, 2011, ISBN- 1449393578.

Rockis, Gary J. and Mazur, Glen A. *Electrical Motor Controls for Integrated Systems*, Amer Technical Pub; 4 ed, 2009, ISBN 0826912176.

Valentine, Richard *Motor Control Electronics Handbook*, 1998, McGraw-Hill Professional; ISBN 0070668108.

Device Interfacing

Fischer-Cripps, Tony *Newnes Interfacing Companion: Computers, Transducers, Instrumentation and Signal Processing* Newnes (December 20, 2002), ISBN 0750657200.

Valvano, Jonathan W. *Introduction to Embedded Systems: Interfacing to the Freescale 9S12* CL-Engineering; 1 edition (April 23, 2009), ISBN 049541137X.

Introduction to PCI Express : A Hardware and Software Developer's Guide; 1st Ed; 325 pages; 2003; ISBN 978-0-9702846-9-3.

Complete PCI Express Reference: Design Implications for Hardware and Software Developers; 1st Ed; 1056 pages; 2003; ISBN 978-0-9717861-9-6.

PCI Express System Architecture; 1st Ed; Ravi Budruk; Don Anderson; Tom Shanley; 2003; ISBN 978-0-321-15630-3.

GPU

Kurzak, Jakub; Bader, David A.; Dongarra, Jack (Eds) *Scientific Computing with Multicore and Accelerators CRC Press; 1 edition (December 7, 2010), ISBN 143982536X.*

Sheppard, Andrew *Programming GPUs* 2011, O'Reilly Media, ISBN 1449302351.

GPS Spoofing

Humphreys, Todd E. et al, "Assessing the Spoofing Threat: Development of a Portable GPS Civilian Spoofer, 2008, ION GNSS Conference, Savanna, GA, Sept 16-18.

Humphreys, Todd E. "GPS Spoofing and the Financial Sector," U. Texas at Austin, June 2011.

DSP (from Wikipedia)

Oppenheim, Alan V., Schafer, Ronald W., Buck John R. *Discrete-Time Signal Processing*, Prentice Hall, ISBN 0-13-754920-2.

Porat, Boaz *A Course in Digital Signal Processing,* Wiley, ISBN 0-471-14961-6

Lyons, Richard G. *Understanding Digital Signal Processing,* Prentice Hall, ISBN 0-13-1089897.

Stein, Jonathan Yaakov *Digital Signal Processing, a Computer Science Perspective*, Wiley, ISBN 0-471-29546-9.

Sen M. Kuo, Woon-Seng Gan *Digital Signal Processors: Architectures, Implementations, and Applications*, Prentice Hall, ISBN 0-13-035214-4.

Bernard Mulgrew, Peter Grant, John Thompson *Digital Signal Processing - Concepts and Applications,* Palgrave Macmillan, ISBN 0-333-96356-3.

Steven W. Smith *Digital Signal Processing - A Practical Guide for Engineers and Scientists*, Newnes, ISBN 0-7506-7444-X, ISBN 0-9660176-3-3.

Paul A. Lynn, Wolfgang Fuerst *Introductory Digital Signal Processing with Computer Applications*, John Wiley & Sons, ISBN 0-471-97984-8.

James D. Broesch *Digital Signal Processing Demystified,* Newnes, ISBN 1-878707-16-7.

John G. Proakis, Dimitris Manolakis *Digital Signal Processing - Principles, Algorithms and Applications,* Pearson, ISBN 0-13-394289-9.

Hari Krishna Garg *Digital Signal Processing Algorithms*, CRC Press, ISBN 0-8493-7178-3.

Gaydecki, P. *Foundations Of Digital Signal Processing: Theory, Algorithms And Hardware Design,* Institution of Electrical Engineers, ISBN 0-85296-431-5.

Vijay Madisetti, Douglas B. Williams *The Digital Signal Processing Handbook*, CRC Press, ISBN 0-8493-8572-5.

Stergios Stergiopoulo: A*dvanced Signal Processing Handbook: Theory and Implementation for Radar, Sonar, and Medical Imaging Real-Time Systems*, CRC Press, ISBN 0-8493-3691-0.

Joyce Van De Vegte *Fundamentals of Digital Signal Processing,* Prentice Hall, ISBN 0-13-016077-6.

Ashfaq Khan *Digital Signal Processing Fundamentals*, Charles River Media, ISBN 1-58450-281-9.

Jonathan M. Blackledge, Martin Turner *Digital Signal Processing: Mathematical and Computational Methods, Software Development and Applications,* Horwood Publishing, ISBN 1-898563-48-9.

Bimal Krishna, K. Y. Lin, Hari C. Krishna: *Computational Number Theory & Digital Signal Processing*, CRC Press, ISBN 0-8493-7177-5.

Smith, Doug *Digital Signal Processing Technology: Essentials of the Communications Revolution*, American Radio Relay League, ISBN 0-87259-819-5.

Charles A. Schuler *Digital Signal Processing: A Hands-On Approach,* McGraw-Hill, ISBN 0-07-829744-3.

James H. McClellan, Ronald W. Schafer, Mark A. Yoder: *Signal Processing* Prentice Hall, ISBN 0-13-090999-8.

John G. Proakis *A Self-Study Guide for Digital Signal Processing*, Prentice Hall, ISBN 0-13-143239-7.

If you enjoyed this book, you might also be interested in some of these.

Stakem, Patrick H. *16-bit Microprocessors, History and Architecture*, 2013 PRRB Publishing, ISBN-1520210922.

Stakem, Patrick H. *4- and 8-bit Microprocessors, Architecture and History*, 2013, PRRB Publishing, ISBN-152021572X,

Stakem, Patrick H. *Apollo's Computers,* 2014, PRRB Publishing, ISBN-1520215800.

Stakem, Patrick H. *The Architecture and Applications of the ARM Microprocessors,* 2013, PRRB Publishing, ISBN-1520215843.

Stakem, Patrick H. *Earth Rovers: for Exploration and Environmental Monitoring,* 2014, PRRB Publishing, ISBN-152021586X.

Stakem, Patrick H. *Embedded Computer Systems, Volume 1, Introduction and Architecture*, 2013, PRRB Publishing, ISBN-1520215959.

Stakem, Patrick H. *The History of Spacecraft Computers from the V-2 to the Space Station*, 2013, PRRB Publishing, ISBN-1520216181.

Stakem, Patrick H. *Floating Point Computation*, 2013, PRRB Publishing, ISBN-152021619X.

Stakem, Patrick H. *Architecture of Massively Parallel Microprocessor Systems*, 2011, PRRB Publishing, ISBN-1520250061.

Stakem, Patrick H. *Multicore Computer Architecture,* 2014, PRRB Publishing, ISBN-1520241372.

Stakem, Patrick H. *Personal Robots,* 2014, PRRB Publishing, ISBN-1520216254.

Stakem, Patrick H. *RISC Microprocessors, History and Overview,* 2013, PRRB Publishing, ISBN-1520216289.

Stakem, Patrick H. *Robots and Telerobots in Space Applications,* 2011, PRRB Publishing, ISBN-1520210361.

Stakem, Patrick H. *The Saturn Rocket and the Pegasus Missions, 1965,* 2013, PRRB Publishing, ISBN-1520209916.

Stakem, Patrick H. *Visiting the NASA Centers, and Locations of Historic Rockets & Spacecraft,* 2017, PRRB Publishing, ISBN-1549651205.

Stakem, Patrick H. *Microprocessors in Space,* 2011, PRRB Publishing, ISBN-1520216343.

Stakem, Patrick H. Computer *Virtualization and the Cloud,* 2013, PRRB Publishing, ISBN-152021636X.

Stakem, Patrick H. *What's the Worst That Could Happen? Bad Assumptions, Ignorance, Failures and Screw-ups in Engineering Projects, 2014,* PRRB Publishing, ISBN-1520207166.

Stakem, Patrick H. *Computer Architecture & Programming of the Intel x86 Family, 2013,* PRRB Publishing, ISBN-1520263724.

Stakem, Patrick H. *The Hardware and Software Architecture of the Transputer,* 2011, PRRB Publishing, ISBN-152020681X.

Stakem, Patrick H. *Mainframes, Computing on Big Iron*, 2015, PRRB Publishing, ISBN- 1520216459.

Stakem, Patrick H. *Spacecraft Control Centers*, 2015, PRRB Publishing, ISBN-1520200617.

Stakem, Patrick H. *Embedded in Space,* 2015, PRRB Publishing, ISBN-1520215916.

Stakem, Patrick H. *A Practitioner's Guide to RISC Microprocessor Architecture*, Wiley-Interscience, 1996, ISBN-0471130184.

Stakem, Patrick H. *Cubesat Engineering*, PRRB Publishing, 2017, ISBN-1520754019.

Stakem, Patrick H. *Cubesat Operations*, PRRB Publishing, 2017, ISBN-152076717X.

Stakem, Patrick H. *Interplanetary Cubesats*, PRRB Publishing, 2017, ISBN-1520766173 .

Stakem, Patrick H. Cubesat Constellations, Clusters, and Swarms, Stakem, PRRB Publishing, 2017, ISBN-1520767544.

Stakem, Patrick H. *Graphics Processing Units, an overview*, 2017, PRRB Publishing, ISBN-1520879695.

Stakem, Patrick H. *Intel Embedded and the Arduino-101, 2017,* PRRB Publishing, ISBN-1520879296.

Stakem, Patrick H. *Orbital Debris, the problem and the mitigation*, 2018, PRRB Publishing, ISBN-*1980466483.*

Stakem, Patrick H. *Manufacturing in Space*, 2018, PRRB Publishing, ISBN-1977076041.

Stakem, Patrick H. *NASA's Ships and Planes*, 2018, PRRB Publishing, ISBN-1977076823.

Stakem, Patrick H. *Space Tourism*, 2018, PRRB Publishing, ISBN-1977073506.

Stakem, Patrick H. *STEM – Data Storage and Communications*, 2018, PRRB Publishing, ISBN-1977073115.

Stakem, Patrick H. *In-Space Robotic Repair and Servicing*, 2018, PRRB Publishing, ISBN-1980478236.

Stakem, Patrick H. *Introducing Weather in the pre-K to 12 Curricula, A Resource Guide for Educators*, 2017, PRRB Publishing, ISBN-1980638241.

Stakem, Patrick H. *Introducing Astronomy in the pre-K to 12 Curricula, A Resource Guide for Educators*, 2017, PRRB Publishing, ISBN-198104065X.
Also available in a Brazilian Portuguese edition, ISBN-1983106127.

Stakem, Patrick H. *Deep Space Gateways, the Moon and Beyond*, 2017, PRRB Publishing, ISBN-1973465701.

Stakem, Patrick H. *Exploration of the Gas Giants, Space Missions to Jupiter, Saturn, Uranus, and Neptune*, PRRB Publishing, 2018, ISBN-9781717814500.

Stakem, Patrick H. *Crewed Spacecraft*, 2017, PRRB Publishing, ISBN-1549992406.

Stakem, Patrick H. *Rocketplanes to Space*, 2017, PRRB Publishing, ISBN-1549992589.

Stakem, Patrick H. *Crewed Space Stations,* 2017, PRRB Publishing, ISBN-1549992228.

Stakem, Patrick H. *Enviro-bots for STEM: Using Robotics in the pre-K to 12 Curricula, A Resource Guide for Educators,* 2017, PRRB Publishing, ISBN-1549656619.

Stakem, Patrick H. *STEM-Sat, Using Cubesats in the pre-K to 12 Curricula, A Resource Guide for Educators*, 2017, ISBN-1549656376.

Stakem, Patrick H. *Lunar Orbital Platform-Gateway*, 2018, PRRB Publishing, ISBN-1980498628.

Stakem, Patrick H. *Embedded GPU's*, 2018, PRRB Publishing, ISBN- 1980476497.

Stakem, Patrick H. *Mobile Cloud Robotics*, 2018, PRRB Publishing, ISBN- 1980488088.

Stakem, Patrick H. *Extreme Environment Embedded Systems,* 2017, PRRB Publishing, ISBN-1520215967.

Stakem, Patrick H. *What's the Worst, Volume-2*, 2018, ISBN-1981005579.

Stakem, Patrick H., *Spaceports*, 2018, ISBN-1981022287.

Stakem, Patrick H., *Space Launch Vehicles*, 2018, ISBN-1983071773.

Stakem, Patrick H. *Mars*, 2018, ISBN-1983116902.

Stakem, Patrick H. *X-86, 40th Anniversary ed*, 2018, ISBN-1983189405.

Stakem, Patrick H. *Lunar Orbital Platform-Gateway*, 2018, PRRB Publishing, ISBN-1980498628.

Stakem, Patrick H. *Space Weather*, 2018, ISBN-1723904023.

Stakem, Patrick H. *STEM-Engineering Process*, 2017, ISBN-1983196517.

Stakem, Patrick H. *Space Telescopes,* 2018, PRRB Publishing, ISBN-1728728568.

Stakem, Patrick H. *Exoplanets*, 2018, PRRB Publishing, ISBN-9781731385055.

Stakem, Patrick H. *Planetary Defense*, 2018, PRRB Publishing, ISBN-9781731001207.

Patrick H. Stakem *Exploration of the Asteroid Belt*, 2018, PRRB Publishing, ISBN-1731049846.

Patrick H. Stakem *Terraforming*, 2018, PRRB Publishing, ISBN-1790308100.

Patrick H. Stakem, *Martian Railroad,* 2019, PRRB Publishing, ISBN-1794488243.

Patrick H. Stakem, *Exoplanets,* 2019, PRRB Publishing, ISBN-1731385056.

Patrick H. Stakem, *Exploiting the Moon,* 2019, PRRB Publishing, ISBN-1091057850.

Patrick H. Stakem, *RISC-V, an Open Source Solution for Space Flight Computers,* 2019, PRRB Publishing, ISBN-1796434388.

Patrick H. Stakem, *Arm in Space*, 2019, PRRB Publishing, ISBN-9781099789137.

Patrick H. Stakem, *Extraterrestrial Life*, 2019, PRRB Publishing, ISBN-978-1072072188.

Patrick H. Stakem, Space Command, 2019, PRRB Publishing, ISBN-978-1693005398.

www.ingramcontent.com/pod-product-compliance
Lightning Source LLC
Chambersburg PA
CBHW031609210526
45464CB00004B/1495